# Contents

C000173067

## Illustrations

# RIGHT AWAY!

RIGHT AWAY

# RIGHT AWAY!

## A Train Driver Recalls
## His Railway Career

STEVE DAVIES

THE CHOIR PRESS

First published in the United Kingdom in 2019 by
The Choir Press

All photographs are taken by the author unless credited otherwise.

ISBN 978-1-78963-035-0

# Introduction

When I retired, and initially for my own amusement, I started to jot down some of the high and low points that I had experienced during my 48 years of service in the rail industry and I eventually produced a long series of notes that could be turned into a book, of sorts. I have tried to make it readable not only for those with a working knowledge of the industry but also for those to whom much of the jargon used would be completely incomprehensible without some form of explanation. This I found to be a hard balancing act between appearing to patronise the former versus bamboozling the latter. Accordingly, I apologise to both groups in advance. In an attempt to assist the second group of readers, there is a glossary of some of the more common railway terms, acronyms and abbreviations used starting on page 275.

I have included some details relating to my personal life but only when they have impacted on my railway career or vice versa. Readers should also be aware that I have deliberately omitted or changed some names that, had they been included may have caused some embarrassment or possibly resulted in me being sued! You will also note that initially, I refer to all my former colleagues in the male gender. That is because they all were. It was only much later that female traincrew came on the scene and some of my workmates modified their behaviour appropriately. I still remember one senior driver verbally criticising the policy of recruiting females as passenger train guards, but the first day he worked with one I saw him carrying her kitbag to their train!

I could never be described as a railway expert, far from it, but I believe that my long period of service has given me an insight into everyday operations as seen from an employee's point of view and that is what I have tried to communicate to the reader. I had a great deal of materiel to draw upon relating to my own personal career including the particulars of all the trains I have officially driven including such nerdish (is there such a word?) details as train head-codes and numbers, times, number of coaches or tonnage of freight hauled, all calling points, destinations, delays and any abnormal events, of which there were many; these details were all logged. In total, I completed 148 notebooks from my first driving turn on 15th March 1982 until my last on 28th September 2017. Some pages of this book simply comprise copies of reports that I submitted following some incident or another that I was directly involved in.

I did not start my railway career on the footplate and it was only through a mixture of luck and ambition that I ended up doing the job that – on the good days – I considered to be the best in the world. Like most jobs, train driving was normally routine but it was also occasionally interesting and seldom boring. Of course, there were days too when everything seemed to go wrong and this included my very last day 'in the chair'. The extremely irregular shifts were also a downside especially as they became more tiring the older I got.

I have driven all types of diesel trains from the lowly shunting locomotive restricted to sidings to freight trains loaded with limestone weighing up to 5,000 tons and from single coach passenger trains to driving in and out of London Paddington with class 1 express trains. Driving a heavy freight train requires a different skill set to that needed for driving a passenger train at high speed. I have been fortunate to have done both many times and, I like to think, just about mastered them. I have never worked on a steam engine as British Rail had phased them all out of service before I started in the industry; thank God! I drove an electric train only once; I was learning the route between Fareham and Portsmouth when the driver asked me if I wanted to "have a go" and drive his train. Being keen at that time, I readily agreed and set off with full power applied not wanting to make his train late. When we reached 85 mph the train began to rock and roll about alarmingly and I commented to the driver, "These electric trains ride a bit rough."

Totally calmly he replied, "Yes, perhaps that's why the maximum line speed here is 70 mph." I took the hint and immediately reduced our speed.

I was a staff representative and an instructor train driver and on several occasions throughout my time in the industry, it was suggested to me by both some senior railway managers and ASLEF officials that I should put my name forward for more responsible positions within their relevant organisations. I have no regrets that I didn't. I knew of one union rep that changed sides and 'moved to the opposite side of the negotiating table' and I considered this to be treacherous and I could never have betrayed the organisation that had saved my career. And as for climbing up the slippery pole of promotion within ASLEF, I felt that the role I was playing was just about within my comfort zone and any higher up would have been very difficult for me to deal with.

The role I enjoyed most was simply train driving and getting my passengers safely and, even occasionally, on time to their destinations.

All train movements require a team effort. Not only traincrew but also signallers, station staff, train maintenance and infrastructure engineers are all in the front line when it comes to the running of any type of train and so I am pleased to acknowledge here all of their vital contributions.

Over the years I must have worked with hundreds of other railwaymen and women and I can honestly say that I can count on the fingers of one hand the few that I did not trust or like. The managers I had dealings with were mostly fair and reasonable too; however, I would now need both hands to tally up those that I did not respect.

Throughout this book you will come across many justifiable criticisms of railway management but I also acknowledge that, on occasions, some went above and beyond their obligations in assisting members of staff who had fallen on hard times through no fault of their own, predominantly relating to health issues.

I am also more than happy to highlight the assistance some managers afforded me personally. For instance, I will always appreciate their understanding and consideration when my son fell seriously ill, and then following the death of my father and later my mother. Additionally, my application to become a part-time driver later in my career was sympathetically received. To be fair (and I always am!) under both the nationalised and privatised systems I personally found that most managers treated staff welfare issues with a reasonable degree of compassion.

All staff would moan and complain but when the chips were down, we usually pulled together as a team and despite some managers and politicians trying to introduce some terrible and shortsighted policies, much of the industry has survived and in later years even flourished in some areas.

This book is predominantly my own personal interpretation of events and it is certainly not a glorification of the railway industry, nor the job of train driving, far from it. I have simply tried to record an honest, 'warts and all' account of the small part I have played within it. A few readers may cringe or even be shocked at some of the more revealing episodes but I think that without honesty it would not be a book worth writing and even less worth reading.

Although I have undertaken some research and tried to be as accurate as possible, no doubt some eagle-eyed and knowledgeable readers may find a couple of factual errors; if so, I must apologise and take full responsibility for them.

Here I must place on record my gratitude to my wife Anne for her patience during the many months that I took to write this book and also my indebtedness to my son Gareth without whose technical and editing input I would still not have completed the project.

Thank you in advance for reading my ramblings and if you would like to send me your thoughts, either positive or negative, I would appreciate your comments.

You can contact me at:

*stevedavies.westbury@icloud.com*

# 1

# Early Days

My interest in the railways originated from that much maligned and underrated hobby of trainspotting and that, in turn, came about due to my dislike of school. I felt reasonably happy at the first school I attended, Glasllwch Primary in Newport, South Wales, but when in 1965 I transferred to Duffryn Comprehensive School (Since renamed John Frost High School) on the outskirts of Newport, after surprisingly passing my 11 plus exam, I soon became disinterested in most of the curriculum. However, a few subjects did hold my attention and capture my imagination, not specifically because of the topics themselves but due to the individual teachers who had that rare and unfathomable ability to pass on their enthusiasm to a bunch of kids who would otherwise be bored to death.

Very few of my fellow prisoners in 'Stalag Duffryn' were permitted to venture outside the perimeter fence during the lunchtime break but I soon discovered that one group of people who could achieve temporary freedom were members of the school railway club. When shown to the guards, sorry prefects, on the gate, your membership card would allow you to access the school playing fields that were adjacent to the main railway line running between Newport and Cardiff and this enabled you to indulge in your hobby every day, even when at school. So, simply in order to escape, however briefly, from the oppressive school atmosphere, I became a card-carrying member of the Duffryn High School Railway Society.*
At first, I only showed a passing interest in the passing trains but surprisingly quickly, when other more experienced spotters explained some of the nuances of their hobby to me, I became well

---

* Formed in November 1960, the Duffryn High School Railway Society had an average membership of 50 pupils and also had a model railway section.

and truly hooked and, in time, an expert, literally in the field. Trainspotting lead to me understand such things as the difference between a diesel electric Co-Co locomotive such as the ubiquitous sixty-eight (later classified as a class 37) and a diesel hydraulic B-B Hymek (later classified as a class 35). Without realising it, I was also educating myself regarding British geography by learning, for example, where certain locomotives were based. Old Oak Common was in west London near Paddington, Laira was the depot in Plymouth and, further afield, Tinsley was in Sheffield, Polmadie was in Glasgow and Gateshead was to Newcastle as Bescot was to Birmingham. Locomotive numbers, names, types and depots soon became food and drink to me. I became a trainspotting addict. I was an active member of the school Railway Society regularly submitting items of interest for our monthly news-sheet that was keenly devoured by fellow enthusiasts. The club was organised by a couple of like-minded teachers (notably Mr. Snelling and Mr. Lewis) who also arranged visits for members to such exotic locations as Reading motive power depot and several of the London main line termini.

I left school with no qualifications whatsoever and you will probably realise that by the numerous grammatical and punctuation errors contained within this book! When I say 'left school' I actually simply stopped attending at the age of 15 as this was then the minimum legal age when formal education could be terminated. I am ashamed to say that not only did I fail to officially advise my school of my actions but also my Mum and Dad were initially unaware that I was not going to school any more but bunking off to go trainspotting every day. Inevitably, however, things soon came to a head and I thought the only way out that may satisfy all concerned would be for me to seek full-time paid employment. As far as I was concerned, that could only be within the rail industry and so, on 22nd September 1969 and in my best joined-up handwriting, I wrote to Mr. Tindall the then British Rail Area Manager at Newport High Street station[†] asking to be considered for any appropriate vacancy. I had a prompt reply thanking me for my interest but explaining that there was no suitable vacancy at that time;

---

† Now simply 'Newport' station as 'High Street' was dropped some time during the 1970s.

however, my name would be kept on file should the situation change in the near future. Naturally I was very disappointed but with hindsight I see now that it was a very professional and kind response, as nowadays many prospective employers would simply totally ignore such a plea and not waste their time and effort with any response whatsoever. However, only two days later I received a second letter from the Area Manager explaining that a vacancy had now become available for a messenger boy and if I was still interested, I was to report to his office for an interview. I was excited and very apprehensive when I attended the interview but it was conducted in a friendly and sympathetic manner as he kindly took into account my age and total lack of experience – I was still only 15 years of age. I then had to attend a medical examination and with that passed, I received a letter dated 3<sup>rd</sup> October advising me that I had got the job. It had taken just two weeks from the date of my first tentative enquiry to becoming an employee. How long would a similar process take today, I wonder?

# 2
# Working for a Living

I started my railway career on 6th October 1969 as a messenger boy based at Maesglas, Newport. The job involved walking, or more often cycling, to the numerous railway outposts on the western side of Newport that included signal boxes, shunters' cabins and various offices within the area, of which there were many at that time, delivering miscellaneous railway notices, work rosters, internal personal mail and all sorts of varied British Rail communications.

There were three depots in Newport at this time where traincrew reported for duty: Maesglas where the freight guards were based; Ebbw (pronounced ebb-oo) Junction Diesel Depot which was the location where most of the drivers booked on; and the much smaller depot of Pill that still retained a few drivers and diesel shunting engines (class 08s) used exclusively within the Newport docks complex.

Separate guards' and drivers' depots had some logic at the time as the drivers would prepare their locomotives on the diesel depot and the guards could prepare their brake vans and inspect their trains before the locomotive arrived. However, it soon became apparent that it would make more economic sense for all train crew to report to one location and so the guards eventually moved to Ebbw Junction. The traditional separation of driver/footplate crew and guards was slowly dying out when I started on the railway though it lingered on for many years in particular, for some reason that I could never fathom, it was more prevalent on the southern region, even to the extent of having separate mess rooms within the same depot! I always considered this to be nonsense especially when I later entered the footplate line of promotion; after all, were we not all train crew working together as a team?

It was during my stint as a messenger boy that I was asked if I would work a night shift to cover for the booking-on clerk/time keeper to whom the guards initially reported for duty. I was very keen to experience such an adult and responsible role and so, even though there was some doubt expressed as to the legality of a 16-year-old working a night shift, I did it gladly.

My occupation as a messenger boy did not last long however, as one day, out of the blue, my boss asked me if I wanted to be considered for a clerical officer's position. (The title 'officer' was still prominent within the rail industry at that time due to the historical connection with military and police forms of organisation. Some older railwaymen still refer to signallers as 'officer' or 'bobby' to this day.) Unsure of the full implications but with little to lose, I agreed to take the British Rail clerical officers entrance exam. I was sent to the regional head office in Cardiff and sat the test. While it did not seem particularly difficult to me, I was not aware how high the pass mark was set. Luckily, I managed to get through and so I was soon appointed to the lofty position of Clerical Officer Grade 1 (CO1) at the Ebbw Junction Diesel Depot administration block. This resulted in a pay rise to a little over £7 per week – before tax of course.

My job as a CO1 involved the calculation of the Freight Train Incentive Scheme (FTIS) – a bonus pay agreement introduced for freight train drivers only, as most passenger drivers had been receiving a bonus for many years based on the number of miles driven during a shift. To receive this FTIS bonus, all freight train drivers were required to complete a daily worksheet that recorded the start and termination points of their trains, the number of wagons involved, tonnages hauled and the relevant timings. I was then required to calculate the individual bonus payments due, based on a complicated formula that was supposed to reflect the degree of productivity obtained. This, of course, was nonsense, as an individual driver had no power to influence the weight, number of wagons or the starting/terminating points of his train. However, drivers are no fools when it comes to boosting their income, particularly at this time, when drivers, like most other railway employees, were undoubtedly underpaid. It was soon discovered that some 'liberal interpretation' of their labours on the relevant form could result in a reasonable bonus. It was not what you did but how you completed the form that proved to be the most significant factor. It was during this period that a new drivers' pay deal was implemented and, although their basic wage increased, a reduction in bonus payments was agreed to help pay for it. This meant that I still had to calculate the payments due but then subtract a fixed sum and the remaining balance is what a driver would then receive in his pay packet. One day, I calculated a driver's bonus but after the required reduction found that the result was minus 2d. (pre-decimalisation). I asked a colleague to check my calculations and we were both flabber-gasted when he confirmed the answer was correct. At the end of each week I was required to pin up in the relevant notice case a list showing how much bonus each driver would receive next payday. There was no way to avoid it, so next to the name 'Driver Des Wilkins' I wrote -2d and waited for the storm to break. Luckily for me Des was a very reasonable man but when he strode into our office the following day with a face like thunder, I thought, "Brace yourself, Steve." However, he just walked to my section of the office placed 2 penny coins on the desk in front of me and walked out again without uttering a single word. He made his point succinctly and with style and it left me wondering if I had a worthwhile job.

The first step on the ladder to eventually become a driver was as a traction trainee; however, these vacancies were few and far between as it was a period of general decline within the rail industry so I was surprised to see such a position advertised at my own depot. Until this point, I never believed that I would ever become a driver but now I had to try. I applied for the position; however, my boss then called me into his office for a private one-to-one meeting in order to attempt, very gently and tactfully, to get me to withdraw my application. I explained to him that I had discovered office work was not for me and that while I wanted to remain in the rail industry, I needed to explore other possibilities. He told me that a vacancy would soon be adver-tised for a position at Bedwas near Caerphilly as the rail yard supervisor overseeing trains in and out of the colliery and although mainly an administration role, if I got the job I would also be required to work outside and get my hands dirty from time to time checking that coal wagons were being correctly dealt with. He suggested that I pay the railway office at Bedwas a visit to see for myself if I wanted the position. So, one day the following week I did just that; however, I spent most of my time with the driver on the Bedwas pilot that consisted of a small British Rail shunting engine (later classified as a class 08) 'wagon bashing' as it was locally known at the time. This involved positioning empty wagons for loading and then making up full trains of coal for the 'main line engine', invariably a sixty-eight (later classified as a class 37) to take away to Llanwern or Margam steel works, for example. I loved all aspects of this very small taster of footplate work so my day at Bedwas had the completely opposite effect that my boss had sought and made me more determined than ever to enter the footplate line of promotion.

Again, I was lucky and my application to become a traction trainee was accepted after an interview and a medical. I became one member of the class that started training in Cardiff on 14th December 1970. This exact date was very important, as it then became my footplate seniority date and would stay with me until I retired a little under 47 years later. Most aspects of a driver's career at that time were strictly governed by an individual's seniority date and the date would greatly impact on me personally years later when I was made redundant.

My traction trainee's course at Cardiff was very interesting and enjoyable. Together with the other students, we knuckled down to learn all we could about footplate duties. It consisted of mainly classroom work but there were also some practical experiences of riding up front with drivers. If we passed this course, the next stage was to apply for a secondman's (later called a driver's assistant) position. The secondman's job consisted of:

- Sweeping the cab floor
- Making the tea
- Setting up the headcode*

---

* To set up the correct four-digit train reporting number or headcode on the front of a class 37 the secondman had to go forward from the cab through a small door into the nose end of the locomotive where he had to lower metal flaps to access the four winding handles and then turn the blinds to the appropriate display. There was more essential equipment also situated within this small dark area: an exhauster – necessary for the operation of the original vacuum braking system, a

- Releasing the locomotive's mechanical parking brake before departure and then reapplying it at the end of the shift
- Coupling/uncoupling the locomotive when necessary
- Verbally interpreting and relaying to the driver signals received from the shunter or guard when carrying out reverse shunting maneuvers if due to the curvature of the line the driver could not see these signals himself from his left-hand side of the cab (all our locos were left hand drive)
- When the train was in motion looking back occasionally to ensure that the train was following in a safe and proper manner
- Operating the steam heating boiler on passenger services[†]
- Assisting the driver as required
- At all times acting under the driver's instructions, which in the worst-case scenario could include carrying out protection, i.e. in an emergency situation, implementing the applicable rules and using the appropriate equipment to try and stop oncoming trains

Basically, the secondman was, in effect, an apprentice driver. Mistakenly this concept was abandoned by British Rail in 1988 and, as a consequence, the lack of any previous railway experience that many newly qualified drivers now have, through no fault of their own, may partly explain why some potentially serious operational incidents still occur today.

---

compressor for supplying crucial air pressure for engine control systems, and a blower motor to cool the electric traction motors. Before the diesel engine was started, all would be calm and quiet in the nose end but when the driver pressed the engine start button all three electrical motors would burst into life accompanied by extreme noise and enough movement of air – mainly from the blower motor – to almost knock you off your feet. Some drivers would deliberately wait until their mate had gone into the nose and then start the engine. Very funny – but only from their point of view!

[†] Before the days of electric train heating, many diesel locomotives were originally equipped with a steam-generating boiler within the engine room to supply steam heating for passenger coaches. Ten days of my traction trainee's course involved tuition on how to operate the three different types of boilers (The Stone Vapor Generator, The Spanner Boiler and the Clayton Steam Generator) then in common use. However, as no passenger services were operated by Ebbw traincrew during my time at the depot I had to be retrained much later, during December 1980, as Westbury did, initially at least, have such work.

Provided we passed the exam at the end of our traction trainee's course, we were entitled to apply for any depot in the country that was then advertising a secondman's vacancy. Being still only 17 years old and naive but keen, three of my classmates and I decided that we would all apply for a London depot and then share rented accommodation in the capital. What could possibly go wrong? Well, after I successfully applied for Kings Cross, two of my would-be joint tenants dropped out and the other one ended up at Cricklewood so I was now on my own.

I transferred to London on 18th February 1971 but the only affordable accommodation I could initially find was lodging with an aunt. However, she lived in New Cross and, despite its name, it was seven miles from Kings Cross. For any employee working conventional hours this would not have been much of a problem using London's public transport system; however, I, like all other footplate crew, had to work shifts that would frequently involve starting or finishing a turn of duty at any time between 01:00 and 04:00. During this period there were no night underground trains, very few night busses and then only on a few routes. Of course, I didn't then know any of the drivers at Kings Cross and being naturally a little shy, I felt very much out of my depth and lost. Until then I would have said it was impossible to feel lonely in a city with a population of eight million; however, I was, and very homesick too. I felt all alone, vulnerable and isolated. All my ambitious plans made back in South Wales had come to naught. Eventually, I moved into a hostel for railway employees but transport issues and personal unhappiness persisted. I used up all my holiday entitlement in dribs and drabs to go home as often as possible but I would then dread the thought of returning to London. At my lowest point, I thought about walking in front of a car, not I hasten to add, in an attempt to kill myself but to have a genuine reason to stay at home and convalesce for a long period. With hindsight this would have obviously been a very risky strategy and I am glad that common sense prevailed even when I was at my lowest ebb. I then understood why my Mum had shed a few tears when she and Dad insisted on coming down to Newport station to see me off to London when I first left home.

The method of allocating drivers to trains was then – and still is at some depots – based strictly on seniority, hence the vital importance of an individual's seniority date. At a depot that covered both passenger and freight work as was the case at 'The Cross', the link structure ensured that junior men were allocated to such work as shunting freight wagons, local goods trains, or possibly empty coaching stock moves in or out of the station to and from nearby yards and sidings. Men with a little more seniority could expect to work local passenger or longer distance freight trains and only in the latter part of your driving career would you be entitled to work expresses and long-distance passenger trains. Eventually a driver would progress up to the next link. The top link was always no.1 and the bottom link could be any number depending on the number of drivers at the depot. So, for example, if a depot had 100 drivers there could be 5 links with 20 weeks' work in each; but those numbers could differ hugely. If you started on week 1 in any link, you would work every week from 1 to 20 before cycling around to start on week 1 again. When a vacancy occurred in the link above, the senior man would normally fill it.

At Kings Cross, as was the case at most of the bigger depots, even the secondmen had their own link structure. So, as I was a very junior hand, I was automatically placed in the bottom link so I never worked with a driver to York or Newcastle, for example. My trains were strictly of a local nature: some freight, some empty coaching stock and a few of the shorter distance passenger workings. I did experience the cab of the famous Deltic locomotive (later classified as a class 55) a few times and also regularly worked into Moorgate terminus with what would later become class 31 locomotives.

I applied for a transfer back to Ebbw Junction Diesel Depot and, much to my surprise, it was granted very quickly. It is possible that the local management at Kings Cross may have understood my position, that I was unhappy and would almost certainly never be able to settle in at 'The Cross' and that they helped to speed up my transfer back home. If they did, I am very grateful.

# SCHEMATIC RAIL MAP OF NEWPORT CIRCA 1970
## (Not to scale)

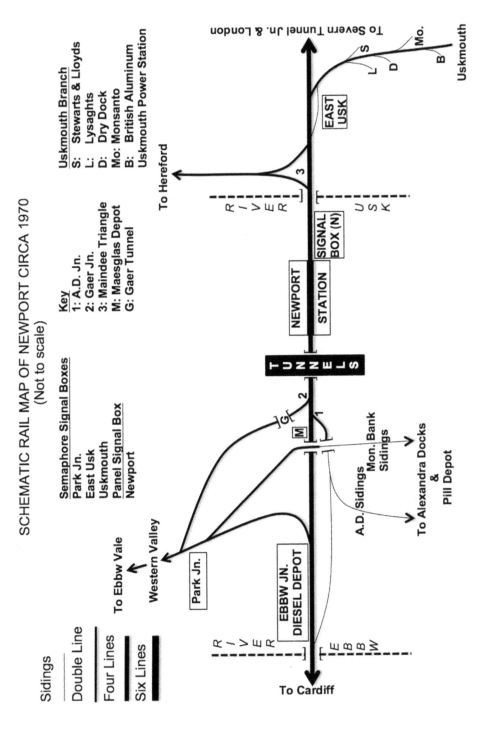

**Sidings**

Double Line
Four Lines
Six Lines

**Semaphore Signal Boxes**
Park Jn.
East Usk
Uskmouth
**Panel Signal Box**
Newport

**Key**
1: A.D. Jn.
2: Gaer Jn.
3: Maindee Triangle
M: Maesglas Depot
G: Gaer Tunnel

**Uskmouth Branch**
S: Stewarts & Lloyds
L: Lysaghts
D: Dry Dock
Mo: Monsanto
B: British Aluminum
Uskmouth Power Station

To Severn Tunnel Jn. & London

Uskmouth

S
L
D
Mo.
B

EAST USK

To Hereford

RIVER

3

NEWPORT STATION

SIGNAL BOX (N)

USK

TUNNELS

G

M

2

1

Mon. Bank Sidings

A.D. Sidings

To Alexandra Docks & Pill Depot

Western Valley

To Ebbw Vale

Park Jn.

EBBW JN. DIESEL DEPOT

RIVER

EBBW

To Cardiff

# 3
# Back to Ebbw – Temporarily

I transferred back to Ebbw Junction Diesel Depot, still as a second-man, on 17th May 1971 so, I was at Kings Cross for only three months but it felt like years. I became a member of ASLEF on 4th June of the same year as I knew by now that is was by far the best trade union to represent footplate staff. I soon became an active supporter and remained so until the day I retired.

Most of the main line work at Ebbw at this time involved the bulk movement of coal, iron ore, steel, or track ballast for railway engineering projects. Passenger work had ceased although we still operated a few parcel trains. We worked coal trains from collieries such as Oakdale, Markham, Rose Heyworth, Abertillery, Six Bells, Llanhilleth, Marine, Celynen North and South, Bedwas / Trethomas, Blaenavon, Hafodyrynys and Llanharan (open cast), to name but a few, predominately to destinations such as Llanwern Steel Works, Margam for Port Talbot Steel Works or Uskmouth Power Station in Newport. Iron ore imports through Newport docks to Ebbw Vale and Llanwern resulted in almost a shuttle service of freight trains after a ship had docked. The iron ore trains to Ebbw Vale needed a banker, i.e. an additional locomotive at the rear of the train to assist the leading locomotive to haul the train up the steep rising gradients in the Western Valley. The experience I gained on these trains stood me in good stead when I later transferred to Westbury, as then, all loaded stone trains heading south also required a banker as far as Warminster.

Many of the drivers I worked with during this period were real characters and all were former steam engine cleaners, firemen and drivers. Rail companies now attempt to mold drivers into their corporate image and try to repress any form of individuality. They would have had their work cut out with some of the old steam men! Senior managers of train operating companies today seek to employ human robots, all thinking and acting alike. Although some recruits do get brain-washed during their driver-training period, the reality of the industry soon becomes apparent when they qualify and start their driving career proper.

It was during this time of my unofficial apprenticeship that I slowly but surely learnt the skill of train driving. Looking back, I now realise that I owe a debt of gratitude to the many drivers at Ebbw Junction who, without any fuss, calmly demonstrated and later instructed and guided me until I too became a competent train driver. Initially, some would let me have a go driving a 'light engine', i.e. a locomotive without any wagons or coaches attached. Then when they and I became more confident and familiar with regard to specific routes, I was allowed to drive empty freight trains, for example, to the docks or a colliery for loading. Eventually after some time, years in the case of some drivers, when I had built up a good working rapport with colleagues who then believed that I could be trusted in their chair, I would usually share the driving equally. In fact, some drivers would rush to the secondman's seat and so, I would do most of their work for them. Most secondmen were like me and very keen to drive and so it was more of a pleasure than a chore. Of course, all of this driving was technically against the rules; however, the management knew it was going on and unofficially supported it as they knew full well that it was a very good way to train the next generation of drivers. However, if anything went wrong it was the driver in charge who ultimately carried the bulk of the responsibility.

The class 37 locomotive was our workhorse at Ebbw Junction Diesel Depot although I also experienced work on the following types:

Class 08   Diesel shunter
Class 25   Normally two in multiple
Class 35   'Hymek' diesel hydraulic
Class 45/6 Known as Peaks
Class 47   Brush diesel electric
Class 52   'Western' diesel hydraulic
Class 53   D0280 'Falcon' that lived out its final days at our depot
Class 56   Diesel electric

Each type was distinctive and had its own different characteristics in terms of reliability, comfort, power, cab and engine room layout to name but a few. For example, all diesel locos were equipped with a hotplate to enable train crew to make tea on the move. Almost everybody drank tea in those days and coffee was normally off the menu, unlike today. The location of these hotplates varied. While most had one in each cab a few had only one and that was located within the engine room. We called the class 52s 'Westerns' because every one of these 74 locomotives was named with the prefix 'Western'. For example, D1020 was named 'Western Hero'. Uniquely these locos had a hotplate fitted in a metal box low down on the right-hand side of the cab. So, the secondman managed the all-important task of making the tea. My first attempt to carry out this most simple of tasks on a 'Western' ended in failure because I put my tea can full of water on the hotplate, shut the cupboard door and switched it on to the high setting. This was a mistake because, although the water eventually boiled, as evidenced by steam escaping from the frame of the metal cupboard, I was unable to open the door and get the can out as the door had then expanded with the heat. My only course of action was to turn the hotplate off, wait for the whole thing to cool down so I could then open the door. This took a considerable amount of time and the little remaining water that had not evaporated was then not hot enough anyway to make the tea. Lesson learned.

The class 37, or the sixty-eight as we originally called them before reclassification, was by far the most common type of loco in service at Ebbw Junction Diesel Depot. They were noisy, dirty and drafty but invariably reliable. The maximum weight of train they could haul, as with all engines, depended upon the gradients en route. When, for example, hauling a train loaded with imported iron ore from Newport Docks to Ebbw Vale Steelworks the distance was only a little over 20 miles but with some steep gradients the engine had to work hard most of the way. Frequently it would get very hot and the automatic fire alarm would sound, ringing a bell in the cab that couldn't be ignored. So, we didn't and, after checking that the engine was not, in fact, on fire, we would simply wedge a K2 (a weekly printed speed restriction and engineering bulletin issued to all traincrew) between the bell and the clapper to deaden the sound. The only other way would have been to stop the train and wait for the engine to cool down enough to stop the fire alarm from sounding and we would not even contemplate that option.

There was a great deal of railway infrastructure still remaining within the area at the time. I say still remaining, as the older drivers would explain to me that what I then saw was just the remnants of what was a much bigger industrial landscape. Many of these drivers had been made redundant at former depots such as Pontypool Road that closed in 1965 and had moved to Ebbw Junction during previous contractions of the rail industry. Little did I realise then that I too would be in the same position in the not too distant future.

The 1970s were a time of major industrial unrest, not least in the rail industry. In an attempt to safeguard jobs and achieve what would now be called a living wage, trade unions called well-supported strikes. We also experienced Ted Heath's infamous 'three-day week'. But my personal life was going well, as during this period, I met and fell in love with Anne and we eventually moved into a first floor flat in a very run-down house in Newport, but at least we were together. Walking to Ebbw Junction from our new home briefly included a view over part of the Bristol Channel and occasionally, I would hear a sonic boom and catch a glimpse of a Concorde heading west, bound for the USA usually at about 18:30.

I don't know if this is a fact or not, but the commonly held belief at that time was that because of the noise that Concorde produced when flying supersonic, it was not permitted to break the sound barrier over land and so the Bristol Channel afforded the earliest opportunity for pilots to start seriously accelerating. True or not, it seemed logical to me at the time and still does.

Both at Ebbw Junction and later during my early years at West-bury, some drivers I worked with had inherited a drinking culture as all had been brought up working on steam engines and having a pint or two when the opportunity arose was normal practice for many. The physical work required on the footplate of a steam locomotive necessitated a substantial intake of liquid and you can only drink so much tea! This did not shock me, as it was common within the industry when I started. Who would say that the footplate crew of a steam engine did not deserve a pint after working an express passenger or a heavy freight train from A to B before working back to their own depot and then perhaps having another drink before going home. While it was not rife in my time, as many drivers would not drink any alcohol at all while on duty, it was also not uncommon. As drivers' assistants, we knew the drivers who liked the odd pint on (and off) duty and because this normally meant that we would undertake most if not all of the day's driving which we enjoyed and gained experience from, we would never dream of reporting such an individual. Of course, the culture has now completely changed and any member of safety critical staff will be instantly dismissed and possibly subjected to legal prosecution if found to be over the alcohol limit which is considerably lower (effectively nil) in the rail industry than the legal limit for driving on the road. A few of the older drivers that I worked with would not last long in their post today due to 'for cause' (after being involved in an operational incident) or random unannounced drink and drug testing. Today discipline in general is much more strict, with train operating companies correctly demanding higher standards and productivity for higher pay. Nowadays, it's a lot more professional but a lot less fun!

Some of the senior drivers that I initially worked with at Ebbw Junction considered certain safety devices fitted to these newfangled diesel locomotives to be unnecessary because they naturally compared these new working practices with the way a steam-engine-powered railway ran. When I started at Ebbw, every train had a crew of three. A driver, his assistant/secondman and a guard and so, because there were then always at least two crew members in the cab, some drivers considered the DSD unnecessary and would promptly isolate it at the start of the shift.

I recall on one occasion when I was driving, I wished that the DSD had been isolated as I nearly caused our guard serious injury. We were working a class 9 train of coal empties and approaching Newport station when I accidentally allowed the DSD to activate. This instantly caused the brakes on the loco to fully apply and consequently, the leading wagon struck our loco with force and this was followed by the ripple effect of every wagon striking the one in front all the way down the train with ever increasing force until it reached the last vehicle which was, of course, the brake van within which our innocent guard was travelling. He told me afterwards that he heard the bang-bang-bang approaching and knew that his brake van would come to a crashing stop so he held on tight. That might have been the end of it if I hadn't made a bad situation worse by my instant and unthinking reaction of stamping on the DSD pedal. This immediately released the brake on our class 37 and the ripple effect on the train then happened again, but this time in the reverse direction. This doubled the impact on the brake van. I slowly regained full control of the train but when we reached the colliery, our guard let me know in colourful language what he thought of my driving ability. Such a scenario would not arise today, as there is an inbuilt time delay before a DSD brake application can be released, ensuring that the train will first come to a complete halt.

It is strange but true that when driving a loose-coupled freight train, there were times when the gentlest way to stop the train at low speed, especially when on a rising gradient, was not to apply the brake at all but to open the power handle instead as this would take the weight of the trailing wagons away from the locomotive and, if timed correctly, the train would stop as one. This was just one of the many freight train driving techniques I learned during my 'apprenticeship' years at Ebbw Junction.

PNB points, or as they were originally called relief cabins, were very basic when I started on the railway compared with the almost luxurious facilities traincrew now enjoy at most locations. In the 1970s, it was common to enter a messroom and be almost overwhelmed by a cloud of tobacco smoke often coming from those engrossed in a continuous card school. There would be a large central coal or wood-burning stove continuously lit whatever the weather; it would be stifling in summer and cold in the winter unless you could get a prime location. Wooden benches provided the only available seating and, in the corner, there would be a phone for the signaller or control office to contact traincrew. Other amenities would include an old cracked sink with only a cold-water tap together with, on a good day, a bar of soap.

Tea-making facilities consisted of a very large heavy-duty kettle permanently in steam (adding to the ambiance) on an old and dirty gas stove. At a couple of locations, outside toilets were still in use. In this all-male environment, swearing and pictures of scantily clad young ladies on the wall were the norm. Political correctness was unheard of. Although steam engines had been phased out before I started my railway career (I'm glad to say) the general atmosphere had not changed much. Old habits die hard and almost all of my colleagues were then still ex-steam men. I have found railwaymen to be a very conservative (small c!) bunch and almost afraid or at least very wary of any changes to their working environment or conditions.

Today's traincrew accommodation is generally first class. Comfy chairs, central heating, air conditioning and large televisions are the order of the day along with full cooking facilities, instant boiling water, male and female toilets and showers. Everyone has a company mobile phone and/or tablet for instant communication (or games!). At some locations a 'quiet' room is also available and very popular they are too when spare on the night shift!

1st January 1976 saw the introduction of a new terms and conditions package for footplate staff and this included a name change for us secondmen. We were now called driver's assistants though the actual job description did not change and life went on as normal as far as I was concerned. Wages for British Rail employees during this period were low on average and so any opportunity to boost earnings was to be welcomed. Normally this was through enhancements, for example, when working overtime, Sundays, nights and, on very rare occasions, at a freight depot for which a mileage bonus was paid when 200 miles or more had been driven within a single shift. We had one turn in the link that normally qualified for all of those enhancements. This was our Sunday to Friday 21:00 engineering turn. The Sunday payment was almost guaranteed, likewise the enhanced pay rates for working nights and overtime and even mileage payments were also common on this particular turn. The trains concerned were made up of anything that the engineering department needed relocating. Usually this was a loaded ballast train from Newport to Acton in London with one or two class 37s depending on the load. New track sections, long welded rail wagons or empty trucks that were required for old ballast and various permanent way department equipment would also be conveyed if and when required. In fact, the load, destination and locos would be unknown to us for certain until we actually booked on for duty. If all went well, we could double our weekly wage on this particular turn and I knew of several colleagues who would try to swap their annual leave to work this very remunerative turn if it coincided with this week. How things have changed. When I retired, there was frequently a shortage of drivers to cover voluntary Sunday work.

I was a secondman to a driver one day when we had an unexpected opportunity to enhance our earnings. We were allocated a class 52 'Western' loco and a train of long welded rail wagons bound for Crewe. I had never been to Crewe on duty before, and didn't expect to that day either, because although my driver signed the road, it was notoriously difficult to get through Hereford and then Shrewsbury without being relieved, as train crews at these depots were also hungry for work. (It was rumored that when Neil Armstrong set foot on the moon a Hereford driver stepped out from behind a rock and immediately relieved him!) However, we slipped through Hereford as quietly as possible and were even more surprised to get the road through Shrewsbury. We had made it! Overtime and mileage payments were now a sure thing. We arrived at Crewe and propelled our train into a siding as directed by the shunter who then told us that our engine was to go onto (Crewe) shed. My driver queried this as he knew that no Crewe-based driver would be qualified to move a Western class 52 and we told the shunter that we should take it back to Newport. (Without the return trip we would not qualify for the mileage bonus payment.) However, the shunter was adamant, so, downhearted, we trundled off to the depot. I was completely lost. (The only time I had ever been to Crewe previously was for trainspotting in my early teens. The station buffet was then well known among the spotting fraternity as the only one in the country open 24 hours a day, 7 days a week – unless dear reader you know otherwise.)

The railway infrastructure at Crewe at this time was considerable with multiple junctions, a mixture of semaphore and colour light signaling and overhead wires everywhere. It seemed like a maze to me. I noticed that my driver was also a little hesitant at times. However, we made it onto the depot without mishap and we were in the process of shutting down our loco when the foreman came running out of his office red-faced and shouting something we could not hear above the sound of our diesel engines.* So, my mate pressed the engine stop buttons. This only seemed to enrage the foremen even more and now we could hear him shouting

"No! No! I don't want that thing on my shed. I'll never get it shifted!"

My driver had been proved correct and so, ever helpful, said,

"We could always take it back light engine."

"Yes. Yes. Clear off!"

And so we did. I phoned the signalman from the shed exit signal and told him that we were to run light engine to Canton. I deliberately did not say Ebbw as he had probably never heard of our small depot, but Cardiff Canton, I assumed, was well known far and wide. The signal cleared and we set off; however, my driver was obviously dubious about our direction of travel and the line we were heading down so he stopped at a line-side phone.

"Give the bobby a ring and make sure we're okay," he said to me. So, I climbed down and contacted the signaller.

"Er … are we heading the right way for Canton?" I asked.

"Where?" Was his reply.

"Canton, Cardiff Canton Depot," I confirmed.

"Oh, when you came off the shed, I thought you said Camden."

We were on our way to London! Now that would have been a mileage payment worth having!

The summer of 1976 was memorable for the hottest and driest ever recorded in parts of the UK and this, in turn, resulted in drought conditions in many areas. Water shortages were severe and so rationing was introduced in many locations with taps running dry for hours at a time. In an attempt to move water to the worst affected regions, the water authorities installed temporary pipes in some specific locations. These pipes, due to their temporary nature, were

---

* Westerns were fitted with two 1,350 brake horsepower engines.

simply laid on top of the ground and sometimes adjacent to railway lines that were used as a convenient pathway. When the rains eventually came and the water shortage passed, all these temporary pipes had to be removed. It was during one such operation that I was involved in my first collision – others were to follow much later. My driver, Pat Kearney, was in the seat as the short journey from Markham Colliery down part of the Sirhowy Valley with a loaded coal train needed the more experienced hand in control due to the gradient and that fact that the train was a loose-coupled class 9. This was normal practice and meant that the only driver-operable brake was that of our locomotive, the usual class 37, and so the speed had to be kept to a maximum of only 10-15 mph otherwise the train could run away out of control. With restricted views ahead along the single line due to the curvature of the track we belatedly saw a large water authority pick-up truck parked at right angles across our track ahead. Pat immediately made a full brake application, which had the temporary effect of marginally increasing our speed as the full weight of our train was then thrown forward against our loco. Both Pat and I sounded the warning horn and we saw the driver of the truck attempt to drive his vehicle over the rails. He failed, the engine must have stalled and the truck just rolled back the few feet to its original position. He tried again and again and by this time it was obvious that a collision, albeit in slow motion, would occur. Pat jumped up and started to shout at the driver to get out. This was an understandable reaction but as the truck driver would not be able to hear him above the sound of his revving engine and our squealing brakes, served no useful purpose. However, just before the inevitable collision he managed to get out and staggered clear. Our class 37 struck the truck and pushed it a short distance before we stopped in a cloud of dust. Pat and I were both stunned by this sudden and totally unexpected turn of events. I jumped down from the cab and spoke to the truck driver who was about my age, in his early twenties. He was clearly in a state of shock and crying. His first words to me were

"I'll get the sack for this – I've only just passed my test!"

I said, "Don't worry about that now, at least you weren't killed – but why didn't you get out earlier."

"I tried, but my boot got trapped under the pedals," he replied.

I thought, "No wonder you're so upset" and tried to calm him down a little. By now Pat had joined us and to my amazement, the truck driver then said,

"I heard someone shouting to get out and it was only then that I realised I was stuck."

(Pat's voice must have echoed throughout the valley!)

The truck was written off but our class 37 only suffered minor damage. Whether or not the truck driver was also 'written off' and lost his job I'll never know, but I hope not.

We worked few trains that did not involve iron ore, coal, or steel, but one exception and one of our more unusual goods trains consisted of wagons loaded with armaments from the Royal Ordnance Factory (ROF) at Glascoed. On Saturday 9th June 1979 I reported for duty at 05:35 and was pleased to find that my driver for the day was gentleman Fred Redmore. Our loco was 37 178 and Fred let me drive the first half of the shift. We ran light engine from our depot to the vast sidings complex at Severn Tunnel Junction and picked up a train of empty box wagons that looked like large windowless garden sheds but with a wheel under each corner and curved apex roofs. We then retraced our journey as far as Maindee East Junction where we left the South Wales main line and headed north in the direction of Hereford. At Little Mill Junction near Pontypool we then took the short single branch line to Glascoed and after a cup of tea, the real work started. Because of the potential risk of fire and then possible large-scale explosions, BR locos were not allowed within the munitions filling factory sidings and the loaded wagons were shunted from the works a few at a time into the adjacent marshaling yard where we were waiting. The ROF had their own fireless steam locomotive for this initial transfer and this was the only place that I ever saw such an engine. Because of the potential volatility of the goods we were to transport, there was a requirement that no two loaded wagons could be marshaled consecutively anywhere in the train. This meant a prolonged period of shunting to ensure that when we departed, we left with an empty wagon leading, followed by a loaded wagon then another empty and so on. I was only too happy to shunt away for as long as it took (I was young and enthusiastic then!). Fred then took over and we retraced our route back to Severn Tunnel Junction where the train would be re-marshaled as required for its onward journey. Then it was back to Ebbw light engine and after we left our steed with the shed men to be fed and watered, Fred offered me a lift home. I gladly accepted as, all shift, Fred had been singing the praises of his Volkswagen Beetle that he had purchased new many years before. Apparently, it was reliable, economic, comfortable, easy to drive, well designed and engineered etc. etc. We jumped in, Fred turned the key and yes, you guessed correctly, it failed to start. The look of astonishment on Fred's face was a wonder to behold. When I finished laughing, I thanked him for an interesting day and walked home.

On one occasion I was allocated a turn with a driver on a special train from Newport docks to Hereford. We were surprised at this because we had never known a contract that required a trainload of locally imported goods that went to Hereford as a final destination. We arrived at Alexandra Dock Junction with a class 47 and discovered that we were to take a trainload of apples to the Bulmer's cider factory at Hereford. The apples were not exactly pristine and were loaded in open wagons previously used for coal. We could smell the rotting fruit from our loco and when we arrived at Hereford, our guard, who had travelled in his brake van at the rear of the train, looked very pale. He said that the smell had drifted back towards him all the way and that he would never drink cider again.

Most rail freight complexes required their own allocated shunting engines to make up trains for mainline locomotives to take away. These were normally the small low-speed and low-geared class 08 diesel locos. However, in the late 1970s and early 1980s, Oakdale colliery would have a class 37 allocated for such work. Most train work to and from collieries was straightforward enough. The train crew would take up a train of empty wagons and return with loaded. These were called out-and-back workings. However, the situation at Oakdale and Markham collieries was a little different. While most of our work to these collieries was indeed out-and-back, due to the requirement for frequent additional movements of coal wagons between Markham and Oakdale and the need for additional local shunts at Oakdale, every weekday a class 37 was allocated to be available there for over 12 hours per day. This involved three sets of train crew. The first would book on duty at 07:10, take a train of empties to the collieries, then shunt as required before eventually being relieved by the second set of men who had booked on duty at 10:45 and travelled up the valley to Oakdale on a public bus. The first set would then catch a bus back to Newport to book off duty. The second set would then carry on with trip or shunting work and later in the day be relieved themselves and travel on a bus back to Newport. The third set of train crew who had booked on at 14:40 and had also travelled to Oakdale on the public bus service would then complete any outstanding shunt or trip working and finally take a loaded coal train down the valley before booking off duty. It was common enough for traincrew to travel by passenger train either before or after working their own trains but this was the only case I ever knew of where traincrew regularly travelled on a public bus.

9E61 was the headcode of one of my favourite trains, even though it never left Newport!

The freight-only branch line that ran from East Usk sidings adjacent to the South Wales main line to Uskmouth Power Station was only a few miles long but provided rail access to numerous industrial plants and factories along its route. These included Stewarts & Lloyds iron and steel tube works, Lysaghts Orb iron works, Monsanto Chemicals, British Aluminum and finally Uskmouth power station. It was the job of 9E61 to provide a daily set down and pick up service of wagons in and out of these works as required. The outward train would be formed up by a class 08 shunter at AD (Alexandra Dock) Junction sidings and then 9E61 would trundle its train the grand distance of four miles to the first siding at S&L Then wagons were detached, shunted and attached as necessary and the same process was carried out at all the other works sidings en route to Uskmouth. This was a time-consuming undertaking but when finished we would return with a train made up of various different types of wagons back to AD Junction. We had been working all day, covered a distance of less than ten miles and not ventured outside the boundary of Newport. Our loco normally allocated to this epic railway extravaganza was ironically one of the fastest and most powerful locomotives then in operation on Britain's railways: the one and only class 53, D0280/1200 'Falcon'. Its 100 mph maximum speed and 2,880 horse power output was totally wasted on a train with a maximum permissible speed of 25 mph and weighing never more than several hundred tons. The reason for this was simple; most of our freight wagons were then only fitted with vacuum operated brakes and by the time Falcon came to us, it was equipped for air-braked trains only. This meant that the only brake available to the driver of E61 was the loco's straight air brake. With little brake force, only a low speed is safe and this resulted in the class 9 headcode.

'Falcon' was eventually broken up in 1976 at Cashmore's, a local Newport scrapyard.

Also situated on the Uskmouth branch line at that time was a railway siding that served a dock on the east bank of the river Usk that handled Bell Line container ships from Ireland. I only once worked a train to this little used railway siding and when we arrived with a short train of empty wagons for containers off the boat, we could see that there were none on the quayside ready to be loaded onto our train and what's more there was no ship in the dock. We made enquiries and were told that the ship could not berth, as the tide was too low. So, we just waited for hours for the waters to rise. We did not object as it was a Sunday and we were being paid overtime rates! Sadly, the ship eventually docked, our train was loaded and we headed off to the local freightliner terminal, which was then sited at Pengam, Cardiff.

We worked a lot of trains loaded with iron ore imported through Newport docks. Some went to Ebbw Vale steel works and consisted of small grey-black rounded pellets. The iron ore that we transported to Llanwern steel works looked completely different. It was rusty red-brown in colour and comprised of small rocks down to dust. The trains to Ebbw Vale departed from Mon (Monmouthshire) Bank sidings and were hauled by a class 37 locomotive, with another class 37 banking from the rear, and ran with headcodes 9A84 and 9A85. The trains to Llanwern departed from AD sidings and were normally hauled by either a class 47 or two class 25 locos running in multiple. These trains were referred to as Cycle 1 and Cycle 2 and ran with headcodes 9A86 and 9A87. On one occasion, my driver was again, coincidently, Pat Kearney and we were working 9A86. I was pleased that Pat had put me 'in the chair' of our two class 25s. We had the maximum permitted load and I struggled to even get the train out of the siding. Then we joined the up relief line where the gradient was against us and we simply came to a halt. Pat's experience told him that there must be a brake dragging somewhere on the train so I jumped down to walk back and check. I didn't have to go far! I soon discovered that the straight air brake was still fully applied on our second loco; I had forgotten to release it after coupling up and before changing ends in preparation for our departure. Pat was forgiving which surprised me a little but it was another lesson learned.

A never to be forgotten experience occurred during my early career at Ebbw with a loaded coal train, this time when coming down the Eastern Valley. Trains that had only the locomotive brake available were classified as class 9, limited to 25 mph and depending on the gradients en route, could be notoriously difficult to control. Prior to entering sections of the route with steep falling gradients these trains would stop and the guard would start manually applying the mechanical brakes on the leading wagons with a brake stick while the train was slowly moving forward. In this way the guard could ensure that although the brake blocks were applied firmly against the wheels to help the driver keep the train under control when it proceeded onto the falling gradient, they would not be applied with so much pressure as to cause the wheels to lock and skid as this could cause damage not only to the wheels on the wagon but also to the rails en route. When the driver considered that the guard had applied a sufficient number of wagon brakes, he would signal to the guard accordingly by sounding the warning horn and with the train still slowly moving forward, the guard would then rejoin his brake van at the rear of the train. At the bottom of the gradient the driver would stop the train and the guard or the secondman – if agreed beforehand – would release the wagon brakes and then the train would proceed having safely negotiated a steep falling gradient section of the line. On this particular day, this maneuver had been successfully completed and we joined the main line heading south at Llantarnam Junction. Away we went and although we had already safely negotiated the steepest falling gradient on our route others, normally less formidable, lay ahead. Unfortunately, my driver underestimated these and we were soon rattling along at an abnormally high speed. Although this was no more than 40-50 mph it soon became apparent that the train was out of control and effectively a runaway despite the full application of the locomotive brake. I and my driver – who shall remain nameless – both new that we were in deep trouble and unless our signals ahead were at green we were heading for potential disaster. I opened the cab door in preparation to jump and awaited events. Luckily, the signals were all clear and eventually my driver managed to regain control of our train with a change of gradient; however, the brake blocks on the locomotive were smoking heavily and the wheels were red-hot. (My only other personal experience of a runaway train came much later in my career and is described in Chapter 14.)

There were several instances of runaway trains locally during my time at Ebbw Junction. One of the most spectacular occurred on 29th January 1975 at Marine colliery with its very steep falling gradient departure sidings, when 37 143 ran through the trap points that protected the Western Valley line and rolled down the embankment and almost into the river Ebbw below before eventually stopping on its side. There were major engineering logistical problems in the recovery process and it remained in this undignified position for so long that I thought that it would have to be cut up on site. However, on the second attempt on 4th August, it was dragged back up, eventually repaired and remained in active service for another 24 years before it was eventually exported, and like many other elderly Brits, spent its twilight years in sunny Spain.

Can you have the opposite of a runaway train? Well yes, in a way. My driver and I were bringing a loaded train slowly down the branch line from Oakdale Colliery one night with our normal class 37 when I heard my tea-can on the hotplate start to spit indicating that the water was boiling and that was my cue to make the tea for us both. My mate kindly switched on the cab light so that I could do the job properly and not scold myself in the dark. I made the tea to my usual high standard, poured out a cup each and we started to gossip. It was some time later that I sensed that something wasn't quite right. I looked forward but in the dark and with little or no artificial light in that part of the valley all I could see was my own reflection staring back at me as the cab light was still on. So, I dropped my side window and discovered that the lineside bushes were not moving past, as they should have been. We had stopped! My driver had not touched the controls since I had made the tea and as the falling gradient had eased slightly, the brake pressure he had previously set had been enough to very slowly and without a jolt bring us to a halt. I advised my driver of my discovery and he simply said okay, turned the cab light off, released the brake and we started to rumble forward again into the night. How long we were stationary we never found out. We completed our journey and nothing more was said. It was like that in those days – very relaxed!

During this period, the output from British collieries was being reduced and those in South Wales were no exception. Pits were going to close and thousands of miners would be made redundant. It was argued that home produced coal was too expensive for the power stations, in particular, and consequently more and more coal was being imported including through the ports of Newport, Cardiff and Barry. The price per ton for this coal was indeed less (even though some of it had to be transported halfway round the world) because it came from open cast mines. However, I do not believe all the implications and full costs were taken into account including:

- Redundancy payments
- Unemployment and welfare benefits
- Tax and national insurance contributions no longer being collected
- The devastating effect on local economies with less goods and services being purchased
- Redundancy costs in the supply chain services
- Retraining costs
- The impact on the UK balance of trade

If all these factors had been included in the final calculations and our home-produced coal received the equivalent in subsidy then former mining towns and pit villages would have flourished for many more years. Numerous areas of the South Wales valleys, like many other former mining areas of the UK, have still not fully recovered from this period of economic madness.

There was at least one beneficial legacy from the wholesale closure of the pits in South Wales and that was a remarkable improvement in some areas of the environment. The river Ebbw is only about 20 miles long from its source north of Ebbw Vale to where it joins the River Usk at Newport immediately before it flows into the Severn estuary. At one time, it was notorious as being the only river in the UK to be officially polluted from almost its source to its mouth. As a boy, I remember it being totally devoid of life and running with different colours depending on which industrial activity was taking place further up the valley. Black with coal dust was the most common but, on some days, it ran a very dark orange colour with iron ore residues caused I believe from the steel works at Ebbw Vale. Today, however, the river is totally transformed. Salmon and trout are among the fish commonly found in its clean-flowing waters. Many types of fauna and flora are now also reaping the benefits of this river that now make it such an attractive feature of the Western Valley. Slag heaps too have not only stopped growing but many have been landscaped and some now blend in with the natural surrounding hills as the greenery of nature takes over. The scenic Cwmcarn Forest is a good example of this process and is well worth a visit if you are ever in the area.

Didcot Power Station was then coal fired and its rail infrastructure was primarily designed to deal with trains arriving from the Nottinghamshire, Leicestershire and South Derbyshire coalfields. Loaded MGR trains would arrive, slowly move along a long gently curved circular siding, discharge their coal automatically through doors in the bottom of the wagons into a pit and a conveyor belt would then transfer it to the stockpile. So, in theory, a loaded train could arrive, unload and depart without stopping as no wagons or the locomotive needed to be uncoupled. However, I think that this rarely if ever happened as there could be a problem with the wagon doors or conveyor belt in the unloading shed or the driver could be due a PNB. But when MGR trains approached the power station from the west, the locomotive either had to run round, unload and run round again prior to departure or an assisting pilot loco would need to be attached to the rear of the train on arrival, haul it 'backwards' through the unloading shed and then detach. This procedure resulted in the original locomotive and train then being in the right direction to depart with the empty wagons. Ebbw Junction crews worked many of these trains from Barry, Cardiff or Newport docks; however, they normally involved a total of three locomotives. The train engine, the Didcot pilot as described above, and, in order to get these heavy trains up the 1 in 100 gradient on the English side of the Severn Tunnel, an assisting locomotive would be coupled in front of the train engine for tandem working and then be detached at Stoke Gifford (now better known as Bristol Parkway).

It was on one of these trains that I experienced my longest ever shift. For various reasons, we were running very late and when we finally arrived at Didcot we had to wait our opportunity in the queue while other trains were being unloaded. Eventually it was our turn but the signalman then told us that the Didcot pilot had broken down and he did not have the capacity for us to run round. So, we waited and waited. We were stationary at the same red signal for eight hours before a replacement pilot loco was found to deal with us. By the time our train was unloaded and we took the empties back to Newport, my driver and I had each been on duty for a total of 16 hours.

During my time as a secondman/assistant driver at Ebbw Junction, I ran a football pools syndicate for several years. This was well before any national lottery came into operation and betting on the outcome of football matches with either Littlewoods or Vernons was the best option for the light gambler. I collected 50p per week from the other eight members of our syndicate that included drivers, guards and other secondmen. Our betting always consisted of trying to forecast which football matches would end in a draw. The maximum prize would be shared out between those who predicted which eight games resulted in a tie. Of course, the more matches that ended without victory to either side the lower the prize money would be. To make life easier for me and my fellow gamblers to check the results, I would put the appropriate number of x's in the same numbered boxes every week irrespective of who was playing who. For us this had nothing to do with predicting results but just a matter of luck, in a similar way that the lotto operates today.

One Saturday I was at home checking our coupon as the results were announced on the BBC and I couldn't believe how our randomly selected numbers repeatedly coincided with drawn games. We had eight out of only nine. I knew instantly that this would result in a massive pay out. I told Anne that we had won big time on the 'pools' but then had to wait for the five late results to be announced knowing that the first prize would reduce with every additional drawn game. Sadly, and unbelievably, four of the five outstanding results were also draws. While I still received a substantial cheque from Littlewoods, by the time I had divided it by nine it was certainly not the life-changing amount it would have been had none of the late results ended in ties.

Anne and I were married on 27th July 1977 and after a few years thinking that things were reasonably settled, we tried for a baby and sure enough Anne became pregnant. It was then that our landlord, who was an alcoholic and lived in terrible conditions on the ground floor below us, died. His family, who inherited the property, wanted to sell it and we were asked if we would buy it. We knew that even at the comparatively low price we could expect to pay, bearing in mind the overall condition of the property and the fact that we were tenants, there was no way we could contemplate such a purchase as my gross pay for the tax year 1979-80 was just £3,825 and so we had to move out. We would have become homeless were it not for our GP who kindly wrote to our local council outlining our position and the possible health implications for Anne and our yet unborn baby. We were offered a council flat three floors up on the huge housing estate of Bettws, Newport, and we immediately said yes, thank you, and moved home on 26th April 1980.

The best day of my life occurred on 6th July 1980 when I watched as Anne wonderfully gave birth to our son Gareth. He was perfect and healthy in every way and although I have never taken any illegal drugs to give me a high, the euphoria I felt at that time would I believe have surpassed any artificial stimulant whatsoever. I have never experienced such a feeling of overwhelming joy and relief, before or since.

But a little over three months later was to be one of the worst days of my life when I was declared redundant. In the meantime, I had the daily commute from our home in Bettws to Ebbw Junction Diesel Depot to contend with at all times of the day and night. This was a distance of a little under five miles. During the day it was two bus journeys each way but at night I had to walk. On some shifts I would catch the depot's mini bus service that ran occasionally between the depot and Newport railway station but was notoriously unreliable so, rather than risk being late on duty, I rarely used it on the outward journey.

The experiences I had and the insights that I gained while at Ebbw Junction would prove invaluable later in my career. I learnt that drivers had to have detailed knowledge in three key areas:

1. **Rules and regulations –**
   Drivers were, and still are, required to have an in-depth knowledge of all the relevant rules to ensure the safe operation of their trains. The rulebook and its appendices are substantial and detailed documents covering all aspects of train operations and drivers are subjected to periodic rules examinations to ensure that their knowledge is thorough and up to date.

2. **Traction faults and failures –**
   Drivers have to ensure that their train is fit for service by carrying out all the necessary safety checks before bringing it into operational service. Further, should a train defect occur en route, the driver is required to go into 'fault finding mode' by diagnosing and if possible, rectifying the fault to minimise delays as far as possible.

3. **Route knowledge –**
   This is probably the least understood but most important aspect of the driver's role. He/she has to have a detailed and thorough knowledge of the route on which they are travelling including the location and type of all signals en route, diverging routes, maximum permitted speeds, gradients, braking points, tunnels, bridges, level crossings and, of course, stations. Sections of line that are prone to possible low rail adhesion must also be taken into consideration.

# 4

# Redundancy

It was less than 18 months after Thatcher became prime minister in 1979 that my world was turned upside down. I reported for duty as normal at Ebbw Junction Diesel Depot on Tuesday 21st October 1980 and was immediately informed by the timekeeper on duty that there was a letter for me and, very unusually for those days, I was asked to sign for it. I did so and when I opened the large brown envelope and read the heading I was completely stunned. It was my redundancy notice! It came completely out of the blue. My local union rep just happened to be in the office at that time and he too was shocked. The timekeeper, who was simply acting as a postman, advised me that he had just received a total of seventeen such envelopes (eleven for the most junior drivers and six for the junior driver's assistants) and mine just happened to be the first he had been able to deliver. When I had recovered a little, I went to see my Local Manager, Gerald Guard, who, after taking one look at me, told me to sit down.

"Whatever is the matter Steve?" he said.

In reply I simply said "This," and passed him the envelope.

He read the first few lines and said to me, "Are there others?"

I replied that there were another sixteen identical envelopes awaiting collection.

"I know nothing about it," he said, which I believed as he had a reputation for being a reasonable manager and I could detect that he was upset at being put in such a difficult and embarrassing position. He had clearly been given no advance warning from more senior management that some of his staff were about to be made redundant. He picked up the phone and called the man who had actually signed my redundancy notice, Jenkins, the Area Manager. I could only hear one side of the conversation when my line manager explained to his boss that I was in his office with my redundancy notice. He didn't say another word on the phone; he just looked blankly at the receiver and put it down.

"Did you hear what Mr. Jenkins said to me?" he asked.

"No," I replied.

"Well after I explained the situation, he just said, 'Oh well, that's life' and then hung up. You know the more I work with that man the less I understand him."

And that was it. I was simply not required any more.

A rumour then started that the area manager would receive a bonus for every redundancy notice he issued. This was probably not true but the fact that it spread so rapidly and some of my colleagues believed it to be genuine tells you all you need to know about staff morale and the downbeat atmosphere that pervaded the depot at that time.

The redundancy notice advised me that I could select any one of the three options listed.

1. Take the redundancy payment on offer and quit the industry.
2. Accept demotion and revert back to a traction trainee's position.
3. Apply for another driver's assistant job at any British Rail depot in the country that was then advertising such a vacancy.

Option one was totally out of the question as I was now 26 years old, married with a three-month-old son at home and our little family was totally dependent on my regular income so, full-time employment was essential. I didn't even bother to calculate what the pay off would be because I knew it would be minimal and the prospects of other employment in the near future were extremely poor as the UK unemployment figures during that period were breaking records almost every time they were published – thanks to Thatcher's policies.

Option two I knew would only be a very temporary solution, as other more senior driver's assistants at Ebbw who were also being made redundant would simply replace me and force me out.

Option three almost certainly meant moving to another part of the country and my experience of this in the past was not one that I wanted to repeat. However, if we were forced to move away, I knew that Anne would be totally supportive and willing to give it a go. I also knew that thanks to previous ASLEF negotiators, a generous financial package was now available to someone in my position who moved home to fill an essential vacancy in the same grade at another depot.

I had seven days to pick an option and return the form. The redundancy notice also advised me that if I had any questions, I was entitled to a personal interview with a British Rail manager who specialised in such matters. Further, I was allowed up to three days leave with pay and rail tickets for me and my spouse to visit other depots that were then advertising vacancies to help us choose which depot, if any, I would apply for.

After talking it over with Anne, we decided that I should request the interview on offer and get some answers as we had cooked up a cunning plan that, if it worked out, could be our salvation. So, I applied for the interview only to be told that because the relevant manager was so busy dealing with the high numbers of redundant staff my interview could only be arranged after the closing date for returning my option form! This was clearly nonsense and I told my local manager this in no uncertain terms. He was forced to agree and eventually it was arranged to postpone the date for me to return the option form and likewise for my other redundant colleagues who had found themselves in the same position.

Ironically, just two days after I had received my redundancy notice, I found myself standing on an unofficial picket line at Ebbw with my redundancy notice in my pocket in a vain attempt to prevent even more redundancies at the depot. Drivers based at Barry were being allocated to trains running to Ebbw Vale and these trains had traditionally only been crewed by staff based at either Ebbw or Aberbeeg depots. So, when an Ebbw driver had been disciplined by being sent home without pay for refusing to pilot a Barry driver to Ebbw Vale, we all walked out as per our union's local branch policy.

I was aware that if I opted to move to another depot to maintain my grade, I would be entitled to receive the generous financial resettlement package so, when I eventually had my one-to-one interview with the redundancy manager on 4th November, I asked him what I thought was a relatively simple question. As I have been made redundant, if I applied to move to another depot to fill a **driver's** vacancy would this be classified as promotion with the resultant much reduced financial assistance package when compared to the entitlement I could claim if transferring simply to retain my grade of assistant driver? I argued that if I moved depots and consequently my home and my family only because British Rail had made me redundant in the first place, I should be entitled to receive the benefits that would apply to a transfer whether on promotion to a driver's post or simply to keep my current grade. He said that he didn't know but would make a couple of phone calls in an attempt to answer my query. To be fair, he did just that and when we reconvened, he said that if I were to transfer to fill a driver's vacancy within the Western Region, I could probably claim the larger amount; however, outside the Western Region then almost certainly not. I thanked him but explained that "probably" was not an appropriate word on which to base my future career.

Anne and I chose to visit three depots: Hitchin in Hertfordshire and Birmingham New Street, that were then both advertising drivers' vacancies, and the only depot on the Western Region apart from Severn Tunnel Junction that was then advertising a driver's assistant's vacancy – Westbury in Wiltshire. We soon discovered that although Hitchin appeared to be a nice area and the type of train work would have been acceptable, the cost of a reasonable house in the town would be unaffordable even on a driver's wage as we had nothing saved by way of a deposit and we were then living in council accommodation and consequently had no house to sell.

Anne felt uneasy in Birmingham partly due to the language barrier! She had a strong Welsh accent and trying to verbally communicate with local people who naturally had an equally strong Brummie accent was difficult for both parties.

Our visit to Westbury town centre left us totally unimpressed. Looking for somewhere to eat, we came across a fish and chip shop that was closed for lunch! The town had, and still has, very little to interest a visitor. It was reasonably well known for two significant landmarks, the carved White Horse on the hill overlooking the town from which there are beautiful views and the since demolished Westbury cement works chimney. However, its rail infrastructure belies its size. Being situated on a junction of the Western Region where the east–west main line from Paddington to Penzance line meets the north–south line from Bristol to Southampton in addition to its substantial freight marshaling yards, Westbury clearly was and indeed still is a significant railway junction with many additional passengers changing trains.* The two local limestone quarries of Merehead and Whatley situated a little south of the nearby Mendip Hills had increased production year on year and as the bulk of their output was transported by rail, more trains and consequently more train crew had been required. Westbury as a rail hub was clearly 'on the up'. When we visited the depot, I asked to see the seniority list because any future promotion or potential redundancy was dependent on an individual's place on the list. When I examined it, I noticed that a line had been drawn between two dates with their respective names and that my seniority date would place me exactly on this line. I asked the friendly supervisor on duty at the time what was the significance of the line. His answer then settled the next 37 years of my career.

"It's simple," he said "above drivers and below assistant drivers."

These few words had a huge effect on me for I instantly realised the implications† and that the cunning plan that Anne and I had previously hatched may be indirectly achieved. If I were to transfer to Westbury as a driver's assistant, I would undeniably be entitled to the significantly larger financial assistance package and yet would also be the very next to be eligible for a driver's position with the substantial

---

* Today Westbury station has an average of 124 passenger trains departing in addition to over 34 timetabled empty stock train movements in every weekday 24-hour period. For a town with a population of about 18,000 this is a significant number of trains. When all the freight train comings and goings are also added, Westbury station is never quiet for long.

† There were also implications for all the names on the seniority list that would then be below mine when I successfully applied for the Westbury job. The person most affected was Howie Reynolds who was next in line to become a driver until I jumped the queue when I transferred into the depot. However, Howie, being the kind of guy he was, did not hold a grudge – at least not for long! In fact, we eventually got on very well, became friends and at one time we both served as reps together on the LDC. Ultimately, Howie retired before me but we are still on each other's Christmas card list, (Luv u lots!)

increase in wages that went with the post. It was a win–win situation for me and my family. It was a good plan but it did not work out quite as well as we had hoped.

After talking over the options with Anne the very next day, I submitted my redundancy notice option form. My first choice was Ebbw. (This was known as a clause 14a transfer and had to be listed if I wanted to keep open the option of returning to Newport should a future vacancy occur. Later, however, I would cancel this preference.) My second choice was Severn Tunnel Junction as, although this would mean commuting a far greater distance, I would not need to uproot my family and move home. My third choice was Westbury. As expected, other more senior redundant colleagues were to beat me to a position at Severn Tunnel Junction; so, Westbury it was and I officially transferred on 15th December 1980.

My rate of pay as a driver's assistant at this time was £64:80 per week and, as I would transfer to Westbury in the same grade, this basic salary would remain similar until I became a driver. I thought that this would happen relatively quickly. However, I was wrong.

# SCHEMATIC RAIL MAP OF WESTBURY CIRCA 1980
## (Not to scale)

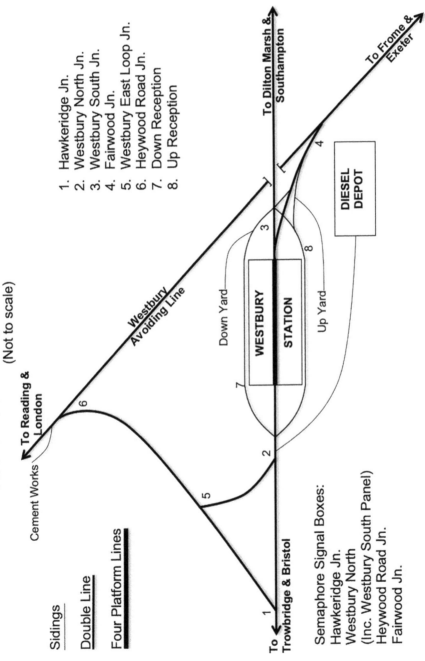

1. Hawkeridge Jn.
2. Westbury North Jn.
3. Westbury South Jn.
4. Fairwood Jn.
5. Westbury East Loop Jn.
6. Heywood Road Jn.
7. Down Reception
8. Up Reception

To Dilton Marsh & Southampton

To Frome & Exeter

Westbury Avoiding Line

To Reading & London

Cement Works

Sidings

Double Line

Four Platform Lines

DIESEL DEPOT

Down Yard

WESTBURY STATION

Up Yard

To Trowbridge & Bristol

Semaphore Signal Boxes:
Hawkeridge Jn.
Westbury North
(Inc. Westbury South Panel)
Heywood Road Jn.
Fairwood Jn.

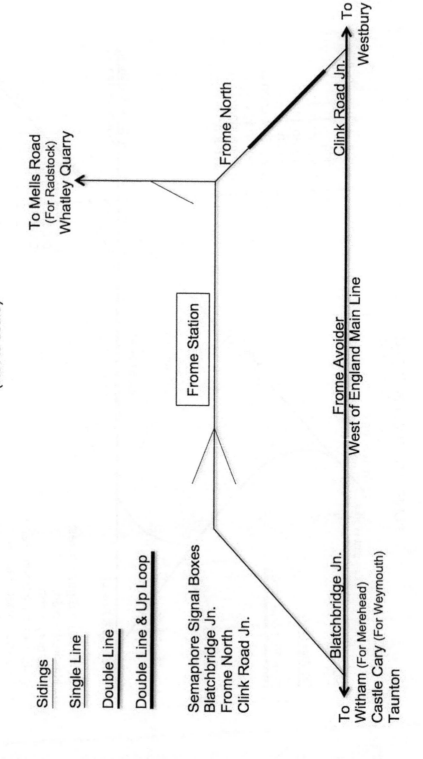

SCHEMATIC RAIL MAP OF FROME CIRCA 1980
(Not to scale)

To Mells Road
(For Radstock)
Whatley Quarry

Frome North

To
Westbury

Clink Road Jn.

Frome Station

Frome Avoider
West of England Main Line

Sidings

Single Line

Double Line

Double Line & Up Loop

Semaphore Signal Boxes
Blatchbridge Jn.
Frome North
Clink Road Jn.

Blatchbridge Jn.

To
Witham (For Merehead)
Castle Cary (For Weymouth)
Taunton

# 5
# Westbury

On 15th December 1980, I officially transferred from Ebbw Junction Diesel Depot to Westbury, less than two months after receiving my totally unexpected redundancy notice. I was forced to move into digs and found a place on Station Road that was, as its name implies, convenient for the station but had little else to recommend it and so when, occasionally, both the start and finish times of my shift allowed me to do so, I would commute by rail to and from my home in Newport on a daily basis.

In an effort to socialise and make the acquaintance of at least a few of my new colleagues, I would occasionally call in at the British Rail Staff Association (BRSA) club that was then situated immediately opposite the entrance to Westbury station. As you would expect, the club served a large range of beers including the then popular Worthington E bitter. One day, as I stood at the bar, two drivers came in and the first ordered drinks for them both by saying to the barmaid in a strong local accent,

"E for E and E for I!"

I have disliked the Wiltshire/Somerset accent ever since.

My first job with a Westbury driver on 16th December 1980 involved taking a loaded train of limestone from Westbury to Botley in Hampshire where each wagon would be individually discharged and then we would return to Westbury with the empties. We had loco 45 062, one of the longest and heaviest diesel locos then in service with British Rail. At Newport, most of our coal or iron ore wagons were fitted with the old-fashioned vacuum brake and were limited to a maximum speed of 45 mph; however, many of the stone trains in the Westbury area used the more modern air brake wagons and were permitted to travel at 60 mph. And so it was that on my very first journey from Westbury, I found myself hurtling south at the breakneck speed of 60 mph and while this was normal for my Driver Jim Rainer, it scared the shit out of me! I later found out that Jim had a reputation for being one of Westbury's slower drivers so heaven help me, I thought, when I have to work with one who is in a hurry.

As we were then living in a council flat in Newport with no savings, we asked the local Wiltshire authority if there was any council housing available. We were advised that because I now had employment in their area, we were entitled to be placed on the waiting list but that no realistic time scale for a house or flat could be offered and so we set about looking for private accommodation either to rent or even to buy at the very bottom end of the market. Then, out of the blue, we had a letter from the local authority advising us that two roads of council subsidised private houses were being built near Melksham, Wiltshire, and as we were on the waiting list, we would be considered as potential buyers if we were interested. We were so desperate for a home of our own that it was only after we replied positively that we found out where Melksham actually was, as we had never heard of the place until then.

After lodging for six months alone in Westbury, the three of us moved into a brand new two-bedroom terraced house in Melksham. We were over the moon to be together again, having a home of our own and a regular income with no realistic prospect of future redundancy. Thanks to the council subsidised price, we paid the builder £15,555 for our house and even though this was well below the genuine market price at that time, we knew it would be a financial struggle to pay the mortgage as interest rates were high.* However, we took heart from the fact that I would be the next driver's assistant at Westbury to undergo the official driver-training course and if all went well and I was appointed to a driver's position, I would receive a substantial pay increase. However, there was an intermediate stage that I had to go through. If I passed the MP12 course, as the six months driver-training period was called, I would then automatically become a relief driver. This meant that while my usual role would remain the same, i.e. as a driver's assistant, I could be promoted on a day-to-day

---

* They were to reach over 15% by the end of that year.

basis should there be a driving turn uncovered and provided I had the necessary route and traction knowledge. As it turned out, I would be a relief driver for nearly five years while waiting for the next driver's vacancy to occur at Westbury.

I needed some form of transport to get me the ten miles from our new home in Melksham to Westbury. Although I had a driving license, we certainly could not afford to run a car so, planning in advance, I bought a small Honda motorbike during my final weeks at Newport. Due to the maximum speed of my 50 cc bike being less than 40 mph, it meant that almost every other vehicle on the road would overtake me. Wind, rain and the slipstream from passing lorries made for perilous commutes. But my worst journey by far occurred during the second week of January 1982 when record low temperatures were recorded locally. One night on my way home in the wee small hours, I almost froze to death. To this day I am convinced that if my bike had broken down in the Wiltshire countryside, I would have not survived. As it was, with temperatures lower than -15 degrees Celsius (-19 was officially recorded in the nearby Wiltshire village of Lacock) combined with the wind chill factor and poor protective clothing, I was suffering from hypothermia by the time I arrived home. Hardly able to get off the bike, I struggled into the kitchen, just about managed to remove my gloves and put my hands under running warm water. Bad move! The pain when the feeling eventually started to come into my fingers was horrendous and as for my toes, I'm surprised that I still have any! Eventually in August 1985, we bought a car, an Austin Allegro to be precise and although it was never voted car of the year by anybody, it did the job of getting me to work in the dry and the warm. Much later, in 1996 in fact, Anne, Gareth and I moved to a house in Westbury and this proved far more convenient when travelling to work. My commute, if I rushed, was then a 20-minute walk but I would always allow 25 or even 30 minutes if I had some bread to feed the ducks on one of Westbury's several lakes.

In 1983, Westbury employed 106 drivers and 46 driver's assistants and, like all depots Westbury, had its share of characters. However, unlike any other depot on earth, we had Driver Ken Butt. He was a one off. His well-deserved reputation was second to none and his antics became legendary. He would embarrass us young'uns by sitting on our laps and serenading us in the messroom. Then he might put on his roller skates (he always kept a pair at work of course) and play darts. Performing on his unicycle was another favourite. Yes, Ken would always put on a show. Unlike everyone else, he didn't have a locker, he had what was, in effect, a props cupboard. From play fighting with oversized boxing gloves to a selection of masks, Ken was always well-equipped for his next prank. Waiting passengers might look up as their train came into the platform and be shocked to see a gorilla driving it! I booked on for duty one day and was not surprised to see Ken performing one of his favourite stunts, hanging upside down from the doorframe of the messroom. He was always very fit and agile for his age. Ken was an unabashed and unique showman. He would lay spread eagle on a messroom table some days just to demonstrate to all his skydiving technique. It was inevitable that one day he would go too far. That was when he decided to put on a mask and pretended to hold up the pay office. He got away with it (not the wages) – how I don't know.

There was no sign of Ken at the depot one day when I was in the messroom and a set of 'foreign' traincrew came in for their PNB and we started chatting. I could not help but notice that they seemed a little anxious and looked up every time the door opened. Eventually, one of them said to me

"Do you have a driver who plays darts on roller-skates?" (Ken's reputation was known far and wide though not everybody had directly observed one of his performances.)

"Oh, yes," I replied, "You must mean Ken Butt."

"Is he er ... all right?"

I knew he was asking if Ken was mentally sound but I pretended to take the question at face value and replied,

"Yes, as far as I know he's not on the sick." Other Westbury colleagues quickly confirmed that Ken was indeed not on sick leave. The foreign train crew just looked at each other, finished their tea and left. They must have been thinking, "They're all nuts at Westbury."

When the American-built class 59 locomotives were first named at a big and lavish ceremony at Merehead on 28th June 1986, to which we were all invited we were honoured by the presence of the then president of the United States of America the one and only Ronald Regan who went around waving to the crowds; or was it Ken Butt in a Ronald Reagan mask?

Ken was actually a very good engineman when he put his mind to it but over the years of knowing him, I got the impression that he found train driving, and indeed life in general, a bit boring so he would play the fool big time in an attempt to make living more interesting for himself and all those he came into contact with. Sadly, he apparently became something of a recluse after retiring but when he passed away, early in 2017, his local church was full and standing as relatives and former colleagues said their farewells. Yes, there was only one Ken Butt.

While Ken was unique, there were a few others at Westbury at this time who I am still able to recall, though often for the wrong reasons. "The Miracle of Westbury North" was an anecdote often retold and while it must contain some element of truth, it has almost certainly become enhanced with every retelling.

There was a certain member of the Westbury station staff (let's call him Ron – because that was his name) who was not often fully aware of passengers needs or indeed what was happening under his very nose at times.

As there was then no lift to the subway, when a wheelchair-bound customer needed to change platforms, station staff were required to escort them to the north end of the station and use the barrow crossing to access another platform or to exit the station. One day, Ron was pushing a wheelchair over the crossing when a train suddenly appeared on the scene because he had failed to check with the signalman that the crossing was safe to use. The first person to react was the elderly person in the chair who, seeing the train bearing down on him leaped up and ran for his life, leaving Ron holding onto an empty chair. Ron could apparently cure the disabled!

During the 1980s, there were frequent light engine movements from Westbury to Cardiff Canton maintenance depot. A day's work could consist of taking locos away for repair or when a major exam was due and returning to Westbury with replacements. Unfortunately, the class

56s were not as reliable as they should have been* and so trips to Wales for repairs were commonplace, sometimes towing or being towed by a class 37 or 47 or two and also often stopping off at Bristol Bath Road Depot to attach or detach one or two other locos. While this work was known as LDM (light diesel movements) and not without interest, the class 56 at speed would ride very rough over certain stretches of track, sometimes to an alarming degree.

Westbury Diesel Maintenance Depot was a very busy place, especially on the night shift when locos would be lined up waiting their turn to be refueled, have coolant topped and sand boxes filled. This was known as an FPX (Fuel Point Exam) that every loco that came 'on shed' would undergo as a minimum. The fueling point itself was uncovered but two sheds were available for locos undergoing repairs or more thorough servicing. When I was on the night-shed turn, both my driver and I would be in constant demand moving locos to and fro. I recall that, on several occasions, we barely had time for tea! A serious situation indeed. However, when, initially, the privately-owned class 59/0s and later the 59/1s locomotives were introduced, it resulted in a gradual decline on the maintenance workload at Westbury depot as the 59s were serviced and maintained at new purpose-built facilities at Merehead and Whatley quarries. Westbury depot gradually declined and effectively closed in 1993.

The biggest job I ever observed being undertaken by the Westbury maintenance team occurred on 9th April 1991 when a complete bogie was replaced on 50 049 'Defiance'. This may have been just a routine job at a major depot but for a small shed like Westbury it was a significant undertaking and I got the impression that the guys relished the challenge to demonstrate what technical engineering skills they were capable of. First a road low-loader turned up carrying a replacement bogie that had apparently come from previously withdrawn 50 016 'Barham'. Then a road crane arrived and was immediately set to work unloading the 'new' bogie and unceremoniously dumping it on waste ground. After the necessary bogie disconnections had been carried

---

\* As an example of just how unreliable the class 56s were at times, 56 048 broke down in service on three consecutive days during August 1983. I know because I was on board on every occasion.

out, hydraulic jacks were used to lift one end of 50 049 and the bogie was hauled out manually with cables. The road crane was then used to place it on the low loader and then lift the replacement bogie off the dirt and lower it gently onto the rails in front of 50 049. It was then manhandled into place and connected to the body. The whole operation was carried out without a hitch and was a credit to the maintenance staff involved who were normally never required to carry out such a heavy duty and technical operation.

Westbury Diesel Maintenance Depot closed during March 1993 as a direct result of privatisation. Initially and primarily due to the introduction of privately-owned locomotives and later post-British Rail when freight and passenger operations were split into separate businesses because the two companies could not agree on who would pay what for its running costs, despite the fact that both would have benefited greatly from a local maintenance depot and, if they had acted quickly enough, the basic depot infrastructure would still have been in place. It was a loss to the industry in general and a great loss to Westbury in particular.

On 24th March 1987 a head-on collision took place at Frome North junction. Both trains were manned by Westbury-based traincrew. The two trains involved were the 06:55 Yeovil Pen Mill to Cardiff Central (2B77) and the 07:08 Westbury to Whatley Quarry (6B03).

2B77 consisted of five vacuum braked coaches hauled by loco 33 032 and 6B03 had 30 air braked empty stone wagons with 47 202 leading. The Westbury signaller had cleared the signal for 2B77 to proceed, correctly giving it priority over 6B03 that was to be held at the signal protecting the junction. However, 6B03 failed to stop at that signal and the collision took place. Derek Masters and his mate Andy Noyes* on 33 032 saw that a collision was imminent and after making an emergency brake application, quickly left the cab for the comparative safety of the engine room. The driver of 6B03 also made an emergency brake

---

\* Andy was driving when the accident occurred and was praised in the subsequent Department of Transport report:

*"It was due to the alertness of Driver Noyes that the consequences of the collision were not more serious than they were."*

application but it was too late. The guard of 6B03 was in the front cab of the class 47 but managed to jump clear after being urged by his driver to do so. The driver himself was less fortunate as the impact then crushed the front of his locomotive towards the engine room bulkhead, effectively trapping him in the cab. It was three hours before the emergency services were able to release our badly injured colleague from the remains of his cab.

Fortunately, there were no fatalities. Fourteen of the fifty passengers on the Cardiff train were taken to hospital as were the traincrew but luckily none of them was seriously injured.

The cause of the accident was due to the fact that 6B03 had passed a signal at danger, although its driver later had no recollection of doing so.

Both 33 032 and 47 202 were deemed to be beyond repair. The 33 was cut up at Eastleigh Works later the same year but 47 202 languished for more than four years at Bristol Bath Road depot before finally being scrapped.

Later, Westbury Driver Trevor Bradley and I took 47 125 light engine to the site to assist in the operations to clear the line. We shunted one coach into sidings at Frome and while we were waiting for further instructions, I took the opportunity to enter the leading cab of 47 202 and was amazed by what I saw. I could not believe how anyone could have survived the impact. The driver's control desk had been smashed so far back into the cab that there were less than six inches between the power handle and the engine room bulkhead. There was only one possible area that the driver could have been to survive such an impact and that was on the cab floor behind the assistant driver's seat and it was from there that the driver was eventually freed.

We 'play around' with trains all day long and it is only when you see derailed and wrecked locos, coaches or wagons that you realise the potential enormity of what we are dealing with. The huge destructive forces of hundreds or even thousands of tons of metal travelling at speed and then derailing or colliding is a sobering thought indeed.

# 6

# Driver Training

Steve Truman and Mike Shields from Bristol, John Evans and Dave Douglas from Swindon, Nigel Miles, Rodney Selman and Mike Badger from Westbury, Mike Brinkworth from Gloucester, Phil Battishill from Plymouth and I all started our MP12 course together on 16th March 1981 at Bristol and, for me at least, it turned out to be the best six months that I was to ever experience during my 48 years on the railway. This was the official British Rail training course that had to be passed in order to become a qualified train driver. We were a good mix of distinctive characters that made for a favorable learning atmosphere. We all got on well with Traction Inspector Jim Machin our class instructor though there was one member of the class – isn't there always – who occasionally gave the impression that he did not want to be there.

I and another Westbury colleague, Mike Badger, soon created a reputation for being the awkward squad which I thought was particularly unfair as we just wanted to be thorough and sought clarification on all aspects of the topic under discussion. Everybody made their own individual contribution and we bounced ideas and interpretations repeatedly off one another. We all had some fun while still taking care of the task in hand. Mike Badger had a very wicked and dry sense of humour. He would come up with some brilliant one-liners that made me laugh out loud, although he would only gently smile at his own jokes and my reaction to them.

The first five weeks of the course involved learning all the relevant rules and regulations. Jim would often use blackboard and chalk to illustrate the operation of a particular rule that he was trying to get across to us and it was on one such occasion that fellow Westbury trainee Rodney Selman jokingly criticised one of Jim's matchstick-men type drawings.

"Well I'm no Picasso," said Jim in his own defense.

To which Rodney replied as quick as a flash, "You're no artist either."

I laughed 'til I cried. It still makes me chuckle even now when I think of it.

Rules were followed by three weeks of route learning, both theory and practical, that involved us all individually drawing, in great detail, the 44-mile route from Bristol Temple Meads to Taunton. Every line, set of points, junction, station, signal, speed restriction, gradient, bridge (under and over) tunnel, crossing, ¼ mile post, sound warning board, embankment, cutting and significant lineside feature had to be mapped, recorded and then retained in our personal training files.

Then from 18th May came traction training; we were to study the class 47 diesel loco until it became so familiar, we could recite its technical details in our sleep, not only which parts did what but also where they were situated, how they worked and what we could do about it if they failed. This became our 'basic traction' and every other type of diesel loco we were to learn later in our careers (and there were many) would consist of very much shorter conversion courses.

On 13th July, we started what was everybody's favourite part of the course – ten weeks of practical train handling, one of which had to be on nights. We were spilt up into pairs each with a traction inspector to mentor, guide and supervise us. I was very lucky as I was paired up with Rodney Selman who, from that day to this, has remained a good friend. Although at that stage we had only learned about the class 47, we were given free range on the types of trains and routes we could drive over – always subject to the booked driver's permission of course. In reality, they were more than glad to have a break while we took over temporary control of their train. So, our Traction Inspector Reg Fox, Rodney and I would have a different footplate experience every day. For example, on Friday 28th August, we drove from Bristol T.M. to Birmingham New Street and after some lunch and a stroll around the market, drove back to Bristol. Both were class 1 express passenger trains. I drove loco 46 026 from Bristol to Cheltenham where Rodney took over for the rest of the outward journey. Then we had 47 421 on the return trip and, again, we shared the driving. Other destinations, in no particular order, included Newton Abbott, Paddington, Exeter, Salisbury, Cardiff, Cheltenham, Reading, Weymouth, Weston-super-Mare, Taunton, Southampton, Old Oak Common, Eastleigh and Merehead. Traction types included the following classes: 31, 33, 37, 43(HST), 45, 46, 47 & 50.

On one occasion during our week of night shifts, while Rodney was driving, I fell asleep standing up. Rodney and Reg couldn't believe it as we were on a rough riding class 33 at the time. I was oblivious to everything including their evident amusement until I woke up in a state of shock when we encountered a particularly rough section of track, which they then found even more entertaining. Rodney, Reg and I would all enjoy these weeks. It was not hard work for Reg due to the fact that Rodney and I already had very many hours' driving experience under our belts, albeit unofficially, and he soon knew he could trust us to just get on with it.

It was during my driver training course that I gave up my digs in Westbury as Anne, Gareth and I were then able to move our family home from Newport to Melksham on 4th July.

Our MP12 class then reunited for one week to revise all we had studied and to learn from one another's experiences before going back to our respective depots at the end of September 1981. We returned to our driver's assistant's duties and awaited our final three-day exam. I was not allocated my test until the first week of December. Day one was a rules exam, day two consisted of practical class 47 traction knowledge including theoretical faults and failures and the final day was practical train handling. In my case, on day three, I was simply asked to drive a class 1 express passenger train hauled by loco number 50 034 named 'Furious' from Gloucester to Bristol TM. Luckily I passed all three parts (I felt like 50 036; 'Victorious'!) and so became a relief driver, which meant that while my normal role remained as a driver's assistant, I could be promoted to driver on a day-to-day basis if there was a driver's turn vacant that I could work. However, this could only happen if I had both the necessary route and traction knowledge, and also my rostered working hours for the day were within the relevant parameters. For us relief drivers, this meant the more routes we signed as being competent to drive over and the greater the number of types of locomotives we were qualified to drive the better our chances were of being promoted for the day with the consequential increase in pay. I quickly signed off the route to Cardiff as, naturally, this was very familiar to me together with some of the more local routes and, after I attended several traction conversion courses, I began to be allocated driving turns reasonably often.

As the years passed, in addition to the class 47, I later became qualified to drive the following traction types:

- 'Heritage' DMMUs (Diesel Mechanical Multiple Units)
- Class 143 'Pacer' units
- Class 150, 153, 155, 158, & 159 'Sprinter' units
- Class 08, 31, 33, 37, 50, 56, 59 and 60 locomotives

Likewise, over the years, my route knowledge also grew and at various times, I was qualified to drive over the following routes:

- Westbury to Cranmore, Merehead and Whatley quarries
- Westbury to London Paddington via Newbury or Swindon
- Westbury to Gloucester via Bristol
- Westbury to Cardiff Central/Canton via Bristol Temple Meads
- Westbury to Weymouth via Yeovil Pen Mill
- Westbury to Southampton Central via Redbridge and Eastleigh
- Westbury to Portsmouth Harbour via Southampton/Fareham and Eastleigh/Fareham
- Westbury to Brighton
- Westbury to Taunton via Bristol

# 7

# Driver Davies

I was now a qualified train driver and classified as a relief driver. My first official train driving turn occurred on 15th March 1982 when I was upgraded for the day and rostered to book on duty at 14:40, travel as a passenger to Cardiff and drive 6Z31 back to Westbury. I was now 28 years old and about to realise a dream. I am happy to report that all went well. My guard for the day was Pete Smart and we travelled to Cardiff Canton, had some refreshments and waited for our train to turn up from the oil refinery at Llandarcy. It duly arrived, I relieved the driver who I knew from my time at Ebbw Junction and after Pete replaced the taillight that had failed, we departed at 19:30. Our loco was 47 309 with a load of 10 air braked wagons with a maximum permitted speed of 60 mph weighing a total of 390 tons and officially classified as dangerous goods – all bound for Furzbrook in Dorset. We had to stop three times en route at red signals and were held in Severn Tunnel up loop for 33 minutes to allow passenger trains to precede us through the tunnel. We eventually arrived at Westbury at 22:10. I booked off duty and went home at 22:30 well satisfied that I had achieved a significant milestone. Coincidently, I was to drive train 6Z31 again the following day, this time with 47 243 up front.

From the date I passed my final driving exam (4th December 1981) to the day I was appointed to a driver's position (11th August 1986) I slowly expanded my route and traction knowledge.

The class 47 was my basic traction and I then qualified for other loco types as follow:

Class 08 on 18th May 1984 after a one-week training course
Class 56 on 25th May 1984 after a one-week training course
Class 33 on 20th July 1984 after a one-week training course
Class 37 on 29th September 1984 after a one-week training course
Class 59 on 23rd May 1986 after a one-week training course

After I was appointed to a driver's position, I also qualified to drive the following locomotive classes:

Modified class 47 901 on 5th November 1986 after a one-day conversion course
Class 50 on 6th February 1987 after a one-week training course
Modified Class 37 7/9 on 12th January 1990 after a one-day conversion course.
Class 60 on 27th September 1991 after a one-week training course.
Class 31 on 28th November 2003 after a one-week training course.
D.O.O. train operations on 11th November 1985 after a one-day briefing.

With regard to multiple unit trains, I passed out to drive the old BR DMMUs during October 1986 after a three-week training course. Then, from April 1988, my unit traction knowledge gradually increased as follows:

Class 155: Qualified 22nd April 1988
Class 150: Qualified 12th May 1989
Class 158: Qualified 6th May 1992
Class 153: Qualified 21st September 1993
Class 143: Qualified 8th June 1995

Later, all Westbury drivers were issued with a traction guide outlining the operational differences between class 158 and 159 units, following which we were also expected to drive the 159s that were then being hired in from SWT to help relieve the constant shortage of units on FGW/GWR.

On Wednesday 11th June 1986, I was upgraded for the day and worked two trips between Westbury and Merehead quarry. This was significant for me as it was the first time that I would be in charge of one of the new class 59 locos and it was also the first time I had driven a train under DOO conditions.

I booked on duty at 10:30 and was told to work 6B29, a train of empties that had previously arrived from Theale. The loco was 59 001 (later named 'Yeoman Endeavour') with a load of 31 wagons and a total train weight of 707 tons. I was then required to drive 6A22 back to Westbury with a 38-wagon train weighing 1,998 tons bound for Wotton Bassett.

My second trip consisted of more empty wagons that had started their journey at Eastleigh. This was 6V42, a 37-wagon train weighing 597 tons and the loco was 59 004 (later named 'Yeoman Challenger' and then renamed 'Paul A Hammond'). My last job of the day was 6A20 from Merehead Quarry back to Westbury heading for Brentford. It consisted of 43 wagons loaded with limestone and weighing in at a total of 2,282 tons.

It was not until 11th August 1986 that I automatically filled the next driver's vacancy at Westbury and then, at last, I officially became Driver Davies and on that very first day, I took a loaded stone train of 1,459 tons from Westbury to Fareham and returned with the empties. My loco was 47 220. The train was fully fitted, as were most by this time and although I had a guard in the back cab, I was all alone in the front as an assistant was not deemed necessary on this particular train because I was allocated a PNB at Fareham and the combined efforts of my guard and the Fareham shunter fulfilled all the safety requirements for shunting in the yard.

Unlike most other depots at this time, Westbury had non-progressive links. Historically a driver would start in the bottom link with local work and gradually progress up through the links based on his seniority. The top link normally took the longer distance, express and higher paid (mileage bonus) work. But at Westbury, the only significant difference in the links was route knowledge. While some routes were generic and applied to all links, e.g. Merehead and Whatley quarries, others that involved less work, e.g. to Cardiff, Gloucester, or Exeter, were link specific to ensure that drivers who signed for these routes drove over them more frequently in order to retain their knowledge.

The LDC placed me in driver's link 'A' and that required me to have the following route knowledge:

Westbury to Paddington via Newbury and Swindon
Westbury to Cardiff (inc. Bristol TM, Bristol Hallen Marsh, Cardiff Tidal sidings & Cardiff Canton)
Westbury to Southampton/Eastleigh/Fareham and Totton
Westbury to Gloucester via Bristol
Westbury to Whatley (including Radstock) and Merehead (including Cranmore) quarries
Westbury to Weymouth

Later I would also learn the routes to Portsmouth Harbour, Brighton, Bristol via Swindon and Taunton via Bristol.

When you signed the road, this included all potential destinations en route. So, for example, between Reading and Paddington you were expected to know the intermediate stations, yards and depots that included Slough, Langley, West Drayton, Hayes, Southall, Brentford (stone depot via Southall), Ealing Broadway, Acton and Old Oak.

My weekly rate of pay when first appointed to a driver's position was made up of the following:

Basic salary £133.20 (£3.41 X 39 hours)
I.U.P. £16.75 (Irregular & Unsocial Hours Payment of £3.35 for every shift worked)
V.R.P. £3.20 (Variable Day Rostering Payment of 64p for every shift worked)
Total £153.15 Gross.
Additional payments of £7.69 per day were made if you worked a train without a guard (DOO).
There were also enhancements for working overtime, nights, Saturday and most of all Sunday working – then paid at time + ¾.

Prior to privatisation, Westbury drivers, like those at many other depots, were multitalented in that they would drive both freight and passenger trains. Comprehensive route and traction knowledge, versatility and flexibility were the norm. For example, a Westbury driver could have carried out the following week's work during this period:

**Sunday:** Drive a multiple unit from Westbury to Weymouth to Bristol and then back to Westbury.
**Monday:** Drive a loaded stone train to Brentford, unload and return with the empties.
**Tuesday:** Drive a Speedlink mixed goods train from Westbury to Gloucester and back.
**Wednesday:** Shunt and re-marshal trains as required in Westbury freight yards with a class 08.
**Thursday:** Take a light engine to Cardiff Canton depot for repairs and return with two others.
**Friday:** Drive a class 1 express to Paddington and return with an empty stone train from Acton.
**Saturday:** A well-deserved day off!

My dad had said to me that one day he would like to experience a ride in the driver's cab and so I unofficially arranged for him to meet me at Cardiff Central station on 19th February 1987, as I was rostered to work the 10:55 from Cardiff to Bristol TM on that day. I thought that a run through the Severn Tunnel would be of particular interest to him. My train consisted of 47 410 with five coaches. Dad turned up, but much to my surprise so did a traction inspector with two trainee drivers! No problem, as this was still in the days of British Rail and so I explained to the inspector why my dad was in the cab and he didn't mind as long as I didn't mind him and the trainees also hitching a ride. So off we set with the five of us up front. It was all very relaxed and friendly; everybody got what they wanted out of the journey and we all went our separate ways at Bristol.

This would never happen today. I would have to ask dad to leave the cab when the inspector turned up. He would be obliged to report me for having an unauthorised person in the cab and then I would have been annoyed and refused permission for his trainees to ride in my cab. I ask you, which outcome is best?

Another example of the relaxed but practical approach to train driving under British Rail, when compared with today happened to me on 21st April 1989 when I was driving 2086 from Westbury to Weymouth with a 3-car 'Heritage' DMMU set number C 986. Three of the small stations en route, Thornford, Yetminster and Chetnole, were all request stops. These were consecutive stations situated on the single line between Yeovil Pen Mill and Maiden Newton. At that time, the guard would verbally advise the driver if passengers wished to alight at any of these halts and if not and there was no one waiting to join the service, the train was not required to stop. As I had not been advised that a stop at Thornford was required and there were no passengers waiting on the platform, I simply drove slowly through the station non-stop. However, before we reached the next station, Yetminster, the guard belatedly advised me that we had over carried a passenger for Thornford. So, when we stopped at Yetminster, I simply changed ends and drove the train the short distance back to Thornford for the solitary passenger concerned. Despite the fact that we were on a single line, there was no danger whatsoever with this unorthodox move as I had possession of the single line token. I then changed ends again and resumed our journey to Weymouth. Now what I have failed to mention so far is that I was being assessed by an inspector on this particular journey. Technically, what I did was against the rules, nonetheless I carried out this brief shuttle without any reference to the inspector who did not comment either way. It is true that we arrived into Weymouth a few minutes late but our Thornford passenger was happy and this was before the phrase 'customer care' had even been thought of. Again, this would not happen on the railway of today.

When I started driving freight trains at Westbury, they were nearly all fully fitted with a continuous brake throughout the entire length of the train, doing away with the necessity of a brake van at the rear, the exception being the occasional engineering train. The last class 9 train I drove was as late as 1989 when, on 11th February, I took 9Z11 from Bristol East Depot sidings to a permanent way engineering worksite east of Bath. My loco was 47 033 and the small train consisted of nine wagons weighing 356 tons.

When the class 59s first entered service in 1986, we were very impressed by their ability to haul with apparent ease the heaviest trains then running in the country. Loaded stone trains from Westbury heading south to such destinations as Eastleigh, Fareham, Botley or Totton had always required an additional banking locomotive on the rear as far as Warminster due to the steep rising gradients at the start of the journey. However, with a class 59 on the front, no additional loco was necessary. They would power these loads away without any obvious difficulty. Computer-controlled power output produced a wheel creep system called 'Super Series' and it was this innovation (combined with automatic sanding) at low speed that proved to be the perfect combination for starting away trains weighing up to 5,000 tonnes on some routes. Furthermore, the class 59s soon demonstrated an almost 100% reliability rate and the General Motors EMD engineers who initially accompanied the traincrew on all class 59 hauled services were justifiably proud of their product and hoped to sell many more locomotives in the UK – which they eventually did – the now ubiquitous class 66. The class 59 cab ergonomics were also excellent when compared to the other locomotives we were driving at that time.

Loaded trains were normally propelled out of the sidings at Merehead quarry in order to gain access to the single branch line that joined up with the West of England main line at East Somerset Junction. This maneuver was not easy as it involved propelling up a rising gradient combined with a severe curve. This resulted in the need for a second engine to assist the heavier trains out of the sidings. The maximum load for a class 59 unassisted was 3,774 tons; however, when assisted it was a little over 5,000 tons. If an assisting loco was also required to start the train away, it could be any one that just happened to be at the quarry at the time. It was very common for Foster Yeoman's own American built 'switcher' loco (EMD SW1001 'Western Yeoman II') to provide this initial assistance. When a train was ready to depart, the train brakes would slowly be released and, at the same time, the train engine and the assisting engine would power up. Very slowly, the train would start to move and both engines would then gradually increase power until both were at their maximum. The train speed then gradually increased and when its driver was confident that no further assistance was required, he would signal to the assisting engine whose driver would simply stop as the two locos were not coupled. The FY switcher was not permitted to operate outside the confines of the sidings as it was 'out of gauge' and did not conform to British Rail parameters. As shunting engines went, it was a giant.

Later, when the class 60 heavy freight loco came into service, they hauled some of our trains that had previously used either a class 56, a 47 or two class 37s in multiple. Not long after Westbury drivers had been trained on the class 60, I was at Merehead and the small group of staff present devised a little unofficial test just to see how powerful they really were. Could their performance match that of a class 59 when propelling out of the quarry? We agreed the switcher would not assist but would be in attendance and available if the class 60 failed to propel a class 59 load out of the sidings. The class 60 passed our little test with flying colours and although it was slow to respond when the driver opened the power handle, when it eventually did so, it could match the power and performance of a class 59. All of us who played a part in this little 'test drive' were greatly impressed as we were previously of the opinion that we would never see another engine that could match the class 59.

I think I am correct in saying that, during this period, the heaviest train in Europe hauled by a single locomotive was 7A09/7E62 or 7L44. (The headcode varied depending on the final destination of the first portion of the train.) It was one of our stone trains that ran from Merehead quarry to Acton in west London. This was a combined service normally made up of three loads ultimately bound for different destinations. Initially, running as a single train from the quarry, it would be divided on arrival at Acton sidings with each section then going forward as individual trains. The locomotive would always be a class 59 as it was capable of hauling a 5,000-ton train unassisted up gradients as steep as 1 in 132 that were encountered near Savernake between Westbury and Newbury on the Berks and Hants route. I drove this heavyweight many times and, while it did not always weigh in at the maximum permitted 5,000 tons, it was rarely considerably less.

On 14th September 1987, I drove 7E62 DOO from Westbury to Acton. My loco was 59 002 (then named 'Yeoman Enterprise') and the trailing load was 56 wagons equal to 101 SLU weighing a total of 4,527 tons. (At the time, this train was permitted to run at a maximum of 60 mph and not the normal 45 mph that a class 7 was usually restricted to.) I left Westbury at 04:50 with the power handle wide open and there it stayed for the next 53 minutes! Due to the gradients, lack of any relevant permanent or temporary speed restrictions and the fact that every signal I encountered was displaying a green aspect, the speed of my train did not reach 60 mph until I had passed Savernake and started on the descent towards Newbury.

All I was required to do for nearly an hour was to reset the deadmans/vigilance device pedal every minute with my foot. A chimpanzee could have been trained to do that! However, from Savernake to Acton, where I arrived at 07:40, I think that Mr. Teeny (for all you Simpsons' devotees) may have needed a little help.

I think that this is as good a point as any to thank fellow Westbury Driver Phil Marshman for saving my life.

On Christmas Day and Boxing Day, no trains ran but a few drivers were still required to be on duty 24/7 to ensure that stabled trains did not freeze up if the weather was extremely cold and also to act as security. Volunteer drivers normally covered these turns. Some drivers were happy to work over the Christmas period, as the enhanced payment for doing so was then substantial. However, if insufficient volunteers were forthcoming, a driver could be obliged to work either Christmas Day or Boxing Day or both and one year I was booked out to work on 25th and 26th December. Anne was not happy (and neither was I) as the Christmas holiday was always a special time for our family. Anne informed me that she would kill me if I worked both days and when I told Phil of my impending fate, he kindly volunteered to work on 25th in my place. Thanks Phil!

The heaviest freight train that I ever drove was on 26th November 1993 when I was working 7A09 from Westbury to Acton. My loco was 59 004 (then named 'Yeoman Challenger') and I had a trailing load of 50 wagons = 100 slu (640 meters) with a total gross weight of 5,065 tons. This was approximately 3,800 tons of actual limestone being taken from Wiltshire to London by a train crew of just one. It would have taken about 120 lorries to shift the same tonnage by road. As usual with these mega trains to Acton, this one was made up of wagons bound for three separate ultimate destinations. On this occasion, they were heading for Purfleet, Woking and Purley. I departed Westbury at 08:10 and arrived at Acton yard at 11:20 having been recessed in Woodborough loop for 16 minutes, stopped by a red signal at Reading West for 4 minutes and encountered a 20-mph temporary speed restriction due to a track defect. Oh, and there was fog all the way from Bedwyn!

While the total weight of a freight train was normally the limiting factor that any given loco could haul over a particular route allowing for the gradients encountered, the maximum permissible length of the train also had to be taken into account. For example, a locomotive may be able to haul 5,000 tons from Westbury to Acton but if that load is conveyed in wagons that exceed 100 single length units then it would be too long to be recessed in some of the passing loops en route.

During 1998, Westbury depot was allocated passenger train work to Brighton. Initially this was with class 158 units but later and then only briefly with two class 31 locos and coaching stock.* I was pleased at the prospect of driving trains to Brighton as I imagined the route along the south coast from Cosham would be as picturesque as the scenic section of line along the sea wall at Dawlish. Boy was I wrong! Not only was it a difficult road to learn that included 40 level crossings in the same number of miles, the only time the sea was visible was when passing by Shoreham docks, not particularly picturesque. Having said that, I enjoyed driving trains over the route, as it required great concentration due to the complexities along the line and the great number of trains operating over the West Sussex coast. I never found driving the Brighton line to be tedious.

Later, when we were involved in working trains to Brighton under the Wessex Trains franchise, our uniform included the option of a pink

---

* On 23rd January 2004, the two class 31 locos working 1098 to Brighton didn't quite get there. They both ran out of fuel at the same time at Southwick just five miles short of the terminus. This resulted in a total of over 2,000 minutes of delays, 23 full or part train service cancellations, the cost of several buses and taxis, overnight accommodation in London for some Eurostar passengers, plus £2,467.50 to hire in a class 73 and its driver to haul the train back to Salisbury for fuel.

tie. I made sure that I always wore mine when on the Brighton run as it gave the opportunity for my southern brothers and sisters to pull my leg when I joined them in the messroom and that helped to create a good-humored atmosphere. The traincrew messroom at Brighton station was upstairs just off the concourse adjacent to platform 1 and it was here that we were diagrammed to take our PNB. Late running or not, I always insisted on taking a PNB not only because I needed at least a short break from driving with the opportunity to relax a little, partake of food and drink and to use the toilet facilities but my experience as a driver's rep had also taught me that if a driver was later involved in any form of serious incident, the resulting enquiry would always initially focus on the following:

- Was the driver sufficiently rested after his/her previous shift?
- How long had he/she been on duty before the incident occurred?
- Had a PNB been taken?

To deliberately forgo a PNB could be detrimental to a driver's career.

There were two particularly memorable events that took place while I was in the messroom at Brighton. The first occurred when, after a late arrival, the supervisor came in when I was drinking tea and asked me if I intended to depart on time, in other words cut short my PNB. I advised him that I would not. Within five minutes he was back to tell me that if my train did not depart on time, my unit would be blocked in by a terminating Southern train service and consequently my departure would be very late indeed. My single word reply, which seemed to astonish my guard, was "Whatever". I then explained the reasoning behind my actions or rather inactions to my train crew colleague who then better understood my position.

On the second occasion, the same supervisor, poor fellow, again interrupted my PNB to advise me that my train was on fire! (Staff based at Brighton had little to do with diesel units, as most trains on their patch were electric third rail powered.) I told him I doubted that very much as I always stopped the engines immediately on arrival, not only to save fuel but mainly to reduce noise and diesel fumes within the station complex. However, to double-check, I strolled out to the top of the stairs from which a panoramic view of all the station could be obtained (see photograph). Sure enough, there was my class 158 unit belching out black smoke from underneath its two coaches. I immediately recognised the cause. The diesel fuelled pre-heaters had automatically cut in but within seconds, as I expected, they stopped again and the smoke trailed off. Within less than a minute I had returned to the mess room and told the supervisor not to worry as I had put the fire out!

## I MISS THE ENGINE AND COACHES
### Dedicated to Jim Lanfear *(See note 1)*

I compiled the following just for a bit of fun after the loco and stock workings from Bristol to Weymouth finished in 2004. These trains were always crewed by staff based at Westbury.

I hope that all the notes help to make sense of the story.

I miss the engine and coaches;
I didn't think I would,
But when I stop and think of it,
They really were quite good.

I know that on the bad days
The engine might just stop
Or the coaches may be faulty,
Not clean and need a mop.

But after all is said and done,
I know you will agree,
At least it was a real train
Unlike a 1-4-3. *(see note 2)*

We leave Bristol Temple Meads
8:30, dead on time,
The 'Sand and Cycle Explorer', *(see note 3)*
I'm glad the weather's fine.

Our first call is at Keynsham'
We stop without a jolt.
Here Joe Winter may get on; *(see note 4)*
Next stop is 'Howie's Halt'. *(see note 5)*

8:49 we're at Bath Spa.
Wild children piling on.
Then Alfie waves his old green flag. *(see note 6)*
A cloud of smoke – we're gone. *(see note 7)*

See the flasher at Bathampton. *(see note 8)*
The signal not the man!
Then it's up the valley Limpley Stoke *(see note 9)*
At 60 when we can. *(see note 10)*

Bradford's starter is at red; *(see note 11)*
We must avoid a SPAD *(see note 12)*
And stop before the signal post
Or Spiller will be mad. *(see note 13)*

The junction signal is now green;
Around the curve we slow.
Arrive right time at Trowbridge.
All on? Then off we go.

The platform's full at Westbury
So, Jackie can't be seen. *(see note 14)*
The train is really filling up
With kids eager and keen.

Dave James gets on and Alfie off. *(see note 15)*
He's had enough of this,
But Margaret Maughan is after him *(see note 16)*
And Howie with a kiss. *(see note 17)*

The RA is pressed at 9:18; *(see note 18)*
Next port of call is Frome.
More passengers are waiting;
There can't be much more room.

Dash down the bank at eighty; *(see note 19)*
Bruton's coming fast.
It's time to brake full service
Or the station will be passed.

Now 'Sticky' passes on the up. *(see note 20)*
He too is dead on time
With a 1-5-0 from Weymouth; *(see note 21)*
It's the 8:39. *(See note 22)*

Next stop now is Castle Cary,
The feather we require *(see note 23)*
Then we're on the single line;
Hope the engine won't expire.

Yeovil Pen Mill has not changed;
The signalman we've woken.
We're in the land that time forgot
As we collect the token. *(see note 24)*

Thornford, Yetminster and Chetnole
We stop at on request. *(see note 25)*
Then down the hill from Evershot
The brake we have to test. *(see note 26)*

Coasting into Maiden Newton
At 15 miles per hour
We stop, give up the token.
Still no sign of a shower.

Some get off at Dorchester
But many more entrain.
Passengers now have to stand;
Can we take the strain?

Now Jamer's working up a sweat
And that's a rare event
But he's selling lots of tickets,
Commission heaven sent.

As we near Upwey station,
Our first glimpse of the sea!
Buckets and spades are gathered up;
Kids can't contain their glee.

So, we arrive at sunny Weymouth;
Our journey is now done.
The invasion of the beach begins
To laugh and play and run.

We've been right time all the way
And so, deserve to boast,
It's 80 miles from Temple Meads
To the southern coast.

All the way the sun it shone,
Each signal was at green,
No problems were encountered;
A journey quite serene.

The perfect trip? Of course, you know,
It's not what it may seem.
You could never have a run like that –
You've guessed – it's just a dream.

Yes, sad but true, the 37s
Have passed their sell by date, (*see note 27*)
The coaches have seen better days –
The train we love to hate.

But after all is said and done,
I know you will agree,
At least it was a real train
Unlike a 1-5-3 (*See note 28*)

## Notes:

1. This is a tongue-in-cheek reference as Jim Lanfear was a Westbury driver (now sadly passed away) who strongly disliked driving this type of train compared to the more modern 'Sprinter' diesel multiple units.
2. A class 143 diesel multiple unit had a bad reputation with traincrew for its poor ride quality, due to the fact that each coach had only a single axle at each end and not the normal more modern arrangement of twin axle bogies and air suspension. Their original build quality and ergonomics (improved after refurbishment) also left much to be desired.
3. Introduced in 1996, the 'Sand and Cycle Explorer' ran during school holidays and was designed to relieve overcrowding on the regular service trains to Weymouth – with their very limited cycle accommodation – and to encourage day trippers to use the train and not their cars. On days when the weather forecasters had predicted good weather, the train would be very popular indeed.
4. Joe Winter was the Westbury-based Conductor Manager who lived in Keynsham and frequently commuted to Westbury on this train.
5. Howie's Halt was the nickname commonly used by Westbury traincrew when referring to Oldfield Park station as Westbury-based driver Howie Reynolds (now retired; see also note 17) lived nearby.
6. Alfie Borg: originally from Malta, was a Westbury-based conductor who

had a volatile temperament and a famous zero tolerance for passengers who wanted to put their bikes on his train. Consequently, he was frequently asked for reports following some incident or another that he had become embroiled in.

7. Not actual smoke but excessive diesel exhaust that the old class 37 loco-motives were prone to produce when powering away from stations and even more pronounced when the engine was started from cold.

8. A flashing yellow signal on the approach to Bathampton Junction indi-cated to the driver that the route had been correctly set and the train may proceed through the junction but at the reduced speed of 40 mph.

9. The Limply Stoke Valley incorporates the River Avon, the Kennet & Avon Canal and the rail route from Bathampton Junction to Bradford (on Avon) Junction.

10. 60 mph was the maximum permissible speed over this section of line for all trains other than 'Sprinter' diesel multiple units.

11. The signal controlling the section of line between Bradford Junction and Trowbridge.

12. Acronym for Signal Passed at Danger; Normally as a result of driver error.

13. Ken Spiller: Popular Driver Manager based at Westbury.

14. Jackie Crease: Then Westbury station supervisor.

15. Dave James: Then a Westbury-based conductor and local staff representa-tive. Frequently the conductors work schedule (diagram) for the day would indicate relief at Westbury – though the driver usually worked through!

16. Margaret Maughan: Then Westbury-based conductor and, at times, acting Conductor Manager.

17. Westbury driver and, for many years, a local staff representative, Howie Reynolds was one of the great railway characters. Always clowning around including his panache for randomly hugging and kissing his colleagues – both female and male!

18. The RA or Right Away is a signal provided at some stations to indicate to the driver that all station work has been completed and that the train can safely depart. (They are now in less common usage as most trains are fitted with guard / driver communication equipment.)

19. "The bank" is a reference to the steep falling gradient (1 in 81) called Brewham bank (named after the long closed Brewham signal box between Witham and Bruton). However, the steepest gradients on the route are encountered later in the journey. (The 1 in 50 between Chetnole Station and Evershot Tunnel and between Bincombe Tunnel and Upwey Station.)

20. 'Sticky': Weymouth and former Westbury driver Brian Stickland; another notable character.

21. A class 150 two car 'Sprinter' diesel multiple unit.
22. The 08:39 departure from Weymouth was a regular service to Bristol Temple Meads.
23. The 'feather' is a term commonly used by drivers when referring to a junction indicator signal that illuminates when a train is routed off the primary route.
24. Before any train can enter the single line between Yeovil Pen Mill and Maiden Newton, the signaller must issue its driver with a 'token' – a large key-shaped metal object designed to prevent conflicting train movements. This safety system has been in operation for well over a century.
25. Trains only stop at these three small and little used stations on request. Should passengers wish to alight they must advise the conductor who will then instruct the driver accordingly, and if passengers need to join a train, they can stop it by giving a clear hand signal to the driver as the train approaches at reduced speed.
26. A running brake test, i.e. an application of the brake when the train is running at speed to satisfy the driver that braking power remains adequate; it is a rulebook requirement under certain conditions.
27. Normally a dated type class 37 diesel locomotive was provided to haul this train.
28. A class 153 is a single coach diesel multiple unit designed for use on lightly used branch lines but due to rolling stock shortages, they were frequently drafted in for use on the main line with consequential over-crowding and passenger complaints.

# 8

# Train Driving Techniques

Officially there is only one correct way to drive a train and that is as the driver's company policy dictates. Right, having got that out of the way now let's have a look at the real world. For a start, while most companies have similar policies and the national rulebook must be the basic template, many now also have their own set of supplementary rules that take into account issues that may not apply to all train operating companies. These variations did not apply before privatisation as British Rail did not muddy the water and had a one size fits all when it came to rules and regulations. So, while a driver must operate his/her train within the rules, the actual technique employed by individuals may differ considerably. Only in extreme cases would a passenger notice this as most variations in driving skills relate to subtle use of the controls that would impact only marginally on their overall journey experience. However, freight train driving calls for a totally different approach when compared to the operation of passenger services.

Having had a great deal of experience of driving both freight and passenger trains, I have been asked which was the most challenging and my reply was that it would all depend on the specific circumstances. With regard to freight, the most significant factors are the total weight of the train, the brake force available to the driver and the gradients en route. Passenger train drivers need to concentrate more on speed, running to time and stopping distances. All drivers also need to have a thorough knowledge of the route and take into account the weather and railhead conditions etc. as these considerations are essential no matter what type of train is being driven.

### Freight train driving at Ebbw Jn.

The classes of locomotives involved were 08, 25, 35, 37, 45, 46, 47, 52, 53 & 56.

Officially I couldn't drive any type of train when I was based at Ebbw Junction Diesel Depot because I was not qualified to do so. However, I frequently did.

When I started in the industry, most freight trains in South Wales were either loose coupled or only had a vacuum brake head. A loose-coupled freight train is one that has only a brake on the locomotive at the front and the guard's brake-van at the rear and was classified as a class 9.

Driving such trains loaded with coal down some of the South Wales valleys was a skill if not an art that I never did fully master. Although the tonnages involved were considerably less when compared to some of the monster freight trains running today, their drivers had to have a 'feel' for the train and an in-depth knowledge of the route, paying particular regard to the changes of gradients. Too little power and the train would simply stop, too much and the train would soon get out of control and possibly become an unstoppable runaway.

Another important factor for the driver to take into account with any freight train that had a guard's brake-van on the rear was the necessity of starting the train very slowly and gently until all the couplings were taut, otherwise a huge snatch would be experienced by the guard in his brake-van that, unless the guard was holding on tight, could cause him injury and the driver's reputation to be damaged. Likewise, stopping the train also required skillful manipulation of the controls to ensure all the wagons' buffers came together gradually and as gently as possible. Of course, it was not only during the starting and stopping of the train that the driver needed to exercise caution but also during slowing down for restrictive signals or a speed restriction and the necessary acceleration afterwards. All drivers are different and some appreciated more than others the comfort and safety of their guard. A few were so heavy handed that guards would brace themselves for regular impacts en route but most would exercise a gentle driving technique so subtle that the guard may not be disturbed from his slumbers (only joking!) for the entire journey.

A crew of three was the norm at this time and consisted of the driver, his secondman and the guard who all worked as a team and assisted each other as necessary. Eventually this was initially reduced to two and today the driver is routinely the only traincrew member on almost all freight trains. Trains conveying certain dangerous goods are the exception.

Fully fitted freight trains, i.e. a goods train that has a brake pipe connection running the entire length of the train and is operable from the driving cab, were either vacuum or air brake and became increasingly common as time went by. This advance had a significant impact on railway operations as it meant that these trains no longer required a separate guard's brake-van at the rear of the train as its primary purpose had been to stop the rear portion should the train become divided during its journey due, for example, to a defective or broken coupling.

The proposed abolition of the traditional brake-van resulted in a significant industrial dispute as the guards considered this, correctly as it turned out, to be the first stage in an attempt to do away completely with guards on freight trains. A temporary compromise was found whereby, for fully fitted freight trains that did not require a brake-van at the tail end, the guard would be positioned in the rear cab of the locomotive where he could check that the wagons were following in a safe and proper manner and alert the driver if, for example, he observed fire, sparks, smoke or a derailed wagon on the train. It was during this period, when on one day we would have a brake van at the rear and the following day we may not as the train was fully fitted, that I was made to look a fool – again. Part of the secondman's job was to periodically look back along the train to ensure all was well. This was particularly necessary at the start of the journey, because when slowly departing from a siding, the guard would hand signal the driver's mate meaning that he had rejoined the brake-van and the train was in order to proceed. This was commonly referred to as the 'tip from the guard' and was essential as otherwise he may not be on board or there was a problem with the train in which case a red flag would be displayed. We were departing East Usk sidings in Newport one day with a train of loaded oil tanks for Ebbw Vale steel works when my driver asked me if I had got the 'tip' from the guard yet. I immediately realised that I had forgotten to check on this important procedure, quickly dropped my side cab window and looked back to the rear of the train. As soon as I put my head out of the window, I heard my driver laughing and immediately realised that he had played a practical joke on me as our train was fully fitted so we had no brake-van at the rear and the guard that I was looking for out of the window was actually standing behind me in the cab. He joined in the fun at my expense and gave me the 'tip' from about two feet away. I went bright red but had to admit that they had caught me out good and proper.

## Passenger train driving at Ebbw

This will be a short section, as I didn't do any – even unofficially. There was no passenger train work at Ebbw Junction during my time although, initially, we did work a parcels train during the night from Cardiff to Gloucester and back normally with a class 45 or 46. However, I do recall that on one occasion, we were waiting in the down goods loop at Pilning for a gap in the passenger services that would allow us the opportunity to pass through the Severn Tunnel and into Wales when my driver and I observed our points repeatedly moving to and fro but the signal remaining at red. As there was no in-cab radio communications in those days, I called the signalman from the signal post telephone who told me that he kept moving the points in an attempt to attract our attention as a Paddington to Cardiff service had failed west of Patchway tunnel and needed our assistance. We were to secure our freight wagons, detach our locomotive, proceed up the down main when authorised, couple up to the stricken express and tow it to Cardiff. What excitement for us freight jockeys! The first part went well but when we reached the down London, its driver informed us that his train was air braked but we had a vacuum brake only class 35 Hymek. What to do? The three of us started to scratch our heads as none of us had any experience in this situation before. I climbed in-between the two loco-motives and waited for instructions from either of the two drivers but none were forthcoming. Normally, I would have coupled our air brake pipe to the leading one on the class 47 but, as our Hymek didn't have one fitted, this proved to be difficult to say the least. So, in the end, I simply threw our screw coupling over the hook of the failed class 47 and we departed on a wing and a prayer. Luckily, the class 47's engine was still running so it could maintain the air brake pressures. Our plucky Hymek struggled with the load up the 1 in 90 incline on the Welsh side of the Severn Tunnel but going was not the real problem, it was stopping! Because of the differences in the two braking systems, the only brake available to my driver was the straight air brake on our locomotive. He had no control over the brake on the failed class 47 or any of the coaches. However, with a mixture of caution, experience and the class 47 driver assisting with the braking we successfully got the train to Cardiff despite the fact that no direct communication was possible between the two drivers. This was an unforgettable learning experience for me observing two skilled drivers dealing with a unique situation that neither had encountered before but handling as if it was an everyday occurrence.

My only other connection with passenger train operations while I was based at Ebbw occurred on 21st April 1980. I booked on at 01:00 spare and was advised that the Cardiff-based driver on the Swansea (Milford Haven?) to London Paddington sleeper service had been forced to isolate the DSD due to a fault and, therefore, an additional traincrew member was now required in the cab to satisfy the safety compliance protocols. The train was stopped on the mainline directly adjacent to the depot and I climbed aboard 47 547 and accompanied the driver all the way to Paddington via Gloucester after which I travelled back to Newport arriving at 09:30.

## Freight train driving at Westbury

The classes of locomotives involved were 08, 33, 37, 47, 56, 59 & 60.

The majority of our trains conveyed limestone from the quarries of Merehead or Whatley both in Somerset, for use in the construction and road building industries. These trains supplied many stone distribution depots spread throughout the south and south east of England including those at or nearby the following locations:

Acton (West London), Allington (Kent), Angerstein Wharf (Port of London), Appleford (Oxfordshire), Ardingly (West Sussex), Ashford (Kent), Banbury (Oxfordshire), Barking (East London), Bat and Ball (Kent), Botley (Hampshire), Brentford (West London), Chesterton Jn. (Cambridge), Chislehurst (South East London), Crawley (West Sussex), Dagenham (East London), Eastleigh (Hampshire), Fareham (Hampshire), Hallen Moor (South Gloucestershire), Harlow Mill (Essex), Hayes (West London), Hothfield (Kent), Luton (Bedfordshire), Banbury Road (Oxfordshire), Padworth (Berkshire), Purfleet (Essex), Purley (South London), Salisbury (Wiltshire), Theale (Berkshire), Thorney Mill (South Bucks), Tolworth (South West London), Totton (Hampshire), West Drayton (Middlesex), Woking (Surrey), Wolverton (North Bucks) and Wootton Bassett (Wiltshire).

This list is not exhaustive!

Some of these depots were only served by short-term temporary contracts such as that at Hallen Moor (see photo.) It was purpose-built solely to supply material for the construction of the M49 in connection with the Second Severn Crossing and was in use for only about a year from June 1993. Others were long-term and include, for example, the depot at Fareham that is still active today.

We were also involved with trains loaded with railway ballast from Meldon Quarry (Devon) that were normally destined for Tonbridge or Hoo Junction, both in Kent. A single class 33 or two in multiple, when heavier loads were conveyed, usually hauled these trains. Additionally, in our portfolio of work were tank trains to and from the oil refineries at Llandarcy in South Wales and Fawley on the south coast. Some liquid petroleum gas trains that were classified as dangerous goods were also manned by Westbury traincrew for part of their journey between Britton Ferry (South Wales) and Fawley.

Early on we also worked British Rail "Speedlink" services to Eastleigh, Bristol, Newport, Severn Tunnel Junction and Gloucester. These were normally lightly loaded trains hauled by class 47 locos.

Local work included tar or bitumen tanks to and from Frome and

Cranmore. To enable these wagons to be emptied of the now partially solidified tar, gas burners that were incorporated into the wagons had to be ignited to heat the tar to turn it into a liquid. This process produced some smoke and a considerable smell that was liked by some but loathed my many.

Other nearby sidings that were then serviced by Westbury train-crew included the wagon repair shops at Radstock, Somerset and the Ministry of Defence base at Warminster that received the occasional train loaded with tanks or other types of military vehicles.

Driver's load slips and, if necessary, Exceptional Load Certificates (No. 29973 forms) had to be issued to drivers prior to the commence-ment of all freight train journeys. He/she was then obliged to check these documents to ensure that the tonnage, brake force and length of the train were all within the prescribed limits for the route that the train was scheduled to take.

Speed limits were governed by the following: maximum permitted speed of the wagons being conveyed, line speed (this is the overall maximum speed over a given section of line) and both permanent and temporary speed restrictions that may be in place en route. So, for example, a loaded train from Westbury to Eastleigh with a maximum permissible wagon speed of 60 mph would initially not be able to achieve this speed due to the gradient and after slowing again for the 35-mph permanent speed restriction through the platform at Warmin-ster could then be required to reduce speed again to typically 20 mph for a temporary speed restriction because of a section of defective track, for example. Further restrictions could also apply if an Excep-tional Load Certificate was issued. For example, all 100-ton wagons had a route availability (RA) number of 10 but the routes over which they were to travel may have only been cleared for wagons with an RA number of up to 8 and so for reasons of safety, the permanent way civil engineer could impose additional restrictions that would apply only to these trains. Typically, this might be an additional 20 mph speed limit over a particular bridge. Given all these restrictions, the theoreti-cal 60 mph maximum was sometimes only achievable over short distances.

Initially, the trains that served Merehead quarry were made up of the smaller vacuum braked wagons but, with increase in demand, larger and more modern air braked wagons were required, the first of which to enter service at Westbury were PGA aggregate hopper wagons weighing in at 50 tons each when fully loaded. The maximum permissible axle weight of 25 tons had been reached. However, even more efficient wagons were introduced later that were 100 tons each when fully loaded. These PHA wagons rode on two bogies with two axles on each so the maximum axle weight of 25 tons was still not exceeded.

From a driver's perspective, while the air brake on the PGA wagons was very efficient being quicker to apply and release when compared to the vacuum system, the couplings between the wagons had not significantly improved and still consisted of the old-fashioned manual three link instanter coupling. However, the middle link of the three was now almost D-shaped, so that, when horizontal, made coupling/uncoupling physically easier and, when vertical, took up more slack thus reducing the maximum distance between a pair of buffers on any two wagons. Despite this marginal improvement it still meant that there was not an inconsiderable amount of slack between coupled wagons and the more wagons on the train the greater the total slack the driver had to contend with. Even though a brake van at the rear of the train was now a thing of the past, caution had to be exercised when starting and stopping freight trains. While heavier wagons were very unlikely to jump off the track and become derailed due to careless driving, snapping the couplings, especially if applying power before the last wagon brake was fully released, was a real danger. I know this from experience (see Chapter 12).

Driving very heavy and long freight trains required extremely careful train handling through some sections of line as the train could be traversing three different gradients simultaneously. The area through Hungerford was one such section that always stood out as being particularly difficult to negotiate without the weight of the train producing severe and repeated snatching of the couplings. This was a notorious 'black spot' as far as freight drivers were concerned. There were two, but both difficult, ways of safely negotiating this section of line. Either way, considerable concentration and forward planning by the driver was required.

Option one consisted of keeping all of the train's couplings taut by gradually applying full power just at the right time. But to achieve this, while at the same time ensuring that the maximum permissible speed of the train was not exceeded after passing through Hungerford, the train had to be braked and slowed a considerable distance beforehand. The other method was to keep all the couplings slack by the well-judged use of the brake. However, this method could result in an extremely slow transit through the Hungerford area. I tried both methods and came to the conclusion the first technique, if applied correctly, increased the likelihood of a smooth transit, but if you got the timing just a little wrong the severity of the resulting snatch would almost knock you out of the seat.

Some types of diesel electric locos would overload if the driver tried to apply too much power at low speed with a heavy trailing load. Class 37s in particular were well known for this characteristic. When the driver opened the power handle, the engine revs increased accordingly and the electrical power then generated was supplied to the traction motors on the wheel axles and would be displayed on the ammeter gauge in the cab. Too little and the train would not move, too much and an overload would occur resulting in a sound similar to a small nearby explosion. This BANG was the telltale sign of a heavy-handed driver. When an overload took place, the ammeter gauge would instantly drop to zero and the only way to regain power was to fully close the power handle, wait while the engine revs returned to idle and try again with a little less power to prevent another overload from taking place.

Acton yard in West London was a regular terminating point for loaded stone trains from Westbury and, consequently, a starting point for the returning empties. Combined loaded trains would initially terminate, be divided as necessary before setting off again to their various destinations. However, Acton itself was the final destination for some trains as it also had an unloading facility for stone trains. At Westbury we would frequently work this 'Acton stone' train and before the class 59s came into operation, we would normally have a class 56 or two class 37 locos working in multiple. We were required to shunt the wagons through the 'hopper house' and correctly position them over the pit so that when the wagon bottom doors were opened, the stone would fall into the pit and be taken away by conveyor belt to the nearby storage facilities. This called for some delicate maneuvering by the driver and good coordination by the shunter who was positioned in the hopper house, and would instruct the driver via a two-way radio system, or walkie-talkies as they were commonly known. During the last week of October 1981, I was the driver's assistant on the Acton stone for three days. Each day, I had a different driver but always with two class 37 locos. My first two drivers of that week were Fred Tucker and Dennis Shell and they showed me how it was done but the third (who shall remain nameless) made a right pig's ear of the job because, when he received instruction to reposition the train, he would apply two much power to our locos (37 224 & 203) and an overload would occur; instead of then waiting for the engine revs to reduce he would slam the controller shut and immediately open up again resulting instantly in another overload. To make matters worse, the two engines appeared to be producing slightly different amounts of power so that, on occasions, the leading one would overload but the trailing one would not and vice versa. The effect was that the wagons were banging and crashing in and out of the hopper house and the poor shunter was getting more and more exasperated as he tried in vain to verbally position the train correctly. Consequently, it took us far longer to unload the train than it should have done and by the time we got back to Westbury with the empties, we were on overtime ... Ah, it all becomes clear now!

On 24th September 1988, even though I was a fully qualified driver at the time, I was booked to act as assistant driver to Mark Peters who, ironically, was then a relief driver. Such rostering was not uncommon and all depended on the availability of drivers on the day. We were working a loaded stone train from Westbury to the distribution terminal at Wootton Bassett, west of Swindon but, in order to access this siding, trains from the west had to first pass through Wotton Bassett Junction, continue on the up main line to Swindon, run round in the sidings and then return to Wootton Bassett as there was no connection into the stone terminal from the up line. We had a full load for our class 56 locomotive and Mark was driving. He handled the train beautifully without us experiencing any snatches throughout the journey and so, as we were slowly entering the sidings at Swindon, he just had to say, "How's that – all the way from Westbury without a single pluck." But no sooner had he uttered these words of self-praise when we experienced a slight snatch from the train. This made us both chuckle until a few seconds later a more severe tugging was felt and then, almost immediately, we came to a shuddering and very abrupt stop. Our attitude changed in a flash from one of mild amusement to that of extreme concern, as it was obvious that something had gone seriously wrong. We both looked back along our train and saw a cloud of dust rising from several wagons that had derailed towards the rear of our train. Unfortunately, only the front portion of our train was in the sidings, the rear was still blocking both the up and down main lines. While Mark contacted the signaller, I grabbed the track circuit clips and detonators and rushed towards the rear of the train in an attempt to carry out protection but, due to the position of our wagons, I could only access the up main line at the rear of our train. Thinking anything was better than nothing I placed the clips on the main line hoping, correctly as it turned out, that the normal signaling system was still operating correctly and fully protecting our train so that there was no chance of any other train colliding with our wagons. When the dust had literally settled, we discovered that the cause of the derailment was a section of defective track in the siding. The rails had spread apart due to lack of maintenance as our heavy wagons had entered the sidings. Mark Peters was completely and correctly exonerated of any blame whatsoever by all concerned, except me, as I would pull his leg from time to time about his standard of driving!

In recent years, many freight wagons and locomotives have been fitted with the automatic buckeye coupling system that provides a far more rigid connection. As a consequence, the whole train handles almost like a single unit. This had been the case on passenger rolling stock for many years.

The train with the slowest maximum permissible speed that I ever drove on a main line was on Saturday 12th May 1990, when I hauled a train with 33 116 from Reading to Woodbourgh that included a small shunting loco that was operated exclusively by the British Rail permanent way department on engineering sites. 97 654 (previously PWM 654) had a maximum permissible speed of 20 mph and it was to be used the following day for nearby engineering work.

I drove my last freight train on 9<sup>th</sup> March 1995, as this was immediately before rail privatisation took place after which I would only drive passenger trains. The train consisted of 40 empty stone wagons from Westbury to Whatley Quarry hauled by 37 803 (see photograph). The headcode was 6Z82 and I departed Westbury down yard at 00:55 and arrived at the quarry sidings at 01:28. I returned to Westbury with 37 803 running light engine and arrived at 02:07.

## Passenger train driving at Westbury

Over the years, I have driven many different types of passenger trains at Westbury including

- DMMU – Various 'Heritage' classes
- DMU classes 143, 150, 153, 155, 158 & 159
- Loco classes 31, 33, 37, 47, 50

The first passenger train that I ever officially drove was on 2<sup>nd</sup> January 1987 when I drove a DMMU three car set number B472 on 2B79 the 06:15 departure from Frome to Bristol TM. These were old vacuum braked units and were also the only trains that required the driver to change gear manually. At the time, some of these trains were serviced at Cardiff Canton maintenance depot and one of our turns involved working the last train to Cardiff Central station then running the very short distance empty stock to the depot. After a PNB we would then prepare two or three serviced sets, depart early AM and run empty stock all the way back to Westbury where the units would be uncoupled and provide the first services of the day.

On one occasion, I had arrived at Canton and was driving my empty train into the depot building when there was a bang on my interior cab door that made me nearly jump out of my skin. I stopped my train now half in and half out of the shed and opened the door behind me to find a young man standing there. Before I had the chance to question him, he said, "Are we at Cardiff yet?"

I replied that Cardiff station had come and gone and that he should not now be on the train. He explained that he had fallen asleep and it was only the noise of heavy rain on the windows that had recently woken him.

I thought what rain? It was a clear night, but then the penny dropped. As all trains did at that time before entering the sheds, we had just slowly passed through the automatic carriage washing machine – hence the "rain". I told him to sit back down, continued to drive into the shed and then escorted our sleepy passenger to the depot supervisor's office. We explained the situation to him and, after we had all had a chuckle, the supervisor called for a taxi to return our erstwhile customer to the station.

On and off over the years at Westbury we drove not only multiple unit type passenger trains but also locomotive hauled coaching stock. Before the High Speed Train sets took over all the Westbury to London services, we regularly drove the 06:50 departure to Paddington – head code 1F15 stopping at Pewsey, Bedwyn, Hungerford, Kintbury, Newbury, Thatcham, Reading West and Reading. My first time was on 12th March 1987. The load was 11 coaches and my locomotive was 50 040 named 'Leviathan'. Sadly, it is no longer with us as it was scrapped in 2008. We departed Westbury three minutes later than advertised and then encountered two 20 mph temporary speed restrictions imposed as a result of poor track conditions. We were routed on the up relief (slow line) from Reading to Maidenhead and then we were stopped by a red signal for two minutes at Maidenhead. We arrived eight minutes late into Paddington at 08:51. I was content with both my and 'Leviathan's' performance with an arrival time of less than ten minutes late despite all of the delays en route.

In my final years at Westbury, I drove nothing other than 'sprinter' type trains and while their reliability had improved considerably since they were first in operation, they had also been modified in numerous ways particularly with regard to additional equipment in the cab.

Again, there was only one official way of driving these trains but individual drivers would implement their own methods and this was accepted provided that they kept within 'management-approved parameters'. As an example, it was considered that a train's speed should be reduced to no more than 20 mph at 200 yards on the final approach to a red signal. This company policy was considered by many of us to be only a recommendation but still a good guideline for trainee or recently qualified drivers but unnecessary for more experienced drivers – at least when rail conditions were good. I have, albeit accidently, been 200 yards from a red signal at 40 mph and still stopped in time although I wouldn't recommend it!

A classic case of an overzealous and unworkable management policy confronted my driver colleagues and me when the class 158 units were first introduced at Westbury during 1992. These trains have a higher maximum speed of 90 mph, are fitted with disc brakes and WSP (wheel slide protection) that is designed to operate in a similar way to A.B.S. (anti-lock braking system) on modern cars. Some manager or other who obviously had no understanding of the practicalities of train driving decided our services that were to then operate with class 158 units could be speeded up with running times between stations reduced. Notwithstanding the fact the majority of the route miles we encountered at Westbury did not have a maximum line speed of 90 mph and moreover where this speed was permissible it may not be achievable due to the frequency and short distance between station stops, drivers were instructed to use a new braking technique that was not only unworkable but, in certain circumstances, could be downright dangerous.

The drivers brake handle on a 90 mph class 158 operates in a similar way to that fitted to the 75 mph class 150. It has four positions that, put briefly and simply, operate as follows:

- Release. No brake pressure is applied.
- Step 1 brake application. Approximately 1 bar of air brake pressure is applied on all wheels.
- Step 2 brake application. Approximately 2 bar of air brake pressure is applied on all wheels.
- Step 3 brake application. Approximately 3 bar of air brake pressure is applied on all wheels.

- Emergency. Approximately 3 bar of air brake pressure is applied on all wheels but the brakes cannot be released until the train has come to a complete halt.

Unlike vacuum or air braked loco hauled coaching stock, there are no intermediate stages of brake application available to the driver. When driving a class 150, I would start braking in step 1 and, after a short delay, increase to step 2 and adjust my approach speed to a station stop by using only these two steps. If I found the brake to be more effective than average, I might even release the brake altogether to avoid stopping short and then try to bring the train to a gentle stop by using step 1 and release as necessary. I would use step 3 infrequently and then only if I had made a misjudgment and my approach speed turned out to be too fast. In this way, I would normally have step 3 'up my sleeve' in reserve. Some drivers would approach stations at a much faster speed than me and would need to use brake step 3 every time.

When drivers were initially trained on class 158s, driver managers were told that all drivers were required to adopt a new braking technique that went as follows:

Assuming the train was running at its maximum permissible speed, at a fixed and predetermined point on approach to a station stop, the driver must immediately select brake step 3 without pausing in step 1 or 2. Then as the train slowed, the driver must partially release the brake to step 2 and then immediately before stopping select step 1. What could be simpler, 3-2-1- stop. This would speed up services and WSP would ensure that deceleration would remain the same irrespective of railhead conditions. I and many other drivers never implemented this foolish policy. Our objections were firstly that the sudden deceleration resulting from the immediate selection of brake step 3 could result in any standing passengers losing their balance or send the catering trolley with its attendant flying down the centre aisle. Secondly, if the approach speed was even slightly faster than normal or the driver reacted just a little slower, the station could easily be passed and although WSP proved to be very effective, the stopping distance always increased, albeit marginally, when it operated. In short there was no margin for error and the drivers who initially did try to implement this crazy management decree must have been a bag of nerves wondering if their train would be able to stop at the next station or overshoot it. It took several station overruns before the inevitable management climb-down came about and a more realistic approach was introduced.

This example is one of many policies that management tried to introduce over the years to either save money or speed up services without thinking through the implications or even consulting with the staff involved.

In another chapter, I referred to the fact that when working for British Rail I had never been asked for an explanation for lost time during a journey. You may think that this should not have been the case, as drivers ought to be accountable when running late. Well yes and no would be my response as, believe it or not, individual drivers are seldom responsible for the late running of their train. Most delays are due to restrictive signals, temporary speed restrictions, train faults, infrastructure problems and now increasingly due to train congestion. Yes, you can have traffic jams on the railways too. For example, it is not uncommon for two or three trains to be held in a queue at their respective red signals all waiting to enter a station that is temporarily blocked by a train with a fault or one that is simply running late or awaiting train crew. All trains are allocated a 'path' in the timetable. That is, at a specific time, it should be at a specific location if running to the preplanned timetable and if only one train is running outside its programmed pathway the result can be that many other trains are delayed. This knock-on effect can play havoc with the timetable. The basic problem is too many trains trying to operate on too little track. So, while British Rail management understood all this and the blame game was not usually played, it is totally different on the privatised railway of today. Time is money and someone, somewhere has to pay someone else for any late running trains. So, if the cause of a delay to a train is not known or not admitted by either a train operating company or the infrastructure management company Network Rail, questions are asked. The traincrew are usually first in the firing line and I have known a driver to be asked for a written report before going home after a long and tiring shift to explain why his train lost one minute between two stations six or seven hours previously. Putting drivers under such pressure is unnecessary and the more they try to make up time or minimise delays, the more corners may be cut and that, in turn, could, potentially, have an adverse effect on safety.

Because the train operating company doesn't want to pay the bill or if they have to, they now want to allocate the cost/blame to a specific department or even a single individual, all the administration costs involved in the necessary detective work would, in many instances, be greater than the fine itself. This crazy system is typical of the way today's railway is run under the privatised franchise arrangements and does not help the passenger one jot.

All drivers attempt to run their trains on time though the first priority is not punctuality but safety. There are hundreds of reasons why a train may be running late and although a few minutes delay may be recovered before the train reaches its final destination, anything more than 5-10 minutes is usually impossible to recoup. On the other hand, reaching a station early is not only unnecessary, it can be counterproductive. For example, if my train is running ahead of time and is approaching Bristol Temple Meads, the chances are it will be held at signals before reaching the station as other trains running on time are still occupying my train's scheduled arrival platform or other trains are timetabled to proceed through Bristol's numerous junctions ahead of my train. So, to reduce the possibility of my train being brought to a complete stop by signals with Temple Meads station in view, it is far better to proceed at reduced speed from the previous station as this will increase the chances of running non-stop into Bristol. Passengers on board are unlikely to notice that their train is running 10-20 mph below its normal maximum speed but will always be aware, become concerned and possibly anxious that they may miss their connection or be late for work if their train is stationary for any length of time. I have used this argument on numerous occasions and while most managers who were former drivers accept this reasoning, others may not appreciate the logic and have accused me of delaying trains that are running behind mine. My tongue-in-cheek reply to that charge was always the same simple one, "I may be good but even I can only drive one train at a time!"

Some readers will be able to recall when smoking was still permitted in a few sections of a train. When a total ban was introduced, I still used to enjoy the occasional cigar and there was a brief period of time when, although it had been banned in all public areas of a train, smoking was still permitted in the driving cabs. I would fiendishly relish my cigar all the more knowing that the people behind me who were paying my wages couldn't smoke no matter how desperate they may be for a drag. I was aware that the smell of my cigar smoke would permeate almost every part of at least the first coach. The reason I knew this was that when someone locked themselves into the toilet for a secretive smoke, I would often be able to smell it in my cab. In later years, this occasionally included the smell of cannabis.

## Dealing with fatigue

Fatigue was and still is a major issue for all train drivers to contend with, especially when in charge of freight trains with comparatively lower maximum permissible speeds, over long distances and often at night. Shift work is common in many industries and the normal working time bands are considered to be 06:00-14:00, 14:00-22:00 and 22:00-06:00. Not so for train crew. Work schedules may require a driver to start work at any time of the day or night. At Westbury, almost all of our freight turns of duty and even some of our passenger turns could have been considered 'antisocial' with some exceptionally bad shifts. I recall we had one turn of duty that required the driver to report for duty at 03:33, then drive a loaded stone train from Westbury to Theale, unload and return with the empty wagons to Westbury. When I first worked this turn, I tried to treat it as a night turn and only go to bed on the completion of the shift. However, remaining awake until about 02:30 before preparing for work proved to be impossible and, like most others, I soon found that the best way of coping was to sleep in two shifts; after work from about 12:00 till 16:00 and again from about 22:00 to 02:00. Of course, drivers who had a much longer commute to work than I did found the shift even more difficult to manage. Also, the opportunity to sleep during such odd hours would very much depend on individual family circumstances. Personally, I found that working nights during the winter afforded improved opportunities for good quality sleep as it was frequently still dark when I crawled into bed and, since local kids were in school for most of the day and the weather was poor, they were far less likely to be playing noisily on the street below my bedroom window.

At the end of one seemingly never-ending week of nights at Ebbw, I got home at about 08:00 on the Saturday morning and decided that I would not go to bed then as it would be a waste of the day. So, I utilised the day usefully, watched 'Match of the Day' on the box until about midnight and then turned in, well and truly knackered. The next thing I recall was looking at my bedside clock that told me it was 4 o'clock. I thought that it must have stopped for some reason at 4 am It had not and was displaying the correct time of 4 pm I had slept continuously for 16 hours. So, I had saved Saturday but lost out on most of Sunday instead! I could have only slept for so long when I was younger as nowadays waking up in need of a pee is a normal occurrence.

While I believe that everyone's body clock is at least slightly different, we all naturally find the time most conducive to sleep is at night. There are the 'larks' who tend to rise early but then struggle towards the end of the day and the 'owls' who can't wake up properly in the mornings but are still full of life late in the day. When I was younger, I was an 'owl' but now the situation has reversed and I am often ready to get up before dawn but I now need to record 'Match of the Day' as I find myself nodding off when watching it live. (That's what Arsenal does to everyone!) However, I still need the same total number of hours sleep albeit during a different time window.

In certain circumstances, staying awake whilst train driving can prove a real challenge and experiencing a micro-sleep is common. This is a short, sometimes very short, period of uncontrolled unconsciousness and though potentially very dangerous when driving a road vehicle, it is less of a danger on the railway, the reason being that there are now so many safety devices built into the driving cab environment that unless the driver reacts in a prescribed and timely manner, one or another of the safety devices will activate an emergency brake application and the train will come to a sudden stop. However, this does not fully exclude the possibility of an incident occurring due to a driver's failure to concentrate on the task in hand as has happened on numerous occasions. Conversely, however, it is not possible to fully focus for 100% of the time for hours on end. If you did you would become mentally exhausted well before reaching the end of your shift. Circumstances will dictate the necessary levels of attention. For example, it's daylight, the weather is good, your train is on time and you can see nothing but green signals ahead so, in these favorable circumstances, it is time to relax a little and possibly glance sideways to admire the passing countryside. But then, when you start approaching a station or a complicated junction with the option of multiple signals, it is time to sit up, take more notice and fully concentrate on the task in hand.

On 12th December 1988, a multiple train collision took place near Clapham Junction during the morning rush hour that resulted in the deaths of 35 people and injury to hundreds of passengers. Anthony Hidden QC chaired the enquiry into this horrific event. The initial cause was found to be a wrong side signal failure. One of his many recommendations involved the strict control and reduction of excessive overtime by safety critical railway employees that was then commonplace on Britain's railways. This was a watershed moment for the industry and subsequently any such employee, including all drivers, have not been permitted to work a shift longer than 12 hours without the strictest safety precautions first being put in place and the company involved obliged to register all such breaches of 'Hidden' and the circumstances involved. Furthermore, safety critical workers must now have a minimum of a least 12 hours rest/off duty from the end of one shift until the start of the next and are not permitted to work 14 consecutive days. While the management of train operating companies have overall responsibility for restricting the hours of their safety critical employees to comply with the Hidden recommendations the individual employee is also obliged to advise his/her relevant manager should they believe that any such breach may occur. The railway trade unions too play an important part in the management of fatigue by highlighting the issue to a train operating company if they believe that the potential risk from fatigue is increased due to the proposed introduction of any inappropriate work patterns.

While this has greatly reduced the possibility of accidents attributed to fatigue, it has not eliminated them completely. Freight train drivers, in particular, are still vulnerable in this area due to the more unpredictable nature of their work and some poor conditions of service.

## Bad weather driving

Fog is a particular problem for train drivers. One minute you could be driving your train in bright sunshine and the next you can't see anything through the windscreen. Your train is running at its maximum speed between stations 'A' and 'B' when, without any warning, you hit thick fog that reduces visibility to almost zero. "Don't panic," you say to yourself, "I know this road like the back of my hand" – and you do, but fog is a great leveler. No problem, you know exactly where you are in relation to the next station and are confident that you will be able to cope. You look down to check the speedo and when you look ahead again, suddenly you don't know where you are. Your confidence has vanished in a flash and anxiety takes its place. What to do? Despite the restricted visibility, trains are expected to maintain their running times if the signals are green; after all that is one of the advantages that train travel is supposed to have over the car. Experience has told me the best action to then take is to close the power handle and select brake step one. Your speed will immediately start to reduce and then you can concentrate solely on picking up any passing familiar landmark. This could be a bridge, a signal, a level crossing a cutting or even an adjacent building. In an instant, you will then be confident again of your exact location and so you can either continue to brake or accelerate as appropriate. You may have lost a few seconds but so be it. The situation would be different if you were to encounter a yellow signal in thick fog. Delay is then unavoidable as you reduce speed considerably more than normal when straining eyes have to locate the red signal ahead.

However, the worst visibility I have ever driven a train in was not in fog but during a sudden but brief snowstorm in February 1996. I was just a few miles outside Weymouth when I experienced a short but very intense blizzard. Due to engineering work, my up train was actually running on the down line and the snow made me reduce speed more than would be considered normal. It was as if a huge white mottled sheet had been placed over my windscreen with the wipers having no effect. Visibility was effectively nil. It didn't last more than a minute but during that time it was very unsettling.

The night of 13th–14th February 1991 was abnormally cold with freezing fog and a severe frost. At 07:00, I found myself at Whatley Quarry with 59 102 waiting for the local ARC shunting locomotive to bring my train, 6A17 to Theale, from the loading sidings to the departure yard. However, the ARC engine could not move the 2,567-ton train as it was frozen to the rails! This was the only time that I ever came across such an occurrence. I was asked to assist with my class 59 and between us we managed to shift it.

Snow, frost, dew and condensation, not to mention those infamous leaves on the line, can all result in low rail adhesion. At most times it's predictable, based on the weather, time of year, ambient temperature, location and frequency of trains. I personally found that the time of year when rail conditions were normally at their worst was during the last two weeks of October and the first two weeks of November. But it could also catch you by surprise at any time. Heavy rain was not a problem, unless, of course, it caused flooding, as a downpour would wash the railhead clear of any contamination.

Certain sections of the line are well known as potential flood zones. Cowley Bridge Junction east of Exeter and the Chipping Sodbury tunnel area are both on the GWR main line and notorious for such problems. However, a blocked culvert or suchlike can also cause similar but far less predictable problems at almost any location.

During early 2014, the Somerset levels were flooded due to repeated heavy rainstorms that caused the local rivers and their drainage channels to become totally overwhelmed.

The main line between Bridgewater and Cogload Junction east of Taunton was closed completely in February but, during the previous month, I drove several services from Bristol Temple Meads to Taunton and back and what surreal experiences they were. For several miles, the track ran on top of an embankment through the flooded country-side but none of the usual farm animals or even their fields were to be seen. It was like driving a train over an ocean. Water as far as the eye could see with hedges, fences and roads all submerged and out of sight. Treetops looked like isolated islands. The line too eventually succumbed to the ever-rising waters and then westbound services were terminated at the aptly named Bridgewater station. The floodwater penetrated many of the lineside cabinets that housed electrical relays controlling the signaling and did a great deal of damage. To prevent a possible reoccurrence, these cabinets are now situated not on the ground but on a platform at least a metre high and are adjacent to – almost comically now that they once again overlook verdant green fields – lifebuoy rings.

My personal best (or should that be worst) passenger train delay was 2 hours 57 minutes late arriving at my final destination.

The weather on the night of 8th December 1993 was atrocious. West-bury station was closed from 17:00 to 19:00 due to the roof being damaged by storm force winds and, though my train had been cancelled, my guard Rob Fox and I were later ordered to travel to Bristol T.M. and work 1B65 to Cardiff Central and 2C83 back to West-bury.

We departed Bristol at 20:15 with unit 158 815 then running only 13 minutes late. The wind did not let up and by the time we reached Wales, the rain had also become torrential. The windscreen wipers, even on their high-speed setting, could not cope. My notebook shows that Guard Rob Fox and I were held at Severn Tunnel Junction for over an hour. When we stopped at the first red signal, I opened the powered door and tried to get off the train to call the signaller on the SPT but the wind was so strong and blowing against our exposed train with such a force that Rob had to push against it just to keep it open. In all we had to stop at ten red signals between STJ and Newport, each one taken out of action by track circuit failures. We had to be autho-rised by the signaller to pass them individually after stopping at every one. This involved proceeding at caution and being prepared to stop short of any obstruction as stipulated in the rulebook. This was almost impossible due to the pitch-black night, the pouring rain and a poor headlight. We departed Newport at 22:46 but then encountered six more signals out of action. Our eventual arrival time at Cardiff was 23:28 compared with the scheduled time of 20:45. After a well-deserved cup of tea, we departed Cardiff Central at midnight and headed for home with 2C83 made up of six cars; 158 838+158 841+150 251. There was a slight improvement in the weather but many signals were still out of action. We were authorised to pass five between Cardiff and Newport and eventually arrived at Bristol T.M. at 01:40. We then had four more red signals to negotiate before Bath and finally arrived back in Westbury at 03:23 a little under three hours late. We had passed a total of 25 signals at danger during our perilous expedition and I later discovered that a wind gust of 86 mph had been recorded in Cardiff that night.

Correction to the above! Reading through my notebooks again I have now come across one of my trains that ran later still! Sunday 4th January 1998 was another date when storm force gales played havoc with services. The timetable was abandoned and trains ran if and when they could. I was booked to travel to Bristol TM, relieve the driver on the same train and drive it to Cardiff Central. However, by the time 1F26 arrived at Bristol it was already over three hours late. I was then advised that the Severn Tunnel had been closed and the train was to be diverted via Gloucester. I then had to give our control office more bad news – I no longer signed the road to Gloucester (another direct consequence of privatisation) and so I waited for a pilotman. Eventually a Gloucester driver arrived to show me the way but by the time we had traversed both banks of the River Severn, our arrival time into the Welsh capital was 4 hours 24 minutes later than that printed on my diagram. My return working had been cancelled a long time since so I was dispatched in a taxi to Bristol where the last train to Westbury departed only 20 minutes late. I finally booked off duty at 01:40.

I don't know if it was just me but I discovered a strange phenomenon when train driving at night. If I passed a single yellow signal at speed on a straight section of track so that its associated red stop signal was clearly in view ahead I would, as usual, brake the train accordingly to stop at the red, continuously judging the remaining distance. However, if the red signal then cleared to display a yellow or green proceed aspect it would seemingly instantly jump further away leaving me with the feeling that I had slowed the train excessively to stop at the signal even if it had not changed to a less restrictive aspect. Has this optical illusion or 'retreating signal phenomenon', as I call it, ever been experienced by any other driver I wonder?

## ASLEF INFORMATION PAPER FOR TRAINEE DRIVERS

March 2009

**Q.** CAN I JOIN A TRADE UNION? – WHAT ARE MY OPTIONS?

**A.** Yes. You have two options.

    **1.** ASLEF – The Associated Society of Locomotive Engineers & Firemen. (More than 95% of FGW train drivers are members of ASLEF.)

    **2.** RMT – The Rail, Marine and Transport Workers Union.

**Q.** IS TRADE UNION MEMBERSHIP COMPULSORY?

**A.** No. There is no longer a 'closed shop'.

**Q.** WHY ARE OVER 95% OF FGW DRIVERS MEMBERS OF ASLEF?

**A.** ASLEF is widely recognised as one of the most influential and effective trade unions in Britain today.

FGW recognise that both ASLEF and the RMT may represent drivers – including trainee and instructor drivers, but uniquely ASLEF negotiates only on behalf of these driver grades. **ASLEF is a specialised Trade Union.** The RMT represent many other FGW grades including on train staff, station staff, some clerical and maintenance staff as well as other employees from different companies, e.g. signallers employed by Network Rail. Additionally, the RMT represents workers from other industries such as road transport and the Merchant Navy.

Drivers' Divisional Council is an FGW/Trade Union negotiating committee and currently six out of the seven drivers elected onto this committee are ASLEF members.

*See below for more details.*

**Q.** HOW IS ASLEF ORGANISED?

**A.** ASLEF is a democratic organisation whose policies are decided annually at the 'Annual Assembly of Delegates'. This AAD is made up of individual driver members elected at local branch meetings. Briefly ASLEF is organised as follows:

BRANCH MEETINGS

Every member is encouraged to attend his or her local branch meetings. These take place normally once a month, or as agreed locally. Full details of branch meetings – date, time, venue and agenda etc. – will be found in the ASLEF notice case at your depot. At these meetings, members will be updated by their Branch Secretary on all correspondence received – including circulars from the ASLEF General Secretary. Members will also have the opportunity to hear reports from, and to question, their local representatives; to elect branch officials; propose motions to the local ASLEF H&S representative; agree on how branch funds are to be spent and debate and vote on all relevant issues. Guest speakers may also be invited.

## DRIVERS' LOCAL REPRESENTATION

Every depot has its own elected local driver representatives. These drivers are often referred to as LSRs (Local Staff Reps) or more traditionally as LDC (Local Departmental Committee) reps. Their role is to negotiate local agreements, compile links (work rotas), oversee annual leave arrangements and to assist all trade union driver members as necessary. Furthermore, should you require representation, for example on a disciplinary charge, assistance in pursuing a claim or a complaint concerning an individual grievance, the local ASLEF officials/reps will advise, assist or represent you accordingly.

## DRIVER REPRESENTATION AT COMPANY LEVEL

Driver Divisional Council/Company Council Representatives represent all drivers collectively at a company-wide level on issues such as driver pay and all conditions of employment. They report to the ASLEF Executive Committee and at ASLEF branch meetings. They also negotiate with senior management to resolve any issue or individual (TU members only) claims unresolved at local level and will be assisted by the ASLEF District Organiser if necessary. (See *below*)

Currently the Driver Divisional Council representatives are:

FGW – West (Former Wessex): Drivers Steve Davies & Steve Newton.

FGW – LTV (London & Thames Valley): Drivers Ian Finn & Martin Boreham.

FGW – HSS (High Speed Services): Drivers Bob Morse, Dick Samuels & Tim Earl.

**It should be noted that while both local and divisional council representatives represent all drivers collectively, individual drivers are only represented provided that they are either an ASLEF or RMT member. Therefore, it follows that if you want your voice to be heard, join a trade union.**

## ASLEF DISTRICT ORGANISER

Stan Moran is the current ASLEF District Organiser for our area. His constituency covers a large geographical area that includes FGW and several other train operating companies. He is one of eight full time officers employed directly by ASLEF and is, therefore, outside the influence of any individual TOC. He deals with major company-wide issues, and normally represents members charged with the more serious disciplinary offences. If necessary, the District Organiser may request the ASLEF Executive Committee (see below) for access to the large pool of ASLEF resources and funds in support of an individual member – for example, at an employment tribunal or for legal advice and assistance.

The ASLEF District Organiser represents ASLEF members only, reports to the ASLEF Executive Committee and is elected by individual members in an independently controlled postal ballot.

## THE ASLEF EXECUTIVE COMMITTEE

The Executive Committee (EC) is the top governing body within ASLEF. It is made up of eight driver members elected on a geographical basis. All EC members are drivers and are elected by individual members in an independently controlled, postal ballot.

The current EC member for our district (No. 7) is Brian Corbett.

The role of the EC includes carrying out the policy of the AAD. It can also dismiss ASLEF officials and members and, if necessary, order ballots for industrial action.

The EC also instigates campaigns to highlight issues within the rail industry and to seek improvements to the status and working conditions of all ASLEF members at all TOCs.

## THE ASLEF GENERAL SECRETARY

Keith Norman is the current ASLEF General Secretary and is responsible for carrying out the instructions of the EC concerning correspondence, accounts and the implementation of ASLEF policy. He is frequently the spokesperson for ASLEF when dealing with the multitude of railway companies and organisations, the media and government departments etc.

The General Secretary is elected by individual members in an independently controlled postal ballot.

## OTHER ASLEF COMMITTEES INCLUDE
- Women's Consultative Committee
- Race Equality Consultative Committee
- Lesbian, Gay, Bisexual, and Transgender Consultative Committee
- Retired Members Section
- Trustees

**Q.** WHAT WILL I GAIN BY BECOMING A MEMBER OF ASLEF?

**A.** Being a member of a respected, democratic and recognised trade union strengthens your position.

By negotiating collectively for improvements in pay, conditions and a safe working environment, great progress has been achieved.

You will also be entitled to:
- Attend meetings of your local branch – resolutions from which may influence local and national ASLEF policies.
- Advice and assistance locally, or when necessary the support and representation of an experienced professional representative – the District Organiser.
- Free legal advice should you or your dependents require it.
- Free legal representation as necessary, concerning any incident or accident.
- A free wills service.
- Receive, each month, a copy of the 'Loco Journal' the in-house ASLEF magazine.
- Receive, annually, a diary that includes your representative's contact details and other useful information.'

**Q.** HOW MUCH WILL IT COST ME TO BECOME A MEMBER OF ASLEF?
**A.** Please see the enclosed letter from the ASLEF General Secretary explaining the current subscription rates.

**Q.** WHERE CAN I GET MORE INFORMATION?
**A.** Contact your Local Branch Secretary, your Local Drivers Representative or the appropriate Driver Company Council representative (as listed above) or check-out the ASLEF web site: www.aslef.org.uk

**Q.** HOW DO I BECOME A MEMBER OF ASLEF?
**A.** Firstly, if you are currently a member of any other trade union you must resign your membership as duel memberships are no longer permitted. Then complete the enclosed ASLEF 'Application for Membership' form and hand it to your Branch Secretary.
Note: Your Local Representative will assist you with this if necessary, as the Branch Secretary may not be an FGW employee but a driver with another Train Operating Company. The Branch Secretary will then place it before the next branch meeting for recommendation. If your application is then accepted, you will receive a 'Welcome Pack' directly from the ASLEF General Secretary.

# 9

# Bosses, Brothers and Others

My enthusiasm for trade unionism in general and ASLEF in particular was as a direct result of my ability to draw upon the generous financial package that was available to staff like me who had been made redundant at their home depot but were prepared to up sticks and move their home and family to fill a vacancy at another location. The benefits that I claimed and received were very fair, some would even say generous. Having said that, if I hadn't been made redundant in the first place, I would have gladly spent my entire railway career at Newport.

Many years before, farsighted ASLEF officials had negotiated the agreements under which I and very many others had transferred and, therefore, I felt a debt of gratitude to them and the union that I wanted to repay in any way I could. Some of the benefits I received included my mortgage being subsidised for 10 years, reimbursement of all legal and household removal costs in addition to a lump sum payable under the clause 'disturbance allowance' that was to cover such basic items as carpets and curtains in the new property. Without receiving these benefits, we could never have afforded to move and, therefore, I would have been unemployed.

Here I should place on record my personal thanks to Bob Gilham who was then the Westbury-based Area Administration Officer but more commonly known as Chief Clerk. Mr. Gilham assisted me greatly when I transferred to Westbury, helping me through the labyrinth of red tape to successfully apply for the above financial assistance to which I was entitled.

1982 was the year when my union ASLEF and the British Rail Board became embroiled in the most acrimonious industrial dispute I have ever been involved in during my career. That old chestnut of pay versus productivity was at the heart of it. Footplate staff had been working a basic daily eight-hour shift for many years, since 1919 in fact, but British Rail wanted to introduce 'flexible' or more accurately 'variable day' rostering to increase productivity. ASLEF were having none of it, believing the eight-hour working day to be sacrosanct and, after a series of 24- and 48-hour strikes earlier in the year followed by inquiries that failed to resolve the now increasingly bitter dispute, things came to a head when ASLEF announced an indefinite all out strike starting on Sunday 4th July as BR had threatened to impose the new rosters at several depots. We all received individual letters from Peter Parker, the then British Rail Chairman, outlining the dire consequences should such action take place. The strike went ahead and was locally well supported. At Westbury even though some members, myself included, thought the strike was unnecessary and found it hard to understand, we were fiercely loyal to our union and knew that we had to be united and support our elected negotiating team. Locally, we had a special branch meeting on the very first day of the strike and almost all the footplate staff at Westbury attended. I was amazed to see all my colleagues together in one room at the same time. If I recall correctly, while some reservations were expressed, there was also the fear that it would be the thin end of the wedge if we capitulated and we passed a motion supporting the action. We were on strike continuously for two weeks during which time we were subjected by pressure from both sides and we each received another two letters. One was from our Area Manager Joe Mc Entee, dated 16th July 1982, the first paragraph of which read exactly as follows ...

**"If you are on strike next Tuesday, 20 July 1982, a dismissal notice will have to be sent to you. If you come to work on Monday and Tuesday, 19/29 July 1982 and thereafter, this will avoid the dismissal of you personally."**

This was individually addressed and sent to several hundred members of local footplate staff. Now if I were to threaten hundreds of my employees with the sack, I would check the wording to make sure that it was 100% correct. However, the reference to *19/29 July* should have obviously read *19/20 July* and speaks volumes for the slipshod approach and contempt that BR management had for their footplate staff at this time. (The feeling was mutual.)

The other letter was from the local quarry owners and delivered by Royal Mail. This meant that our employer must have provided a third-party private company with our home addresses without our permission and this all added fuel to the fire. The quarry owners feared that they may never fully recover from a protracted rail strike and that, consequently, when we did return to work, some rail contracts may have been lost to the road industry. I don't know if they attempted to persuade BR to settle the dispute or if they only pressurised us.

The strike was called off after two weeks and although we lost our guaranteed eight-hour day from 4th October 1982, allowances and pay were increased and BR failed to implement their original far more wide-ranging goals.

I first became a local staff representative on 18th July 1983, just two years and six months after transferring to Westbury. This was unusual for someone in my position as I was not yet a fully-fledged driver but still a relief driver and nearly all footplate reps at this time were experienced drivers. There were four of us standing for the single vacancy and the result was:

Paul Cousins: 34 votes
Steve Davies: 73 votes
Dave Smart: 13 votes
Ray Naish: 23 votes
Spoilt papers: 3

I was voted onto the committee mainly thanks to the other relief drivers and assistant drivers who wanted someone from their own grade group who could relate directly to their particular grievances. Little did I realise at the time just how much this first simple election would impact on the rest of my railway career.

I and three drivers, Phil Marshman, Tom Rundle and Morris Miles, made up the staff side of LDC B (Local Departmental Committee B – footplate grades) and it was our job to represent our Westbury-based footplate colleagues both individually and collectively during consultation or negotiation meetings with local management. We were also required to scrutinise every diagram to ensure that these daily individual work programs issued by management to footplate staff complied with all of the relevant agreements then in operation and to place them in the appropriate links taking into account, where necessary, such issues as route and traction knowledge requirements, rest day patterns, rest periods during and between shifts, equalisation of potential earnings and weekend work to name but a few. On the rare occasions when we could not reach an agreement with management a 'failed to agree' would be officially recorded in the minutes and the issue would be reviewed and dealt with at the next level up within the machinery of negotiation procedures. It all sounds a bit bureaucratic and it was, but if both parties acted reasonably, most local issues were resolved eventually. National issues were another thing altogether!

During one LDC B meeting where we met with local management, we had worked our way through another long agenda when we came to an issue that I thought would be dealt with swiftly and with little controversy – wrong! Morris Miles had received complaints from some drivers regarding the poor state of cleanliness in our messroom and he was seeking assurances from David Smith our Local Manager at the time that arrangements would be put in place to improve the standard of cleaning. Things soon became heated when Smith appeared to blame drivers for making our accommodation dirty in the first place. Words were exchanged and, in exasperation, Smith accused some drivers of "Behaving like animals". Bad choice of words! I should explain here that Morris was a big sturdy guy whose previous efforts in a tug of war team had earned him a reputation as a strong and robust individual and, in comparison, Smith was certainly not. Morris was out of his chair in a flash and was making his way at some speed to the other side of the table. Fortunately for all concerned, Smith reacted quickly and headed away from Morris who was now verbally threatening him with a promise of putting him through the window. (It was closed and we were not on the ground floor!) Luckily for all parties, Morris failed to make contact with Smith who left the room in a hurry while the rest of us were trying to calm Morris down.

Needless to say, that was the end of the meeting and, as far as I am aware, apart from local industrial relations reaching an all-time low, there were no repercussions either way, which, on reflection, was about right as neither party behaved well.

Our local ASLEF branch was, to be honest, not well supported at times. That all changed when we were 'invaded' by the Aberystwyth mafia. This was the collective name we gave to the gang of three: Dave Griffiths, Steve Clements and Simon Weller who all transferred together from Aberystwyth and British Rail's last remaining steam-operated line. This was the wonderful narrow gauge Vale of Rheidol railway that ran from Aberystwyth to Devil's Bridge. All three were strong trade unionists and collectively they provided our branch with the shot in the arm that, quite frankly, it needed. Dave went on to become our Branch Secretary and Simon deservedly ended up as the ASLEF National Organiser.

Of course, it was not always an ASLEF dispute that resulted in industrial action on the railway and we drivers could also become embroiled in other trade union disputes. The biggest and most obvious was during the miners' strikes when ASLEF proudly gave the NUM as much support as was legally possible at the time.

The RMT were also fond of calling the occasional strike and it was during one such day of action, when the guards were on strike, that I had an incident that resulted in some embarrassment for me. The company was trying to run a skeleton service with a few managers who were, on paper at least, qualified to act as guards. As ASLEF were not technically in dispute we were obliged to work as normal; however, due to the fact that very few trains were actually running, most drivers were not called upon to drive on RMT strike days and after reporting for duty in the normal way, most were allowed to go home after just a few hours of drinking tea or perhaps catching up with any outstanding paperwork or other non-driving duties. It was simply the luck of the draw for the few unfortunate drivers who were called upon to work trains with managers acting as conductors. On this particular occasion, I was one of the unfortunate few and was ordered to drive a special (the timetable was null and void) from West-bury to Bristol TM and back stopping at all stations with two class 158

DMU 'sprinters' with a manager based at Portsmouth acting as my guard. Off we went with a well-loaded train but my 'guard' was too keen and, at a couple of stations, released the doors a little before the train had come to a complete stop. This resulted in a full emergency application of the brake and consequently the train stopped suddenly and with a jolt. I, like most other drivers, would try and stop the train as smoothly as possible so if the actions of the guard prevented this it reflected badly on the driver as most would think that poor driving was the cause of a sudden stop. I let it go twice but on the third occasion at Oldfield Park when we stopped yet again with a jolt despite my best efforts, I had had enough and stormed back down the platform and told my guard/manager what I thought of his performance in no uncertain terms. He apologised, said that he would not do it again and with my point well and truly made, I marched back up the platform to return to my cab. Calamity! In my haste to leave the cab I had slammed the door shut and the only way to gain access was with a carriage key and mine was in my jacket pocket hanging up on the other side of the door. I had inadvertently locked myself out. What to do? There was only one thing I could do and that was to ask my guard/manager, to whom only seconds earlier I had given a bollocking, to do me a favour and lend me his key. So, I did and to be fair, he kindly gave me his key without comment but now it was my turn to feel belittled.

Not only have I stood on ASLEF picket lines I have also shown solidarity with my conductor colleagues when their union, the RMT, called a strike, by joining their demonstration and even providing them with some refreshments during their 24-hour vigils. It was such support for each other that contributed to our depot's camaraderie when, win or lose, the dispute was over.

However, on the down side, there were always one or two selfish individuals who would blackleg in an attempt to undermine their colleagues. I have nothing but contempt for them. I recall that the last time the GWR RMT conductors were on strike, they were totally united bar one. Not only did this individual work, he also extended his route knowledge beyond what was required of him so that he could work additional trains that, on the day before the strike started, he would have never worked. Bastards such as he are loathsome creatures in my eyes.

On Monday 15th July 1991 I booked on duty at 01:31 and, after working a train of empties to Whatley quarry, I was supposed to return to Westbury with a loaded train. However, the Transport & General Workers Union were then on strike and, as they had members at the quarry, I was asked by a T&GWU union official not to cross their picket line. I phoned my local ASLEF branch secretary, spoke to my fellow local driver's rep and we agreed that we would support our brothers and sisters in the T&GWU. The train that had been ready to depart since Saturday was still there when I set off back to Westbury light engine. If the same situation arose today, my refusal to work normally could be classified as 'secondary action' and therefore illegal.

There were two very controversial issues we had to deal with during my time as a staff rep at Westbury and both involved different aspects of privatisation of the rail industry. The first concerned the introduction of privately-owned locomotives for the first time on British Railways – the class 59. Before the arrival of these giant, USA-built locomotives, our heaviest stone trains had to be hauled by two class 56 locos coupled in multiple, i.e. one driver operating them as a single unit through electrical and pneumatic connections between the two locos. However, the class 56s generally returned poor reliability figures, retention of engine coolant being one of their biggest problems. Seeking a more reliable service than British Rail could then provide with their locomotives, Foster Yeoman operators of Torr Works, the huge limestone quarry at Merehead near the Mendip Hills, initially purchased four class 59 locos (numbered 59 001-4) from General Motors that were imported early in 1986. This would have been controversial at any time but it was during this period that the famous locomotive works at Swindon was being closed. We were worried that, as Foster Yeoman wanted to use their own locomotives hauling their own wagons from their own private quarry to and from stone distribution depots some of which they also owned, they may seek to employ their own train drivers. ASLEF recognised that these locos were a huge investment in the rail industry, however, and provided that only drivers employed by British Rail were used to drive them, co-operation would be forthcoming. The class 59 would be the only time I drove a new train in my entire 46 years on the footplate. That says all you need to know about the lack of investment in the rail industry during this period.

The second area of huge controversy that happened during my time as a staff rep was, of course, privatisation of the entire industry and the impact this would have on its employees. During 1995, our depot along with many others in the country, was split in readiness for privatisation. Westbury depot was divided into two sections while some others were broken up into three, four or, as in the case of Bristol, even five separate parts. Regional Railways wanted 24 of the 76 drivers then based at Westbury to operate their passenger services while all the remaining drivers would initially stay with the Mainline Freight sector of British Rail and drive freight trains only. So, we were each given a simple option form to complete, sign and return by a specific date. This was a big personal career decision to take, as it was not just the type of train that you would be driving perhaps for the rest of your working life but the unknown long-term prospects of the separate companies involved. Some drivers had little doubt as to which option they considered best for them and made their minds up instantly while others agonised for days. Personally, I opted for passenger work for two main reasons. Firstly, I thought that there would always be demand for our local passenger services and I didn't want to be made redundant again and secondly, the shifts would almost certainly be less grueling than on the freight side. The big day came and, being a driver rep, the local manager and I opened all the returned envelopes and put the appropriate tick against a list of all the drivers at the depot. It had been agreed nationally that if there were more applications than there were vacancies then seniority would be the deciding factor. That meant in the case of Westbury, for example, if Regional Railways wanted 24 drivers and 30 opted for that choice then the 24 most senior drivers would be deemed to have been successful while the junior 6 would have no choice but to work only freight for the foreseeable future. I was dreading the outcome, as I knew that if many drivers did not get their first choice there would be a lot of bad feeling and low morale for months if not years to come. I couldn't believe my luck when the manager and I added up the figures. There were 23 drivers who elected for passenger work and this meant that only one (the junior driver who had opted for freight work) was forced to transfer to the passenger side. When I eventually spoke to him, he wasn't too upset and thought that there was good chance that he would not get his preferred option due to his lack of seniority. So, we went from a potential disaster to a near perfect outcome, notwithstanding the whole nonsense of depots splitting in the first place. So, Westbury depot 'split' on 13th March 1995 when the majority of drivers elected to work for Mainline Freight but I became one of 24 drivers transferred to Regional Railways that was, at that time, still part of British Rail until the privatised South Wales & West Railway (later known as Wales & West) took control of operations. However, the owning company Prism Rail needed a huge government subsidy to ensure viability. Prism were founded by a number of individuals from the bus industry; so, no conflict of interest there then. Rail privatisation made a few individuals very rich – thanks to the taxpayer.

As you might expect, privatisation caused an earthquake within the rail industry. Personally, I hated the concept that my primary role had now changed from helping to deliver a public service within a nationalised industry to contributing to the profits of a private company.

After serving my colleagues as their local representative on and off for many years, in 2001, I decided to put my name forward to become a candidate for the next higher level of representation. This was as a driver's representative on Sectional Council (later known as Drivers Divisional Council, which formed part of the full Company Council – the body that represented all grades) and my constituency now covered several depots collectively. For a brief time, I was both Local and Sectional Council rep but, as this was inappropriate and impractical, I eventually resigned from my position as a local rep.

My first partner-in-crime on Sectional Council within the privatised industry was Ernie Whitfield, a driver based at Par depot in Cornwall. Ernie was a big man and a larger than life character too.

We soon built up a good personal and working relationship. Being far more experienced than me, Ernie had an uncanny knack of accurately predicting management's next move in most areas during our negotiations. We soon became a two-man team with Ernie doing the thinking and plotting while I would do most of the speaking and fire the bullets.

I was the staff side secretary and this involved considerable amounts of paperwork, faxes, telephone calls and later e-mails. Life became very hectic attending meetings with management, representing colleagues, consulting with fellow reps and attending ASLEF branches. Agendas before most meetings and minutes afterwards all had to be compiled, checked and corrections agreed. My note books indicate the during one particularly hectic month, I was engaged in train driving for only one day – and that was on a Sunday – while all of the other working days I was occupied on union business representing my colleagues. As my personal contact details, along with all the other companies' driver reps were now quite rightly listed in the ASLEF member's diary I received numerous phone calls every day and even occasionally at night. On more than one occasion, I received a call from a driver who was in trouble with the company over some misdemeanour or another who was so upset he might lose his job that he broke down in tears. My biggest mistake as a rep was that I took all issues personally. My supporters said that this was because I cared so much but my critics said I was acting unprofessionally. On reflection, I think both opinions were correct. Either way I could not have done the job at all without the unqualified support and patience of my wife Anne.

Initially, not having either the technology or the knowledge of how to use it, I wrote all my correspondence by hand. The very first letter I wrote on my computer was as follows and was to one of my drivers who I feared was about to get himself into serious trouble if he did not change his ways. I have deleted his name for obvious reasons.

Dear \*\*\*,

I am becoming increasingly concerned about the number of incidents that you are involved in lately. Not many weeks go by before either a manager or a driver mentions your name to me with regard to an operational, attendance or pay issue.

As your ASLEF representative I feel that I would be failing in my duty if I did not advise you of the possible consequences of your actions on your driving career.

As you may know your depot is currently understaffed, however the management plan to increase the number of drivers to cover the current workload and when this is achieved they may be prepared to pursue, with more vigor than in the past, errant drivers. Please remember that Wales & West do not owe you, me, or indeed anyone a living.

I hope you understand that I have only your best interests in mind by writing this letter to you. It is my desire to try and help if possible, by pointing out some ways that you may be able to help yourself to reduce stress when on duty. I am only too well aware of the pressures that our job can put us under, especially so if like yourself you have been unlucky to have been involved in several accidents over the years.

One of the most difficult parts of our job is to give 100% of our concentration to driving when other, often personal problems are pressing on our mind. Another is to try and keep cool when faced with operational problems such as very late running or traction faults.

So my advice is to try and keep calm in all situations whatever the provocation; take a deep breath and a step backwards. Try and avoid controversial situations with managers, control and other drivers and keep a low profile. It is our task to drive so let management manage, and control organise.

I sincerely hope that you accept this letter in the spirit that it is written as one dedicated railwayman to another.

Yours fraternally
Steve Davies

Driver *** had a terrible reputation due to his frequent inability to control his temper. He was always right and everyone else was wrong – on all issues. He was also one (I encountered several others over the years) who thought that the company owed him a living, that he could not be sacked for poor attendance and the union would always be able to get him out of whatever sticky position he had got himself into. He was wrong on all three counts. Knowing his temperament, I thought that I should word the letter as carefully and as diplomatically as possible. I took a considerable amount of time and trouble over it and thought that not even *** could complain or get upset over its contents. In fact, I was hoping the he would appreciate my efforts to help point him in the right direction. Boy was I wrong! I was told that when he read it, he went ballistic. He did not change for the better; in fact, he got worse and I knew that it was only a matter of time before he would be removed from driving duties. When the inevitable happened, of course, he did not want me to represent him, as I was the devil incarnate in his eyes. Two of my other colleagues then took turns to try and save his driving career but I knew that he was beyond help. Apparently, at one meeting with the management, his rep had to physically restrain him. He lost his driving job, of course, but was employed in another role within the company. I was surprised that he was offered any other position whatsoever but, of course, in his eyes it was all ASLEF's and, in particular, my fault.

Although there were only a few drivers I came across who had a similar attitude to *** they were all memorable – for the wrong reasons. A much later case (March 2006) involved a driver at a west of England depot who had been suspended from driving duties pending disciplinary procedures. I was dispatched posthaste in an attempt to help our member. I knew little of the details of the incident when I initially met with my accused colleague. During our private discussions, although they admitted that they had made mistakes they claimed that there were numerous and indisputable mitigating circumstances and anyway the local management had escalated the whole thing out of proportion. This was not an uncommon situation for me to find myself in and I only asked a few questions to clarify some details in my own mind before I met with the local manager privately and 'off the record'. I was shown the printed readout that had been downloaded from the train's OTDR (black box) of my driver's last and disputed journey. I was horrified at what I saw. It was clear that the driver's level of concentration must have been absent for long periods of time. In fact, the phrase used by the manager was that our driver "Must have been away with the fairies" – repeated and excessive speeding during part of the journey and then crawling along before again using full power followed by very harsh braking for all station stops. But this was not the worst part. The train was scheduled to terminate at a dead end station and, as the driver had overshot the previous station, it was perhaps fortunate that the terminating plat-form was a long one and so the train did not crash into the buffer stops. As it was, it eventually came to a juddering halt well past the authorised stopping point. I asked the manager if he was aware of any personal issues with the driver that may explain this atrocious stan-dard of driving. He told me that the driver would not discuss such matters with the management and had said that it was none of their business. He then showed me the driver's individual safety of the line record that lists any previous incidents that could have had an impact on safety. It was long, detailed and a cause for concern despite previ-ous attempts by the local reps and management to reduce the number of incidents involving this driver. I then phoned the local rep who was not surprised when I explained the seriousness of the situation. Later, I spoke again in private with the driver to give them the opportunity to declare any personal concerns that had impacted on their concen-tration levels. I suspected that there were but if the driver would not open up to the management or me then there was little I could do to help. This was not a good position for me to be in as I was required to try and safeguard my colleague's position as a driver but I also then realised, for the first time, that my responsibilities extended beyond this individual driver and must take into account the potential risk to passengers and other staff alike should our coworker remain driving. I was forced to agree with the manager that it would be best for all concerned if a non-driving position could be offered as the concentra-tion levels required of a driver appeared to be beyond our colleague. Eventually, an alternative position was offered and very reluctantly accepted but from then on, my name was mud in certain quarters.

Over the years, as ever changing greedy private companies took turns to try and milk the rail industry for all it was worth, I and my colleagues were repeatedly transferred from one company to another. British Rail (Regional Railways) South Wales & West / Wales & West, Wessex, First Greater Western and finally Great Western Railway was the list of franchise or company names that I was automatically transferred from and to during my driving career. However, there is no doubt that privatisation resulted in drivers receiving far higher salaries. A driver's basic salary under British Rail was poor considering the responsibility, shift work, knowledge required and skill involved but take-home pay could be increased through overtime payments and a complex multitude of add-ons including such things as IUP (Irregular and Unsocial hours Payment), VRP (Variable Rostering Payment), DOO (Driver Only Operated payment) mileage payments and enhanced payments for nights and weekend work. If a British Rail driver worked any overtime between the hours of 02:00 – 06:00, the enhanced rate of pay he /she received was time (basic rate) plus seven twelfths. I kid you not, it was that convoluted. Post-privatisation when ASLEF was forced to deal with every new company separately, it saw the opportunity to sweep these old pay structures aside and negotiate a new innovative deal for drivers. The man leading the charge for ASLEF was Keith Norman during negotiations with First Great Western. A new driver's pay and productivity restructuring package was agreed that incorporated nearly all of the previous add on payments into the basic wage. This resulted in a far greater and more predictable income, higher overtime rates of pay and perhaps, above all, an increased pension entitlement on retirement. This watershed pay deal became the template for all future pay negotiations and as one company was now paying a far higher wage for a more productive driver, all the others had to compete. As it takes, on average, a year to train a driver from scratch to fully productive, the costs to the employer are substantial so why not try and entice fully qualified drivers from other companies? Post-British Rail there were many different passenger and freight operating companies in competition with each other trying to poach qualified drivers from one another and this rapidly drove wages up and this process continues today.

I often worked with Keith Norman over the years and soon discovered that he did not suffer fools gladly. I found this out the hard way on several occasions.

The first high-level meeting I attended with him involved an annual pay review with Wessex Trains at their head office in Exeter during May 2002. I was a little nervous but trying not to let it show. Naturally, we were seeking as big an increase as possible for our brothers and sisters. Keith and I together with all the other union reps sat at the large negotiating table waiting for the management side to turn up. Eventually they did so and we could not help but notice that Dennis Baker the then Wessex Trains Human Resources Director was carrying an above average sized briefcase. Without hesitation Keith pointed at the bag and said, "I hope that's full of money for us Dennis." I was shocked at such a comment but when everyone started to laugh, I realised that this was simply Keith's way to generate a friendly atmosphere – at least to start with!

Keith later became the ASLEF General Secretary and did more than any other individual to ensure that ASLEF recovered from its darkest ever period: the infamous barbecue brawl of 2004 that took place in the grounds of ASLEF head office then in Arkwright Road, London, and resulted in three senior officials being suspended. Our trade union was in a mess. Legal battles, financial issues, low morale and fierce internal squabbles lead to some members resigning, others reluctant to join, and the rest of us embarrassed over the whole debacle. A few managers could not contain their glee at our troubles and, on more than one occasion, I was asked if I had been to any good barbecues lately.

After Keith was elected General Secretary, he slowly but surely got ASLEF back on track – if you'll forgive the pun. For example, I became personally aware just how attentive Keith was concerning the union's finances when he challenged one of my expense claims. I was mortified to think that he or indeed any other member might suspect that I was claiming money to which I was not entitled. Most meetings that I attended I was being paid my driver's salary by my employer but when I attended ASLEF branch meetings to report to members on the latest issues, then naturally I was not. However, I was then entitled to claim limited expenses from ASLEF, and I did. Over the years, I attended branch meetings literally from Paddington to Penzance and all depots in-between. When I received the letter from Keith asking me to justify one particular claim, I directly wrote back explaining in detail the justification for my claim. I was then immediately paid the full amount due to me but thereafter I was always careful to include full details of any claim and consequently, I was then always promptly paid without question.

You may have gathered that I was opposed to privatisation but if the whole industry had become British Rail plc. in which the public were offered or better still given shares and it had not fragmented into the myriad of parts it's in today, then I am certain that we would now have a better system overall. Today, it appears that any profits go to the private companies but the government/tax payer must pick up the bill for any losses. In my view, the rail franchise arrangements are grossly unsuitable for a national railway network and a totally inappropriate way to manage an essential public service.

Rant over. Moving on.

I and my other staff side colleagues now on the council dealt with issues that impacted on all drivers within the company. We were led by one of the ASLEF full time officers, Stan Moran, and we all reported to the ASLEF Executive Committee. I would describe Stan as a rough diamond but with a heart of gold. He was a real character and I remember that he once told a driver whose outlook was entirely parochial that he should pay a visit to Curry's in order to see a bigger picture!

The major issues we now dealt with were pay, annual leave, all joint conditions of service and, surprisingly perhaps, one of the most contentious of all, staffing levels. ASLEF had a policy that I strongly supported that insisted on all train companies employing a sufficient number of drivers without the need for excessive overtime or drivers working their rostered days off. Rest day working was, and still is, a very controversial issue. Some drivers took the view that if my employer asks me if I am willing to work my day off and I am prepared to do so in order to boost my wages then why should my union try and stop me. This sounds very reasonable until you consider the bigger picture. Let's say a train operating company actually needs 500 drivers to operate all of its services but employs 450 and relies on voluntary overtime to make up the shortfall. The company will have a reduced wage bill overall because, although the average driver will be paid a little more with the overtime payments, the company will save considerably more by not only not paying the extra 50 staff their basic wage but also all the add-ons including sick pay, national insurance, holiday pay, pension contributions, training, uniform and administration costs etc. We believed that companies should be 'encouraged' to recruit and train drivers to agreed establishment levels. The problem was that some companies had no agreement with the unions about what constituted the correct number of staff. So, the policy was that if no agreement was reached on how to calculate the appropriate number of drivers at each depot based on the workload allocated by the company, then ASLEF was not prepared to sanction rest-day working. RDW arrangements were always outside and separate to the contract of employment and were only put into operation as a temporary measure if both sides agreed. So, the first thing we had to do was to work with the management to create a depot establishment formula. This was more complicated than some may think as this mathematical equation had to take into account the workload (number of trains/hours of driving), pending retirements, annual leave entitlements, cover for drivers on sick leave, training, and numerous other reasons why a driver may not be available for duty – including ASLEF representation! There was also a need to add into the formula a percentage for additional spare drivers who may be required during short notice service disruption or to cover for any driver who failed to report for duty for any reason, e.g. overslept, rostering error, accident, domestic reasons etc. If and when such a formula was agreed, the company was then obliged to recruit and train drivers in appropriate numbers and, if they did, then ASLEF would agree to a dated voluntary rest-day working agreement until such time that the agreed establishment levels were reached.

As you may imagine, there were many ups and downs, disagreements and heated debates regarding staffing levels in all train operating companies some of which lead to industrial action. For example, during the summer of 1998, when a dated rest-day working agreement between ASLEF and the Wales & West train operating company expired, it was not extended as requested by the company because ASLEF was not satisfied that the W&W recruitment programme was adequate and that it was producing the necessary additional number of drivers within the timescale previously agreed. As a result, an increasing number of trains were being cancelled and Wales & West sought to pass the buck. The following is an extract from posters displayed at all of their stations that must have been sanctioned by the then Managing Director Mr. David Weir ...

**"Some local Wales & West trains may be cancelled at short notice in the Cardiff, Bristol and Westbury areas because of a temporary shortage of train drivers, aggravated by some drivers at these locations withdrawing their previous willingness to work overtime."**

My interpretation of that was ...

**We can't run the service we advertise because of staff shortages so we will publicly blame the staff we have got!**

I recall that when I was an ASLEF rep working for Wessex Trains, we saw a 20% increase in the number of drivers on their books in a little over a two-year period and a 35% increase by the time the franchise ended. This gave the opportunity for many railwaymen and women then in other grades and also individuals from outside the industry, to apply for a trainee driver's vacancy that we had helped to create.

Over the years, I have occasionally been annoyed by the antics of some managers and also, sad to say, with a few of my own colleagues from time to time. However, on 12th September 2003, when the franchise was operating under Wessex Trains, a local driver manager at Westbury overstepped the mark and left me absolutely furious.

All company-recognised trade unions were entitled to have a notice board prominently displayed at every depot in which the local branch secretary would post TU circulars and other relevant information for members. The Westbury ASLEF notice case was in the messroom and, one day, I read an official circular signed by the ASLEF General Secretary that a long-running and controversial issue had finally been resolved by Network Rail in ASLEF's favour. Pleased by the outcome, I was keen to advise my colleagues of this victory and did so with some enthusiasm. However, when I again visited the messroom a couple of days later, I discovered that the circular had been removed* and placed in my pigeonhole together with a note from Driver Manager Paul Richards stating that he had removed it as he considered it to be inaccurate. I went straight to his office and he confirmed his actions. I just about kept my temper but insisted that he accompany me to Jon Godden's office who was then the Service Delivery Manager and, therefore, the most senior manager based at Westbury. In Jon's office, I let rip.

"How dare a manager remove an official ASLEF notice? The fact that he may not personally agree with its contents could never be a justification. If I took the same attitude and removed management notices that I did not personally agree with there would be very few left. If Mr. Richards had a problem with it, I suggested that he should raise his concerns officially through the correct channels and not interfere with the internal communications of a union of which he was not even a member!"

Jon then asked Paul Richards why he had taken this action to which he replied that, as the company had not advised its driver managers of any change of policy, he could not accept that the ASLEF notice was correct. (It turned out to be 100% correct and it would not be the first or last time that ASLEF would be ahead of the game with regard to information dissemination.) Both Jon and I knew that if I reported this incident to the ASLEF General Secretary, all hell would break out, as industrial relations were again very poor at that time.

---

* Following this incident, we made sure that a lock was fitted to the doors on the ASLEF notice case.

I then advised Jon that I would not take the matter any further and it could be dealt with locally if the following actions were taken:

1. The circular be immediately replaced in the ASLEF notice case. (In fact, I did this myself.)
2. That Jon and Richards both apologise on behalf of Wessex Trains to me on behalf of ASLEF in writing before the end of the day.
3. A written assurance that no manager would again interfere with official ASLEF communications.

Jon must have realised that Richards had let him down and assured me that he would take the necessary action and, sure enough, when I booked off duty later that same day, Jon's appropriately worded letter of apology was waiting for me. I assumed that the matter was now closed but the same evening I received a phone call from the Wessex Trains Human Resources Manager Andrew Page who understood the sensitivity of the situation and sought to calm the troubled waters. This left me in a predicament as I had told Jon that the matter could be resolved locally; however, either he or Richards must have informed senior Wessex Trains management of the situation otherwise Mr. Page would have not known or contacted me on the issue. I then knew that if I failed to advise ASLEF senior officials of these recent events, I could be accused of some sort of cover up as ASLEF head office would expect me to report such gross interference and attempted censorship by a manager with ASLEF internal communications.

I had respect for both Jon Godden and Andrew Page and so I wrote to Jon advising him that, as his side had not kept the incident local, I too was now obliged to report it and, accordingly, I wrote to the then ASLEF District Secretary, Keith Norman. I am not aware of any further actions by either side but I suspect that Keith made a mental note of it for future use or dealt with it appropriately.

A new rail franchise came into operation on 1st April 2006 when Wessex Trains merged with First Great Western who were then already operating high speed services on the former British Rail Western Region together with London & Thames Valley services out of Paddington. This process created a new train operating company.

Things didn't go well from the start and, in less than a year, some services became so bad that many of our local commuters staged a ticket strike on Monday 22nd January 2007. Hundreds got together, refused to pay their fare on the day and produced imitation tickets that replicated the layout of a genuine ticket but included the title 'Worst Great Western' and details such as 'Cattle Class' and 'To hell and back'. This was well publicised in the press and on TV. The management's initial reaction was to warn these customers that they could face a fine of up to £1,000 or three months in prison. Bad move, as this only made commuters more determined than ever to prove their point. The great day dawned and FGW finally came to their senses and, in effect, accepted these fake tickets believing that the bad publicity it had already attracted would be considerably worse if mass confrontation was reported either on trains or at ticket barriers during rush hour at Bristol Temple Meads, for example.

Naturally, we raised the problems our passengers were experiencing at Company Council level and we could have spent the entire meeting on this one agenda item alone but the management side Chairman, Operations Director Kevin Gale, sensibly asked me to put our views in writing to allow him to achieve a better understanding of why staff morale was so low as he considered this to be a contributory factor to the poor service that the company accepted it was then providing. So, I wrote the following letter and personally handed it to the Operations Director the next time we met.

*Dear Kevin*

*FGW – WEST STAFF MORALE*

*You will recall that I promised to provide you with a detailed report concerning the ongoing issues that FGW-West employees have in relation to their attitude towards the company. While I can only formally comment on behalf of drivers, I believe that most FGW-West employees irrespective of their role within the company would support most if not all of the following observations and criticisms.*

## FRANCHISE CONCERNS

It all started to go wrong on the 1st April 2006 – the first day of the new franchise because this was the date that First had the chance to start with a clean sheet of paper but elected not to do so. They decided to continue with the same name and image and gave staff and public alike the impression that First Great Western had completed a takeover of Wessex. This myth has been continued and indeed amplified by the actions of the company ever since. We know that this is not factually, legally or technically correct as ALL employees were transferred on this date under the TUPE arrangements into a new TOC, to operate a new franchise.

The great majority of cuts both in the train service and individual employment opportunities (a diplomatic way of saying compulsory redundancies) have impacted more on former Wessex employees than any other section, and it continues. The proposed diagrams from May would result in the majority of West depots losing route knowledge. How many HSS or LTV depots will receive similar treatment? I suspect none. This is perceived to be unfair and perpetuates the belief that First would have been happier if the franchise did not include the former Wessex area at all.

Very recently one FGW manager said to me he considered it would be promotion for an ex Wessex driver if in the near future, he/she were to transfer to an HSS depot as it would result in a pay increase. This elitist attitude says it all. He clearly believes that ex Wessex drivers are lower down the food chain than his "High Speed" drivers. It is unacceptable that this attitude prevails because any unbiased and responsible manager would realise that all drivers have the same job description and responsibilities and that the pay is only dissimilar due to different conditions of service and historical circumstance.

## RECENT SERVICE PROVISION PROBLEMS

I know that you have been acutely aware that the service provided to our customers (or as I still like to call them "passengers" or "the public" – as we provide a public service) since the timetable change in December has been a shambles and at least you had the good grace to admit as much. However, do you realise just how much damage has been done to staff morale as a result. Trains cancelled or short formed leading to chronic *and sometimes dangerous overcrowding or leaving passengers behind on platforms in the middle of winter, angry, frustrated, cold and late for work or appointments and these are the very people who pay our wages!*

*The lack of advance planning by the relevant managers that led to this debacle was lamentable.*

*However, I do also recognise that there has been some recent improvement to our services along the Westbury – Bath – Bristol commuter corridor but the damage has been done and passengers and staff alike do not now have a good word to say about FGW.*

*I note that the M.D. has now publicly apologised to FGW customers, and this is welcome. A similar view expressed to her employees would also be warranted considering the abuse, stress and difficulties some have suffered from when trying to carry out their duties as a direct result of the company's actions, or more precisely inactions.*

## MOTIVATION – SERVICE V PROFIT

*Front line staff put service before profit. The company has the totally opposite approach. We are not naive enough not to know that profit is every train company's raison d'être. However, FGW should not have put staff in a position to have to explain to a customer, forced to stand or left behind on the platform, that the reason that this train is formed of only one coach is to help maximise FGW profits – on the very same day that the cost of their ticket increased above the rate of inflation!*

## LOYALTY

*Traincrew are on the whole, loyal to the rail industry. This is evidenced by the large number of employees with many years of service to their credit. However, they are not loyal to the Company. How can they be? Since privatisation, companies and franchise operators come and go and many believe that FGWs days are already numbered and will suffer the same fate that recently befell GNER.*

*I once had this debate with a former very senior Wessex Manager who argued that he had the loyalty of most of his staff, but within two weeks he had moved on to seek greener grass with another TOC!*

*TRAINS OR …*

*The units we work are, in the main, not fit for purpose. Passenger complaints about lack of air con and defective toilets are an everyday occurrence. Filthy, uncomfortable cabs that are unbearably hot in summer and in winter are attempted to be draft proofed by the ubiquitous use of sticky tape. Cab heater fans that are so noisy you have to shout to make yourself heard. Worn and dirty seats with the ergonomics of an orange box. Wipers that are so slow that in heavy rain they can't cope but when set on fast speed impact so loudly against the frame of the window that with every sweep they make your brain hurt. Class 158 headlights that would break the trade description act. And what do our employers do about it? They send us all a glossy brochure featuring refurbished HSTs including expensive leather seats for customers. Well lucky them! Such crass insensitivity to the conditions that West traincrew have to put up with only emphasises the widespread belief that we are the 'Cinderella' section of the company and our working environment is not worth investing in.*

*You are aware that Nigel (Nigel Birkett was my colleague on DDC at this time) and I have reported our concerns in detail to the engineering department's management. We submitted a detailed written report and then later, on the 25th September 2006, we had a site visit to Exeter depot. Since then we have had no positive response. No remedial action plan whatsoever has been proposed.*

*… BUSES*

*You will recall the meeting on the 18th October 2006 at Bristol, at which all FGW driver local reps were present, that you were asked what plans FGW had to run additional services during high Summer 2007 to cope with the predictable large increase in demand during the school holidays. In particular would the traditional increase in the number of trains to Brighton and Weymouth be continued? You advised us that this would not be the case and only one additional return train to Weymouth and then only on a Sunday would be provided. When asked how we would cope with such a huge increase of passengers with no additional trains, you answered with one word – "Buses". This made it absolutely clear to those reps in attendance that FGW would not even attempt to provide an adequate train* service during this period on these routes but would oblige the public to use their own cars or travel on FGW hired buses. Either way they would be forced onto congested roads to use a much less safe and greater polluting method of transport to reach their destinations.

I thought that the T in T.O.C. stood for Train and not Transport.

## IF IT AIN'T BUST DON'T FIX IT!

We know that the service provided to the customer will deteriorate if/when the duty managers are removed from locations such as Westbury and Exeter. Most of these individuals are dedicated and long-serving employees who ensure that on a day-to-day basis all operational and traincrew problems are dealt with as and when they arise. This cannot be done efficiently by remote control from Swindon or anywhere else.

The regional type of train services that Wessex provided were not the same as the Inter City FGW high speed services and you can't have a better system than having a local manager with his/her hand on the tiller controlling things on a real-time basis. They have a thorough knowledge of the geographical area, local service requirements and, above all, a personal working relationship with their staff. They will know who to call upon to help out when things go wrong – which has now become a daily occurrence.

Obviously, you will still need some form of central control for the overview but the minutiae of the arrangements that need to be put into place can only be carried out efficiently and effectively if done locally.

For example, I work my train to Brighton and back to Westbury to complete my shift for the day. However, on my return the local Duty Manager says to me;

"Steve we're in a spot of bother. That empty class 150 in platform 3 should have been shunted to the holding sidings 20 minutes ago and the signaller wants the up London in there in 5 minutes. But the Bristol driver booked to make the shunt is still at Bath due to a point's failure and I have had to use my spare driver to cover his back working to Bristol. So could you do the shunt for me before you go home please?"

I could say no but I do not and I make the shunt. Why? Because I personally know and respect the duty manager, we have a good working *relationship and I know that in return he/she will do me a favour if at all possible the next time I ask. This will not happen if the relevant manager is at Swindon. Firstly, with everything else going on he would not realise that an empty unit is blocking a platform at Westbury and even if he became aware he would think that it could not immediately be shunted, as there is no spare driver. This remote manager would not know that I am now the only driver in the vicinity and even if he did he would not be able to contact me, and again if he did manage to speak to me I would say no, because it would just be a voice on the end of a phone and not someone I would sympathise with, relate to, or put myself out to assist.*

*INTEGRATION*
*The next time you are at Bristol Temple Meads pay a visit to the (former Wessex) duty manager's office on platform 7. I am certain that within you will find Bristol West traincrew, either between trains, waiting orders or having their PNBs – despite the fact that superior facilities are available upstairs on platform 5 adjacent to the FGW HSS booking-on point. Why is this? It is because despite the best efforts of some HSS managers and staff alike the West train crew still feel uncomfortable and alienated when using these facilities even though we have been one company now for 10 months.*

*It is unfortunate that an 'us and them' atmosphere still prevails. I sincerely hope and anticipate the current well-defined edges will erode and merge over time and that more of a single team spirit will develop. Obviously the harmonisation of pay and conditions (all grades) is required if this goal is ever to be achieved.*

*If you have taken the time and trouble to read this far – congratulations and thank you. I feel a little better with it off my chest – but after all you did ask!*

*Yours sincerely*
*Steve Davies*

Driver Divisional Council meetings within FGW were normally heavy going due to everybody having different priorities and insisting that their own favourite axe be placed on the agenda, as they wanted to thoroughly grind it. During most of my time on the council, my staff-side brothers were Bob Morse, Dick Samuels and Brian Jones (aka Bald Eagle) representing their respective high-speed train depots, Ian Finn and Martin Boreham from the Thames Valley depots and Nigel Birkett then Alan Chase and later Steve Newton and I representing FGW West drivers (see photos). On the management side, our meetings were often chaired by the FGW Operations Director Kevin Gale and we were all – staff and management sides alike – kept in check by FGW's hardest working, totally dedicated and most trustworthy manager, Resource Analyst Sue Mundy, whose knowledge concerning FGW employees and their conditions of service was second to none.

Every year, the British tabloid press would produce hysterical head-lines regarding an impending outbreak of bird flu that was certain to result in a huge number of deaths. My colleague Martin Boreham had taken all this on board and insisted that we put 'Bird Flu' on the agenda of our next meeting with management that was due to take place on 7th July 2006 and so reluctantly, we did. When it cropped up, Martin asked if the company had considered what mitigation measures it was going to put in place to help safeguard employees should a future bird flu epidemic break out. I had expected Kevin Gale to say something banal to the effect that "The company was in the process of assessing the situation and would be seeking advice on the best course of action should an outbreak occur". Instead he said

"When I saw this item on the agenda, I thought that I would ask an expert to attend the meeting to answer your questions and address your concerns". He then reached down into his briefcase and took out a child's multicoloured stuffed toy parrot and put it on the table. Everyone, except Martin, found this very funny and when the laugh-ter had died down, I took out my handkerchief and used it to wipe the parrot's beak.

"It looks like bird flu is already here!" I said.

You will not be surprised to learn that when the official minutes of this meeting were produced 'Professor Beaky' was not included on the list of attendees.

Kevin Gale and I had an ongoing and friendly debate concerning the status of different groups of drivers within the company. He couldn't understand why some of his drivers and I, in particular, did not want to drive what was then considered to be the company's flagship services that were operated by the High Speed Train fleet. The fact that his HST drivers received more pay than the other two groups of drivers (true) and deserved to have a higher salary (untrue) should be reason enough for me to transfer into this 'elite' group of staff. He didn't understand that there were some of us who were content with our status but would still battle on until parity had been achieved across all driver grade groups in a process commonly known as 'harmonisation' (see below).

Well Kevin, if you ever read this book, I am pleased to advise you that I never did learn HSTs before I retired and so you lost our friendly wager (unfortunately there was no money involved).

However, I confess that I have driven HSTs on three occasions: twice when piloting diverted services from Westbury to Bristol TM and once during my MP12 driver-training course. To me they were just another type of train but with the driver's seat near the centre and not to the left of the cab as was the case with every other train I had driven. It didn't feel quite right somehow and I knew I was not missing anything special from a driver's perspective although, overall, the HST concept and design was clearly excellent.

By far the hardest nut to crack during my time as a Driver's Divisional Council rep on FGW was the issue of 'harmonisation'. The background to this thorny issue was that, in 2006, the government created a new franchise that was to be operated by a newly created company named First Greater Western. This was a new company and should have not been confused – though it usually was – with First Great Western, the company that was already running the high-speed services from Paddington to South Wales and the West of England and the same one that had previously incorporated the Thames Valley services into its portfolio. Now, under the larger franchise arrangements, all Wessex Trains services and staff were also to be merged into the new First Greater Western train operating company. Many managers and even staff already employed by First Great Western viewed this new arrangement as a takeover of Wessex Trains by FGW. This was not the case because First Great Western itself ceased to exist on 31$^{st}$ March 2006 to be replaced by the new train operating company called First Greater Western.

ASLEF had, and still has, a policy that all productive main line train drivers working for the same train operating company should receive the same rate of pay and all other conditions of service that include such basics as number of days annual leave entitlement, guaranteed breaks from driving, maximum length of shift and all rostering and linking arrangements etc. Now you might think it obvious that any two employees doing the same job within the same company should, inevitably, receive the same remuneration package. This was not automatically the case for drivers within several train operating companies that included First Greater Western. The company and the unions inherited three different sets of pay and conditions: FGW high-speed train drivers, the Thames Valley service drivers and thirdly, the former Wessex Trains drivers.

FGW drivers had three different sets of pay and conditions and it was our task as drivers' reps on DDC to persuade the management that all of their drivers should be treated and paid alike.

The stumbling blocks on the way to achieving this goal were many and complicated. I will list here just a few of the basic problems.

- Pay: HST drivers were in receipt of a higher rate of pay than that enjoyed by Thames Valley drivers and considerably more than the former Wessex drivers were being paid. (As the years rolled by without harmonisation being achieved, this disparity in pay became greater when the same percentage increases were paid to all three groups.)
- Holidays: Again, all three groups received a different number of annual leave days.
- Breaks and workload parameters: While similar arrangements were in operation, they would still need to be renegotiated to ensure a common policy for all drivers.

Initially for harmonisation talks, FGW employed the services of a third party by the name of First Class Partnerships Ltd. to try and smooth the negotiation path and, while the very first meeting on 8$^{th}$

December 2006 went reasonably well considering the enormity of the task ahead, the services of this company were soon discarded by FGW. The reason? – We were never told. Our guess was that either their charges were too high or that senior management considered that they were not necessary after all. We then spent well over a year in these on and off negotiations trying to agree a package that would be acceptable to all parties. Eventually we negotiated and agreed a pay and conditions package that DDC, ASLEF and FGW could all recommend to the 800 drivers concerned (soon to grow to over 900). It was a good deal but when we visited all twelve FGW driver depots (Paddington, Reading, Oxford, Bristol, Gloucester, Swansea, Westbury, Fratton, Exeter, Plymouth, Par and Penzance) we received a very mixed response to the proposition. Despite the fact that my DDC colleagues and I reiterated that there would be no improved offer put on the table if the first one was rejected – and there never was – some drivers appeared not to believe us. While others did not accept the principle of the same rate of pay and conditions for all and, I am sorry to say, this attitude seemed to be more prevalent among many though not all HSS drivers. The final result of the December 2007 harmonisation referendum was ...

| | |
|---|---|
| Voting papers distributed: | 782 |
| Voting papers return: | 651 (83%, none spoiled) |
| Votes in favour: | 209 (32% of papers returned) |
| Votes against: | 442 (68% of papers returned) |

This was bitterly disappointing to all of us who had worked for so long and hard during the many months on these very complicated negotiations but ASLEF had to accept the result and was finally forced to officially reject the offer.

Of course, this situation was not unique to the driving grade as the guards and maintenance staff were also in a similar situation. Following the driver's harmonisation package rejection, we were forced to negotiate separate deals and the new 2009 pay and conditions package for FGW West (former Wessex) drivers was again recommended for acceptance. Every driver involved received a personal copy of the proposed agreement and, although it was 88 pages long, the last page still listed an additional 25 separate issues that were to be reviewed and restructured at a later date as they applied to all employees and not just drivers. These included such important matters as collective bargaining procedures, maternity and paternity leave entitlements, health and safety issues, individual grievance and disciplinary procedures, alcohol and drugs policy, etc.

My colleagues and I visited all the depots concerned (Gloucester, Bristol, Exeter, Par, Penzance, Westbury and Fratton) to explain the package and answer any questions that arose. There was then a ballot of the drivers concerned with the result as follows:

288 Voting papers distributed
234 Voting papers returned
192 Votes in favour
41 Votes against
1 Spoiled paper

This was a three-year deal that resulted in the following basic salary for main line FGW West drivers:

December 2009: £35,500 p.a
April 2010: £37,000 p.a.
April 2011: £40,750 p.a.

While these rates of pay were very good, we were now far more productive than ever and out pay still lagged behind that enjoyed by our HST and Thames Valley driver colleagues within FGW who had their own separate discussions.

During these periods of hectic negotiations, occasionally, my DDC colleagues and I were often required to stay overnight in hotels when either the distance we had to travel for a meeting made it impractical to commute for the day or we had arranged for meetings to take place at the same location on several consecutive days. To be fair, the company always used good hotels and both the management and staff reps were equally well catered for. On one occasion, there were about a dozen of us staying overnight at a rather plush hotel when, after the business of the day had finished, we all met up in the hotel's very smart restaurant for dinner. We were all sitting at a single large table well equipped with high class tableware including an array of shiny cutlery, flower displays and sparkling glasses when, as if by magic, the wine waiter suddenly appeared and handed us each a wine list. We all studied our copies intently, pretending we knew what we were considering would be the best wine to select with our choice of food. All went quiet and the wine waiter stood poised ready with his pen and notepad. Nothing happened. The wine waiter then gave a small diplomatic cough as if to say,

"Well – I'm still waiting."

Eventually one of the management team said, "Shall I order the wine for us all?"

Everyone around the table warmly welcomed this offer. (It was the only thing we had agreed on all day!) What a relief we collectively thought, someone who knows about wine, even a connoisseur perhaps.

He took a final look at the wine list, slapped its cover shut, looked up at the unfortunate wine waiter who was still patiently hovering and said, "Four bottles of red and four bottles of white please."

We all burst out laughing and even the wine waiter had a smile.

The food was excellent and more importantly, perhaps, the wine was very nice too!

On one occasion, I surprised myself by writing a letter of support for a manager after he had been sacked but before his dismissal appeal hearing.

A very senior manager (let's call him 'A') had dismissed a middle-ranking manager ('B') for failing to get authorisation from him before hiring in a driver from another TOC to move an FGW unit to Reading depot for heavy-duty under-frame cleaning following its involvement in a fatality.

The use of drivers from other companies was a very controversial one as ASLEF always fought to keep all work 'in house'. So, while 'A' had given no promise that he would not use drivers from other TOCs, in exceptional circumstances and when no FGW drivers were available, he also gave his personal assurance that ASLEF would always be advised and consulted beforehand should the necessity arise.

However 'B' was either unaware of his boss's commitment or, in an effort to get the train cleaned overnight to be available for service the following day and thereby avoiding possible train cancellations, he used his own initiative and arranged for another TOC to move the train, as at that time, it would have required four FGW drivers to do so: one for traction knowledge, another for route knowledge out and then the same back the following morning.

'A' was upset and angry that his promise to the union had been undermined by 'B' and promptly sacked him.

I liked and respected 'B' and he used to be my boss before he was promoted so I wrote to 'A' and while not commenting on the specific issues I advised him that 'B' was well respected by staff and was clearly a dedicated railwayman.

Of course, I did not believe either then or now that my input would make the slightest difference to the outcome of B's appeal hearing but I felt better for doing so and I believed that at least it would do no harm. Eventually 'B' was reinstated but with a substantial demotion.

I still have no Idea how 'B' became aware of my letter of support but when the dust had settled, he sent me a personal thank you note.

Ironically 'A' has now left the company while 'B' is again slowly climbing up the promotional ladder.

Historically, ASLEF and the RMT (formerly the NUR) trade unions had been friendly and occasionally not so friendly rivals when it came to representing footplate employees. Whereas ASLEF only represented drivers and those in the footplate line of promotion, the RMT covered most grades within rail and other transport industries. For many years, the recruitment of new members had been very competitive; however, as ASLEF was a specialist trade union dedicated to drivers' issues alone it had always won the numbers game and by a considerable margin. Some depots had a driver ASLEF membership rate of 100%, most averaged about 95% and I was not aware of any under 90%. There is no longer a 'closed shop' and drivers are free to join ASLEF, or the RMT or neither. However, as only these two unions are recognised by train companies as representing footplate staff, a driver would be very foolish to join any other.

ASLEF is widely regarded as a union that 'punches above its weight' and that is because of its overwhelming support and traditional solidarity from its rank and file members. Is it perfect? No, of course not, and even though membership subscriptions are relatively high when compared to other trade unions, the fact that almost all drivers are members speaks for itself.

There had been a considerable number of trainee drivers employed in recent years and I was permitted by FGW to ask permission from their instructors to address the trainees in their classroom regarding the benefits of becoming ASLEF members. None of the classroom instructors ever refused me permission. On the contrary, they were only too well aware of the advantages of TU membership and wanted the best for their trainees, some of whom were from other grades, notably guards, within the company, but others were new to the industry and had possibly never been trade union members before. On several occasions when I addressed a classroom full of trainee drivers, Tim Earl who was my equivalent within the RMT, accompanied me. We took it in turns to try and persuade them to join our respective unions. We would explain the particular merits of each, distribute membership application forms and answer their questions. Tim had one and only one advantage and that was that his RMT subs were considerably lower than those of ASLEF. If you pay less you must expect less would be my response but I would mainly emphasise the fact that ASLEF was a specialised trade union representing footplate staff only and not diluted with the concerns, however legitimate, of other grades. My last advice to the trainees was to join ASLEF but if you decide not to for any reason then at least join the RMT because as an individual you would be very vulnerable indeed if you were a non trade unionist. Although Tim and I were rivals we were also both drivers and, at the end of the day, there was little animosity between us.

The appropriate RMT representative was always entitled to attend any of our DDC meetings with management when discussing or negotiating matters applicable to all or certain groups of drivers. These were called collective issues and the RMT full-time official was allowed to choose whether or not to put in an appearance. I recall on one occasion we were discussing some driver related technical issue concerning new radio communication equipment being installed in our cabs when, during an adjournment, the RMT rep who was not a driver was frank enough to admit to me that he was out of his depth and frequently didn't understand what we were all talking about. I thought that was a very honest admission but I also wondered what his driver members would think of the situation if they knew; not that I would take advantage as I liked the guy and his honesty.

On 4th January 1989, I was booked to work 6074 from Westbury to Old Oak Common in London. This was the 11:20 from Meldon Quarry near Exeter to Tonbridge in Kent and consisted of an engineer's train loaded with railway ballast with 33 006 + 33 015 providing the motive power. I was advised that it was running late, as the Exeter driver on the first leg of the journey to Westbury was experiencing problems with the train. I knew no more details until I spoke directly to my West of England colleague when eventually the train arrived. The signalman had stopped the train because it had activated an automatic lineside axle hotbox detector west of Castle Cary and, on examination, the driver had found that the wagon concerned had one axle overheating. So, he then proceeded at only 20 mph stopping frequently to check that the wagon was still safe to continue and this had naturally resulted in the very late arrival at Westbury. The Exeter driver's last words to me after I relieved him were ... "If I were you, mate, I'd have it off", meaning that he thought the defective wagon should be detached from the rest of the train and not continue beyond Westbury. That was good enough for me. I advised my supervisor, the shunter and the signaller that the train needed to be reversed back into the up yard for a detachment to be made but I was told not to move the train until a carriage and wagon examiner had inspected the wagon concerned. So, I waited and waited, until about an hour later there was a bang on the side of my cab and this was the C&W examiner to advise me that he could detect no hot box and that the wagon was to continue. I commented that I was not surprised that it had cooled down given the precautions carried out by the previous driver and the time it had remained stationary waiting to be examined. I refused to take 6074 forward with the suspect wagon still in the train. I was ordered by my supervisor to get the train on the move but I stuck to my guns with the previous driver's precautionary words "If I were you, mate, I'd have it off" still ringing in my ears. After all, this driver had been the only person to see the state of the hot box at its worst. Stalemate. Eventually, however, the supervisor sent over another driver to relieve me to take the train to Old Oak Common. I fully explained the situation to this driver but his attitude was that they shouldn't have given the job to a boy in the first place. (This was ten days before my 35th birthday.) He then took the train forward and I was asked for a report to justify my refusal to work. I submitted my report and heard no more on the subject from anyone.

The driver who eventually took 6074 to London was Dave Walker. Better known as 'Melksham Walker' simply because this is the town in which he lived and because it differentiated him from another West-bury driver with the same surname – Den Walker. They were completely different characters. Den was a pleasant and friendly colleague whereas, in my opinion, 'Melksham' was a loud mouthed, self-righteous, obnoxious individual who had no scruples and a very selfish outlook on life. If charity begins at home then Melksham Walker was the most philanthropic person I have ever known! He would study the links and the daily alteration sheets avidly and in great detail because he wanted to know everybody else's business and to be sure that he was not missing out on any lucrative work. On one occasion, he happened to be in town when my wife was also in Melk-sham doing some shopping. He stopped Anne in the middle of the street and said to her, "You had better get back quick as your old man will soon be home and he'll want his tea."

Now if anyone else had said that to her she would have laughed it off as a joke; however, she knew that he meant it. She told him to mind his own business and carried on shopping.

In my introduction to this book I wrote, *"Over the years I must have worked with hundreds of other railwaymen and women and I can honestly say that I can count on the fingers of one hand the few that I did not trust or like."* Melksham Walker was one of these few.

On a more positive note, I cannot close this chapter without paying tribute to the best manager by far that I ever worked under during my entire railway career. Ian Burbidge was naturally gifted with that very rare skill of excellent man management. Always cheerful, helpful and with a sympathetic ear, he was very well respected by every driver who ever met him. His operational railway knowledge and practical approach to solving problems were recognised company wide. He was a driver for many years before he went on to higher things and as a former driver, he appreciated more than most other managers the difficulties any driver could experience that may have resulted in him or her making an error. Although he would implement company policy, he also took the time and trouble to support any driver in difficulty who he knew would benefit from a soft approach rather than just throwing the book at them which is what most managers would do as that was the quick and easy way to deal with an errant driver. He would also try to deal with any issue locally as he knew the best approach to take would depend on the individual involved.

Ian retired a little early because I believe he was not prepared to implement some changes to FGW company policy that he considered unnecessary, unrealistic and grossly unfair. To many of us, he appeared to have been forced out by senior management who considered his management style to be too relaxed notwithstanding the fact that he was considered by drivers to be their most respected manager.

Ian's departure was not only a severe loss to Westbury depot but also to the whole rail industry. At his retirement party on 22nd October 2016, he was presented with many gifts from his colleagues and as everybody had also previously generously donated to his collection, the cheque he received was a fittingly substantial one. A recently qualified driver was in tears as she thanked him for all he had done to help her pass her driving exam.

I did not and still do not understand why some managers think that staff must be subjugated. Ian was one of only a few managers who knew that good staff morale would produce the best results. Most staff want to be proactive and would go that extra mile to help provide a better service for the public but are at best ignored or even condemned for using any sort of initiative by some deskbound manager who often wouldn't know the difference between a class 153 and a steam engine.

One of our Newport workhorses 6989 (later 37 289 and then 37 408) was photographed at Ebbw Junction Diesel Depot on 13th November 1970. A common headcode in use at this time, 9A70, has been set by its secondman. (Coincidently this was my loco 23 years later: see 'Road Block' photo and description in Chapter 2 Working for a Living.)

A class 37 drivers' control desk (this one is 37 233 at Westbury on 2nd October 1983) is almost identical in design to that of the class 55 Deltic. This is not surprising because the majority of the 37s and all of the 55s were manufactured for BR by English Electric at Vulcan Foundry in Newton-le-Willows during the early 1960s.

This photo taken during my trainspotting days shows D9019 (later 55 019) 'Royal Highland Fusilier' departing Kings Cross on 31st July 1967. Little did I know then that 3½ years later, I would be working as a secondman and based at 'The Cross' and that the dominating 1932 signal box would still be in use.

Ebbw Junction: 37 191 (originally D6891) crosses over onto the down relief line from the Western Valley branch with a train of used track sections. The photo was taken on a Sunday morning in July of 1979 and explains why so many locos (inc. 08s, 37s & 56s) are on the depot. Our breakdown vans carrying rerailing equipment and snow-plough are also 'on shed'.
Photo: thanks to Andy Hoare.

The small Wiltshire town of Westbury was known for two prominent landmarks: the huge White Horse carved into the hillside on the edge of Salisbury Plain that overlooks the town and the now demolished 400 ft. high cement works chimney that was frequently used by military aircraft as an aid to navigation.

The other Westbury landmark. The White Horse looks down on an SWT three-car class 159 unit providing the 12:20 London Waterloo to Bristol Temple Meads service on 16th May 2012.

Westbury Driver Bert Casley and me with tea can in hand are about to climb aboard 56 108 in Westbury down yard in preparation for working a loaded stone train to Eastleigh on 8th November 1984.
Photo: Pete Mantell.

The MP12 trainee drivers' class of '81.
Back row L-R: Steve Truman (Bristol), Mike Badger (Westbury), Phil Battishill (Plymouth), John Evans (Swindon), Dave Douglas (Swindon). Middle right: Nigel Miles (Westbury). Seated L-R: Rodney Selman (Westbury), Steve Davies (Westbury), Instructor Jim Machin (Bristol), Mike Brinkworth (Gloucester) and Mike Shields (Bristol). See Chapter 6 Driver Training.
Photo: Nigel Miles.

In the cab of 47 519 (originally D1102) working 2V62 the 10:35 from Weymouth to Bristol TM on 8th September 1988. I am driving through Frome North Junction with full power applied.
Photo: John Philips.

I'm departing Westbury some 38 minutes late on 7th June 1989 with DMMU set C995 made up of two power cars (51436 & 53162) with 2V76, the 16:53 Weymouth to Cardiff Central service.
Photo: John Philips.

19th May 1984: the abandoned Westbury (North) signal box. It and three other semaphore signal boxes were all replaced by the new Westbury panel box that had opened five days previously.
Photo: Rodney Selman

33 101 is hauling 3 x 4 car withdrawn southern region EMUs en route to Margam for scrapping. 5V45 is stopped by a red signal at Bathampton junction on 16th April 1992.

Road Block! On 3rd June 1993 my excursion to Weymouth Quay hauled by 37 408 was blocked by an illegally parked Porsche and the police had to arrange for its removal. See Chapter 17 Odd Jobs for full details.
Photo: The Dorset Evening Echo.

17th August 1993: 59 001 'Yeoman Endeavour' has its 24 x 100-ton wagons of limestone emptied at the temporary depot of Hallen Moor near Bristol providing materials for the construction of the new M49 and the Second Severn Crossing. (The bell was ornamental and would not ring unless you threw a piece of ballast at it!)

This is the last freight train that I would ever drive. 37 803 in Mainline Freight livery waits in Westbury down yard on 9th March 1995.
See Chapter 8 Train Driving Techniques for full details.

158 843 with a Portsmouth Harbour to Cardiff Central Wales & West service passes through flooding at Wylye on 15th December 2000.

Wessex Trains operated some services to Weymouth for several years with two class 31s and Mk. 2 coaching stock. With 'Santa' on board the 08:58 departure from Bristol TM (2085) waits at Frome North on 11th December 2004 with 31 601 'The mayor of Casterbridge' leading four coaches in matching livery with 31 452 (out of view) at the rear — but still working in multiple.

Photographed from the top of the steps leading to the traincrew messroom, this view of Brighton station was taken on 27th October 2008. 158 950, my train to Bristol (1V96) can just be seen waiting on platform 1. It's not on fire! See Chapter 7 Driver Davies.

On 2nd February 2009, through the snow near Wylye appears FGW 150 261 with a Portsmouth Harbour to Cardiff Central train.

12th March 2012. FGW refurbished 150 101 at Frome with 2A87 the 21:02 service to Westbury. The station was opened in 1850, has an overall wooden roof and is a Grade II listed building.

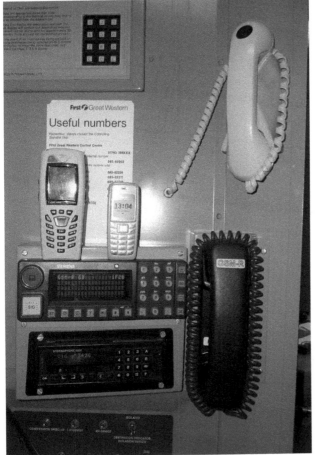

Additional trains to Weymouth were provided in connection with the 2012 Olympic sailing competitions being held at nearby Portland. On 2nd August SWT EMU 450 079 Desiro passes by on the up line with a service to Waterloo while CrossCountry Voyager No. 220 024 and FGW 3 car hybrid Sprinter 158 953 wait in Jersey sidings for their respective return workings. See Chapter 17 Odd Jobs.

Communications!
For many years, drivers had no in cab communication apparatus to directly contact other colleagues such as signalmen or the control office but then, for a brief period, we had four options! Initially NRN was installed but this proved unreliable, so portable IVRS (Interim Voice Radio System) handsets were used as an intermediate measure before GSM-R was fully implemented. The fourth was a company issue driver's personal mobile phone and all are seen together in this photo taken on 14th December 2012 in the cab of an FGW class 158 Sprinter.

Pilning is the last station in England before trains enter Wales through the Severn Tunnel.

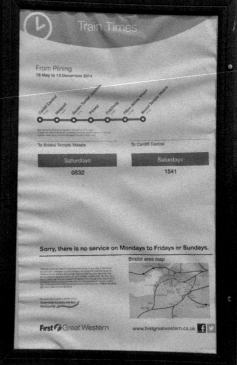

These posters photographed at the station on 25th July 2014 ironically ask, "Where is my train?"
And give the answer,
"The next one is due on Saturday!"

Situated between Severn Tunnel Junction and Newport is Bishton Crossing Box. To access the opposite side of the four running lines, any road vehicle over 5′ 6″ high must utilise the adjacent level crossing and any pedestrian over this height must walk with a stoop! Is this the lowest rail-over-public-road bridge in Britain?

At 14:09 on 10th July 2010, 1C84 the 13:06 FGW HST service from Paddington to Penzance struck a fallen tree near Lavington, nine miles east of Westbury. Despite the 90-mph impact, its driver surprisingly escaped serious physical injury even though the cab of power car 43 041 suffered extensive damage (see below.)
Photo: Halcrow: For the Rail Industry.

3rd February 2010. This front-end damage suffered by my train (158 766) occurred while I was working 1F29 the 17:30 FGW service from Cardiff Central to Portsmouth Harbour after collision with a road vehicle that had 'strayed' onto the line between Wilton Junction and Salisbury. Luckily there were no fatalities or injuries (see Chapter 14 Alarming Experiences).

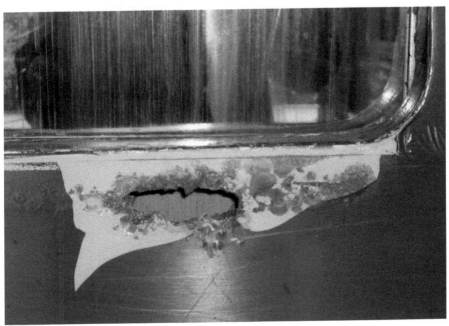

Not all damage to trains is caused by impacts. This was a bodyside hole below the driver's cab side window on FGW unit no. 150 248, photographed on 25th July 2012; it was a result of rust and neglect.

23rd January 2015. This photo shows the single line working apparatus on the up platform at Maiden Newton. Drivers of trains arriving from Dorchester West are required to confirm to the signaller at Dorchester South that their train has arrived complete by pressing the button on the left. (Here this has already been done as the lower lamp is illuminated.) Then permission must be obtained from the signaller at Yeovil Pen Mill to remove a token in order for the train to enter the next single line section. (There are many tokens in this particular machine but it is only possible to remove one.)

I helped to train many trainee drivers during my time as an instructor driver and the following are three of them.

1. 23rd October 1992.
   Trainee Driver Dave Hooper with 59 101 at Whatley.

2. 6th January 1995.
   Trainee Driver Dave Drew in the seat of 59 101 at Acton.

3. 1st March 1995. Trainee Driver Harry Bush on 37 098 with a loaded train of ballast at Yeovil Pen Mill. (See Chapter 12 Instructor Driver.)

The full team of Wessex Trains driver reps line up  at Exeter on 23rd September 2005.
L-R: Dick Chapple (Penzance), Howie  Reynolds & Jerry Cole (Westbury), Chris Meads & Alan Chase (Exeter),
Chris Naylor (Glous.), Steve Davies (Westbury), Tony Kyte (Glous.), Ernie Whitfield (Par), Nigel Birkett (Exeter), Steve Cox (Fratton)
Steve Howard (Par), Mark Cook & Mick Gould (Bristol), Tim Comer (Par).
Photo:Driver colleague.

During an adjournment on 10th October 2007 some members of FGW DDC desperately seek guidance from a homemade Ouija board. L-R: Alan Chase, Brian Jones, Dick Samuels and Martin Boreham.

Happy Chappies, 4th May 2009. L-R: Westbury Drivers Roger Matthews, Howie Reynolds, Steve Davies & Andy Gentle and, in the centre, is former Westbury Driver, now ASLEF National Organiser, Simon Weller.  Photo: Driver colleague.

These two photos were taken at the former ASLEF head office in Arkwright Road, Hampstead, London on 10th March 2009 by an ASLEF brother. This was to be my last visit to 'The Ark'. In the first line-up are the FGW Company Council Drivers' Reps. L-R: Martin Boreham, Bob Morse, Steve Davies, Ian Finn, Steve Newton, Dick Samuels and Howards Rugg.

In the this picture are L-R: ASLEF President Alan Donnelly, District Organiser Stan Moran, General Secretary Keith Norman and FGW Company Council Drivers Secretary Steve Davies (see Chapter 9 Bosses, Brothers and Others).

24th May 2012. FGW Trains Director Kevin Gale presents me with a certificate in recognition of my 40 years' service to the rail industry while Anne received flowers.
(I couldn't resist wearing my ASLEF tie.)
Photo: Event photographer.

Former FGW Weymouth-based Guard and now ScotRail Driver Dave Cornwell, his charming wife Noreen and my wife Anne enjoy a day out together at Windermere on 3rd July 2017 (see Chapter 15 Faults and Failures).

This is the last train that I would ever drive: the 17:06 GWR service from Taunton to Cardiff Central. 2U26 was formed by two car sprinter 150 128 and is seen at Taunton shortly before departure on 28th September 2017 (see Chapter 18, Winding Down and Retirement).

THE RAILWAY INDUSTRY MEMORIAL
IN CELEBRATION OF THE MAGNIFICENT ACHIEVEMENTS OF
THE RAILWAY FAMILY WHO HAVE SERVED THE BRITISH ISLES
WITH GREAT DISTINCTION FROM HUMBLE BEGINNINGS IN
THE NINETEENTH CENTURY THROUGH TO THE PRESENT DAY.

WE SPECIALLY REMEMBER AND GIVE THANKS FOR THE
MANY THOUSANDS OF RAILWAY PEOPLE WHO HAVE
GIVEN THEIR LIVES IN TIMES OF CONFLICT OR PEACE.

DEDICATED 22ND MAY 2012

THIS MEMORIAL WAS COMMISSIONED BY THE BRITISH TRANSPORT PENSIONERS FEDERATION
IT WAS MADE POSSIBLE BY THE GENEROSITY OF ITS MEMBERS FRIENDS AND TODAYS RAILWAY INDUSTRY EMPLOYERS

LEST WE FORGET

# 10

# Passengers Not Customers

Over the years, the use of the word 'passenger' has been replaced by reference to the 'customer' and, while this may be understandable from a commercial point of view, as a driver I personally considered them all to be passengers or, more accurately, long suffering members of the public. This stems from the fact that, under British Rail, we were deemed to be providing a public service whereas, today, under the privatisation philosophy, the number one priority is increasing revenue and thereby profit for the train operating companies.

*Picture this scene: No. 1 (British Rail)*
A passenger is at Bristol Temple Meads station and approaches a porter who is leaning against a Royal Mail trolley smoking a fag. He is scruffily dressed in an ill-fitting uniform.

Passenger: "My train to Birmingham is late. Can you tell me why and what time I am now likely to get there?

Porter: "Dunno mate."

He then flicks his cigarette butt onto the platform and wanders off to the porters' cabin for a well-deserved mug of tea and a read of *The Sporting Life*.

*Picture this scene: No. 2 (Privatised Railway)*
A customer is at Bristol Temple Meads station and approaches a female Customer-Platform Interface Assistant Deputy Duty Manager who is smartly dressed in a well-fitting uniform with a bright pink tabard over the top.

Customer: "My train to Birmingham is now showing 'delayed' on the departure screens. Can you tell me why and what time I am now likely to get there?

Customer-Platform Interface Assistant Deputy Duty Manager: "I am very sorry sir, I am unable to provide you with that information."

She then walks off to her office for a well-deserved expresso con panna coffee, and to read her smart phone social media feeds.

Spot the difference? At the end of the day, both the passenger and the customer are none the wiser but the customer has paid considerably more for his ticket to Birmingham on the privatised railway. Ah progress!

I could not do a conductor's job. I would not have the patience to deal with any yob that had no ticket and refused to buy one or challenged my mother's marital status. I would give as good as I got and this would inevitably lead to further confrontation, train delays and possible police action. No, I would not last long as a guard/ conductor/train manager.

Conductors were the guards I worked with day in and day out for nearly 30 years. While some were more proactive than others, the very nature of their job resulted in inevitable and substantial face-to-face interaction with their passengers; sorry customers.

When things went wrong, and they often did, the conductor was the public face of the company and apparently responsible for late running, overcrowding, cancellations, high fares, toilets not working, or the train being too hot or too cold, most of which, in fact, they had no control over whatsoever. Nevertheless, they had to take the flak. On many occasions, traincrew and station staff have often felt personally embarrassed by the poor or, in the event of a cancelled train, nonexistent service on offer to frustrated punters.

Every guard has been verbally assaulted and many physically attacked. Of course, most turns of duty do not result in confrontations as 99% of customers are mild mannered and well behaved; however, it is the other 1% who may be under the influence of drink or drugs that can make a conscientious guard's job almost impossible. Conductors mainly work trains operating local stopping services with many of the smaller stations en route being unmanned and having no ticket barriers. This results in some passengers being tempted not to part with their money and become genuine customers. The conductor is not only required to check tickets but also to sell ones to customers, including some with no intention of buying or, if caught without one, with the intention of paying as little as possible by either lying about their age, where they boarded or their final destination. Hiding in the toilet is also an old trick to try and escape paying for a ticket. On top of all this, the guards must have adequate route and traction knowledge, understand and put into operation all necessary rules and regulations, cope with the convoluted fare structure, be responsible for the wellbeing of the travelling public and, above all, make tea for their driver!

It is absolute madness for passenger train companies to try and increase the number of trains in operation with the driver being the only member of staff on board (DOO-P). GWR's original proposal for the manning of their new class 800 trains included the provision for more on-board staff and promised to recruit accordingly. However, it is not simply a matter of how many employees are on these trains but what they are able to contribute to the safe operation of them. Catering staff provide good customer service, do a decent job and are hardworking but are of little use should the train catch fire, derail, or suffer any other abnormal incident such as the driver being injured or taken ill. Tea and sympathy are all very well but that won't get the train moving again. GWR's first proposal included the option of running these new trains between London and Bristol or Cardiff/Swansea under DOO conditions should no guard be immediately available. When ASLEF and the RMT challenged this possible scenario, GWR 'clarified' their proposal and announced that all of these trains would have at least one other suitably qualified member of staff on board. In other words, they would not run under DOO conditions and there would be no significant change to the previous manning agreement other than in the method of train door operations.

During all my time at Newport and my early years at Westbury, all staff were paid weekly in cash and every Thursday, a queue would start to form at the pay office window immediately after the security company had made their delivery. This was common at all depots and in most industries at the time.* Unfortunately, and for whatever reason, the delivery system was not always reliable. Paying out was

---

* My last cash pay day occurred on 28th May 1998 though I continued to be paid weekly (through choice) until the day I retired and not four-weekly as the majority of my colleagues were.

frequently late and occasionally, did not happen until the following day. Most employees including myself were finding it hard to make ends meet as rates of pay under BR were generally low and so, cash in the hand every Thursday was an essential part of our personal budgetary requirements. If the pay was not available and an employee had financial commitments that could not wait, the local manager had the authority to issue the individual with a chit to enable him to receive at least some cash from staff in the station ticket office. The relevant amount would then be deducted from his pay the following week. While this procedure was far from satisfactory and should not have been necessary in the first place, at least it could provide some immediate cash for an individual on the day that he justifiably expected to be paid. When I was on the LDC during this period, we had cause to repeatedly complain to our local manager for failing to ensure that staff were being paid within the agreed time scales.

I booked on duty one Thursday, a short while before the pay office was due to close, but discovered that it hadn't even opened as no cash whatsoever had been delivered! I was angry that the reliability of payday arrangements was getting worse and not better so I went to see the boss again who had to agree that the arrangements in place were not good enough. He was unhappy with employees demanding chits from him as this created extra administration work not only for him but also the ticket office staff and with the pay department who had to readjust pay due the following week. After I had let off steam, I too demanded a chit for part payment and collected cash from the ticket office. Now all this took a while and by the time I eventually arrived on the platform to work my train to Southampton, it had been delayed for about 10 minutes. I was still annoyed when we arrived at our first stop, Warminster. So, I used the PA to announce the following:

"Ladies and gentlemen, this is your driver speaking. I would like to apologise for our late departure from Westbury. This was due to the fact that British Rail have failed to pay any Westbury-based employees their wages this week."

All of the 'Sprinter' DMU's were equipped with a public address system that could be used by the conductor to inform, update and advise passengers whenever necessary. Unless the train is running under DOO-P conditions (something I have never done with a train in public use), the driver will not normally have cause to use the PA system. The few times I have used it (in addition to the above), were on the rare occasions that the train was being delayed due to waiting for the conductor or when something untoward had occurred and the conductor was not able to readily access the PA system.

Drivers have very limited contact with the public compared with guards. However, I have been punched in the face once (at Southampton), spat on three times (at Cardiff, Severn Tunnel Junction and Weymouth), and verbally berated on numerous occasions (at many different locations) by passengers. Respectively, these incidents left me with a sore nose, disgusted and exasperated.

I have also had some laughs at, or I should say with, members of the public too. It always annoyed me to see feet on seats. It was not only disrespectful but made the seats dirtier than they already were. If I saw someone with his or her feet up, I would always take the same approach and use the same line: "Excuse me, sir (or madam), would you mind taking your feet off the seats please?"

I considered this to be a reasonable request and surprisingly, perhaps, it always had the desired effect. Not expecting to be challenged, they would be taken by surprise, remove their feet and often mumble, "Oh sorry". Not once was my request refused which, in a way, was a shame because I was always prepared with an appropriate response should they try and excuse their actions by claiming that the seats were already dirty. My reply would have then been:

"I wonder how they got that way?" Unfortunately, I never got the chance to say it.

On one occasion, I was walking along the platform at Weymouth to the leading end of my class 150 unit to prepare the cab for departure when I noticed two adults and two young children in the leading passenger section of the train. The male adult had his feet up on the opposite seat so I quietly opened the door and said to him, "Excuse me, sir, would you mind taking your feet off the seats please?" I received the usual response of, "Oh sorry" and he put his feet on the floor. I then said, possibly in a sarcastic tone, as I was not impressed with the example he was setting his children, "Thank you!"

Then as I went to close the door, I heard his little girl say, "Driver told you off, daddy."

I smiled to myself and thought that his daughter did more to shame him than I could ever have done.

Passengers would naturally approach any member of staff wearing a uniform with enquiries concerning their journey. "What time is the next train to Gloucester?" or "Am I on the right platform for the Exeter train?" would be typical of the questions you could expect to be asked. However, one day, while waiting on the platform at Bristol Temple Meads for the arrival of my train to Taunton, I was approached by a man in his late twenties who had a different question altogether. He said to me, "I've got a problem."

"Oh dear," I replied, "What's that then?"

"Should I go straight home to the wife, or stay and have a few drinks with the boys?"

By his manner I thought that he had already had a few drinks with the boys. However, trying to be diplomatic and thinking quickly I responded with,

"Well, why not go with the boys for a drink but ask the wife if she wants to join you?"

He beamed and said, "Now that's a good idea mate. I'm glad I asked you!"

Another satisfied customer, I thought, as he wandered away. I briefly spotted him once more on the crowded platform when he was talking loudly on his mobile phone. I got the impression that his wife did not think my idea a good one. Time for me to retreat to Taunton!

We were only about five minutes into our journey from Westbury to Bristol when my conductor Derek Stoneham called me on the cab-to-cab phone and explained that he was having difficulties. Apparently, there were two young men on the train acting wildly, upsetting other passengers with loud and vile language and who could not produce any tickets when asked. Derek told me that they were either well drunk or under the influence of drugs. I asked him if he wanted them off our train at Trowbridge, our first station stop.

"Better had," he replied.

As I slowed the train for Trowbridge, I could hear raised voices coming from the coach behind me. I stopped the train at the platform, got out of the seat and opened the internal door into the coach. I saw that Derek had opened the exit doors and was telling the two young men that they had to get off his train. (I always adopted the same course of action on any occasion when my guard was involved in any confrontational situation. I would join him or her but not interfere unless I had to. While it was the primarily the job of the guard to deal with belligerent passengers, I always considered it my role to support my colleagues as best I could. I believed that the presence of a second member of staff may help to resolve the situation and, if not, at least I would be a witness to whatever may develop.) I joined Derek in trying to persuade them to leave the train when one started to act like a deranged wild animal. He began screaming obscenities at the top of his voice and kicking out. He had totally lost control of his actions. Clearly the drugs he had taken were having a horrifying effect. There was no way he would ever listen to reason and there was also no way that we were going to move the train with him still on board. So, it was stalemate. Derek and I knew that if we were to try and physically force the young man off the train and it did not go as we planned, we could end up being charged with assault, so I was about to return to the cab and call for police assistance when a passenger came to our aid. A giant of a man stood up and said, "I'll get him off," and eventually he did. He grabbed hold of the still hollering youth and tried to bundle him out of the door but initially he had a firm grip on a handrail and refused to let go. I had to use both of my hands to prize his fingers apart and then, suddenly, he was face down on the platform. His friend put up no resistance and got off the train 'unaided'. Derek then promptly shut the doors. Now many passengers had witnessed all this commotion and after I thanked our helpful 'bouncer' and was walking through the train back to my cab, I felt that I should try and reassure them that all was now well and try and reduce the still tense atmosphere. So, in a loud voice, I said to no one in particular, "Another satisfied customer." That seemed to do the trick as I heard a few chuckles as I walked past.

There is one final thing that I will always remember concerning this very unpleasant incident and that is what Derek did next. Before he gave me authority to proceed, he asked me if our signal on the end of the platform was still showing green. I assured him that it was and only then did he give me the right-away signal. Despite all the distress and trauma that Derek had just recently encountered, he was still mindful of his obligation to check the platform starting signal. This says a lot about the calm and professional attitude of the man and, from that day on, I considered him to be one of the best guards at Westbury.

Bristol Temple Meads is a very busy station and one that GWR Westbury drivers encounter almost daily. It can also be a little confusing for the public due to the platform numbering arrangements.

No. 1 is a short bay platform at the east end of the station.

No. 2 is a short bay platform at the west end of the station but not open to the public and is only used to stable empty trains (see Chapter 17 Odd Jobs).

Nos. 3 and 4 are physically one single very long platform but divided into two to increase capacity.

Likewise, numbers 5 & 6, 7 & 8, 9 & 10, and 11 & 12.

Platform number 13 is not divided into two but is a terminal platform with stop blocks at its west end.

Platform number 14 does not exist.

Platform number 15 is not divided but is a through line.

All the even numbered platforms are towards the west end of the station and all the odd numbered platforms are towards the east end except 13 & 15 as they are not divided. Still with me? Well done!

The long-divided platforms such as 3 & 4 are not physically divided of course and only a small suspended St. Andrews cross sign indicates the demarcation point for drivers to ensure that they stop their trains at the correct platform.*

When a hopeful passenger arrives at the station, passes through the ticket barriers and on to the platform, logic would dictate that they would then be on platform number 1. No chance, because the first platform they always encounter, as there is only one entrance and one exit, is, of course, number 3!

---

* After many years these St. Andrews crosses have now been replaced by conventional colour light signals.

So far, so complicated. Late platform alterations are not uncommon at Bristol TM. For example, passengers and traincrew alike may have checked the departure display screens and the 17:05 to Weston-super-Mare is scheduled to depart from platform number 4. Regular commuters going back to the seaside town and train crew alike make their way obediently to platform number 4. Infrequent travellers eventually find it. We are reassured by an automated announcement that the next train to arrive on platform 4 will indeed be the 17:05 departure to Weston-super-Mare. Then just as 17:05 is displayed on all the station's clocks, there is another announcement (this time obviously not automated) that there is to be a platform alteration and our train will now be departing from platform 10. Near panic ensues. I then put into action operation 'sweep up'. I make sure that I am the last person to leave from platform 4 and that all the slow-moving passengers, i.e. those with pushchairs, kids, the elderly, and those with lots of luggage or in wheelchairs, have a head start on me. In these circumstances, I would not rush to my train irrespective of how late it may then be. I make my way slowly down the stairs and into the subway making sure that any of the less agile passengers who have taken the lift are still ahead of me. On more than one occasion, I have advised these passengers not to rush (it can be dangerous – especially on the stairs) and they might breathlessly reply, "But I'll miss my train."

"No, you won't," I would reply, "I'm driving it."

The look of relief on their faces would help to make my day. We would then amble along to platform 10 where the train would be waiting for us. I was always determined to do what I could to ensure that no one would miss their train due to a late platform alteration that was obviously our fault and not theirs.

# 11

# Overcrowding

I had serious concerns over many years with regard to overcrowding on trains. While the most obvious relates to passenger discomfort, it can also impact on staff safety. Despite a commonly held public belief, overcrowded trains are not necessarily unsafe – at least not for the public. Many of the diesel multiple unit 'Sprinter' and 'Pacer' trains now in operation have a design flaw that I do not believe would be acceptable if these trains were introduced today; the only exit from the driver's cab is through a public area. This means that, in the case of extreme overcrowding, the cab door can become effectively blocked by standing passengers, luggage, prams, bikes or a catering trolley that can result in the driver being unable to escape from his/her cab in an emergency situation such as a fire or an imminent collision. I had always found this disconcerting and raised it on several occasions with managers at all levels pointing out that if the fire exit from their office were blocked, would they not be concerned? Furthermore, their office is not moving at speed! Their response was always the same; if on the day, the traincrew considers it to be unsafe then their train should not be moved until it is deemed to be so by the traincrew themselves. My response to this policy was twofold; firstly, it could be interpreted as management passing the buck by not issuing unambiguous instructions or even guidelines for traincrew to follow in such circumstances and secondly, such a procedure is fine if you don't have to implement it.

Overcrowding can occur for many reasons including sporting or entertainment events, cancellation of a previous train or simply because it is a Friday evening with commuters and weekenders all wanting to travel at the same time. There are many examples of events within the GWR area that will always result in overcrowded trains.

These include the Glastonbury Music Festival, Henley Regatta, Cheltenham Races, international football and rugby matches at the Principality Stadium Cardiff, various Christmas markets, the Bristol Harbour Festival and the Bath Half Marathon to name but a few. Events such as these are known well in advance and while some additional trains may be possible or service trains lengthened, the lack of rolling stock and traincrew greatly hinder the management of an adequate service provision.

The challenge to provide enough train seats for demands that fluctuate wildly is a tough one. For example, during the school summer holidays, if the weather forecasters predict a warm and sunny day for southern England, we must expect a great demand for train travel for instance to Weymouth. However, if rain is predicted, the numbers travelling on these seaside services will, naturally, be low. So, the normal 2-car class 150 to Weymouth may be overwhelmed by families on a day's outing to the coast one day but be running nearly empty the next. Those managers within TOCs who have to plan many weeks in advance for the provision of trains and traincrew have little scope to adapt such plans at short notice. Again, this is mainly due to lack of resources. In the past, in order to meet expected demand, some train operating companies have been known to hire in rolling stock from preserved railway enterprises. I appreciate the difficulties in this great fluctuation in demand but if we are serious about reducing road traffic and increasing the opportunities for public transport then far greater investment in the rail industry is required and not only on the main lines.

Please don't misunderstand me, high numbers of customers are excellent for the rail industry; however, the investment must have previously taken place to facilitate them and it is this lack of investment that lies at the root of the problem. (I was once rebuked by a woman at Bath station who couldn't get on my train due to overcrowding who asked me why I didn't have more coaches on my train. I pointed out to her that if my employer had provided me with a ten-coach train then I would be happy to drive it but as they had not and only provided me with two, I could do no more.)

Most traincrew deal with overcrowding in the most pragmatic way possible and that is by simply ignoring it, as they can do little or nothing about it. However, if a driver has been forced to evacuate their cab when their train is still moving at speed, as I had to do on one previous occasion, then a different approach is clearly required.

The first time I refused to move a train due to overcrowding was at Bristol Temple Meads when I was part way through my journey from Westbury to Cardiff. It was a year after the huge Ministry of Defence Procurement Establishment at Filton opened in 1996 that now employs over 8,000 staff, many of whom commute by train. A new station had been specially built at Filton on the outskirts of Bristol and numerous trains were scheduled to stop as customer numbers were rapidly increasing. It was the morning rush hour on 8th May 1997 and our next stop after Temple Meads was to be Filton Abbey Wood; however, the passenger numbers were so great that our two coach DMU No. 158 830 (I was diagrammed to have four coaches made up of a 158 + 150) couldn't cope and so I advised my guard and the station staff that I considered the situation to be unsafe – with particular reference to my blocked cab door. Confusion and chaos ensued as standing fare-paying passengers were asked to detrain. While my guard and the station staff advised customers that there was another train behind that they could catch, I used the train's public address system to announce that the train was being delayed, as I did not consider it safe to proceed due to the severe overcrowding. Eventually enough passengers got off to await the next service and we departed about 10 minutes late. On arrival at Filton Abbey Wood, I stopped the train, the guard released the doors and passengers flooded out. They then had to pass my cab to exit the station but one stopped and tapped on my window.

"Are you the person responsible for delaying this train at Bristol due to overcrowding?"

"Yes sir," I replied and waited for the inevitable barrage of criticism.

"Well," he said, "I just wanted to say thank you. This train is always dangerously overcrowded and it's about time someone took some action." And he shook me by the hand. I was thinking that he would want to shake me by the throat for making him late for work. Then, much to my astonishment, another three passengers passed similar comments. It just goes to show you never can tell how people will react.

Much later, I became embroiled in another overcrowding incident, this time at Westbury when I was reported by station staff for unnecessarily delaying my train to Brighton. My local manager wrote to me asking for an explanation. The following was my reply:

*In response to your letter, dated 9th September 2008, requesting my report into the above delay I would like to start by confirming that I was the driver involved, and the service was indeed delayed by my actions.*

*I have used personal note books to record details of all trains worked, station stops, and delays however caused and, on this occasion, I recorded that my train was a two-coach class 158 unit (158 745) and that I departed Westbury three minutes late at 13:30 due to overcrowding but arrival at Brighton was on time at 16:12.*

*From the driver's perspective overcrowding only becomes a problem on class 142, 143, 153 & 158 units as the door to/from the driving cab opens into a public vestibule area. Should this area become congested it will delay and possibly prevent*

- *Rapid egress from the cab should the driver need to escape in an emergency e.g. impending collision;*
- *Rapid egress from the cab should the driver need to carry out emergency protection of the line;*
- *Egress from the cab to enable the driver to use an SPT or carry out other duties such as fault finding.*

*On class 158s overcrowding in this area also increases the risk of a passenger falling from the train should the driver forget to check the doorway is clear and open the door by using the butterfly valve from within the cab if there is a need for him/her to leave the train for any reason.*

*I will not drive a train if I judge overcrowding in the vestibule may increase the risk of any of the above and on this occasion, I made such a decision. After a short delay, customers redistributed themselves elsewhere in the train, none were left behind and my train departed safely.*

*This was my call and I expect to be supported. I will not accept any Station Manager or his/her staff interfering in my responsibilities. They are responsible for the safety of the public on the station. My conductor and I are responsible for the safe operation of our train.*

*You may not be aware but over many years and through successive train operating companies both as a driver's representative and an individual driver, I have staged a one-man safety campaign on this issue. I have repeatedly and unsuccessfully argued (I have the minutes and scars to prove it) for a set definition on what constitutes overcrowding on trains, i.e. when is a train so full it becomes unsafe to move?*

*Over the years, many different senior managers from all the TOCs I have worked for have always responded alike, i.e. 'There is no legislation that we are obliged to enforce and we will not put a fixed limit on numbers, however the company will support traincrew who are best placed to make such operational decisions on the day'.*

*At the risk of arguing against myself, there is some merit in this position as how could any policy logically define unsafe overcrowding? Is it a given number of passengers standing nose to nose, and/or cubic feet of space taken by luggage of all sorts and sizes, and/or number of pushchairs, folding bikes and/or a catering trolley?*

*The ideal solution would be for the company to provide sufficient rolling stock to ensure that overcrowding does not become such an issue in the first place. The return to three-coach 158 units on the Cardiff – Portsmouth Harbour route is very welcome by both customers and traincrew alike. However, my two-coach class 158 to Brighton, on a Friday, during the high summer timetable period was clearly insufficient.*

*Delay attribution has become a blame game. TOCs may blame Network Rail and vice versa. But now it appears that different departments within the same TOC have started to blame each other.*

*I consider myself to be a conscientious and professional railwayman whose primary aim is to serve the public by working as one of a team to ensure, as far as practicable, that passengers enjoy a safe and punctual journey. I leave it to others to judge if I have been successful. Quite frankly I resent the implication that I delayed a train unnecessarily.*

*If you cannot do it safely, don't do it – where have I heard that before?*

*Note: The cab doors on class 150, 153 & 158 units are deliberately designed to be "burst through" i.e. normally open into the cab, but can be forced, in an emergency, like a fire door, to open outwards.*

*The situation on class 142 and 143 units is worse as the cab doors will ONLY open into the vestibule area thus removing the second option for the driver to gain egress.*

*Interestingly SWT have recognised this problem and acted. Their class 158s have been modified to prevent public access, except in an emergency, into the vestibule area immediately behind the driving cab when the driver has a key in the desk.*

*The class 150 units have a small cross-corridor area immediately outside of the cab that can be locked to prevent access from the public saloon.*

*I hope that this response is satisfactory; however, should you need any further information please advise me accordingly.*

*Thank you.*

*Yours sincerely*
*Steve Davies*

I heard no more from the management about this incident and I felt a little better for getting it off my chest!

Following this episode, I adopted my own personal strategy to deal with overcrowding. I only had to apply it on about nine or ten occasions but when I did it worked – albeit with delays to the service.

My tactic was that if I drove into a station where I could expect an excessive number of passengers would attempt to board, e.g. at Bath when a rugby match had recently finished, I would stop the train in the usual location, leave the cab and follow off the train the last passenger who had alighted and wait on the platform for the new customers to board. More often than not, in these circumstances, I could not then regain access to my cab due to the number of passengers who had crammed themselves into the vestibule area immediately outside my cab door. This was irrefutable evidence that if I could not get into my cab then I would also not be able to get out in the case of an emergency. I would then advise the station staff and my guard of the situation and they would jointly help to move passengers from the leading vestibule area to other less crowded parts of the train. However, if all parts of the train were similarly crowded, as happened on several occasions, we were forced to leave some unfortunate would-be passengers behind on the platform.

The above occasions obviously resulted in delays and customer complaints but I was never accused of unnecessarily delaying a train again.

# 12

# Instructor Driver

With the abolition of the driver's assistant grade in 1988, a whole-sale review of how the next generation of British Rail drivers were to be trained was required and as part of a new training programme, it was decided to seek experienced drivers to instruct trainees on a one-to-one basis with regard to practical hands-on driving techniques together with the application of all necessary rules and regulations. (These instructor drivers were initially given the title 'Minders'.) The trainee would stick with his/her instructor driver on their rostered shifts, have the same rest days and drive regular trains in service but strictly under the instructor's guidance.

Although I thought the abolition of the driver's assistant position was a shortsighted policy, I was keen to help would-be drivers, in the same way that I had been helped years before at Newport.

I was interested in the possibility of becoming a minder from the start. I felt that I was now experienced enough to contribute and pass on my practical knowledge to a trainee driver who may be completely new to the industry. This type of recruit was deemed to be 'off the street', a term that I disliked as, after all, we were all 'off the street' at one time or another but, nonetheless, it served its purpose in high-lighting the difference between those who had no previous railway experience whatsoever and others who had transferred from another role on the railway, such as a guard.

Newly recruited drivers had to undergo an intensive training course that lasted at least six months and with all the additional route knowledge they then needed to learn, it was seldom less than a year after they had initially entered the footplate line of promotion before they actually took charge of a train.

The 'off the street' recruits had the most to learn as they would not yet understand even the most commonplace terminology used within the industry. Former guards, for instance, had a significant advantage as they already knew the difference between the up line from the down and the four-foot from the six-foot, for example.

In total and over many years, I attended four interviews and several Minder/Instructor Driver training courses, initially with British Rail and then with three different private train operating companies that I worked for, as franchise boundaries and operators regularly changed. Demand for these positions came and went depending on the numbers of new drivers being recruited at the time.

On one occasion, early in 1992, I applied for one of the several minder drivers' jobs advertised at Westbury and when I booked on for duty on 2nd May, I was advised that another driver would cover the first part of my turn and I was to attend a meeting with two of my local managers. I had no advance notice that this meeting would, in fact, be my interview for a minder driver's position. When the meeting started, I complained, tongue-in-cheek, that they had caught me by surprise and that I had no time to prepare. To this, their response was that that was the whole idea – to see how I would cope. I was asked why I wanted the position and I explained that during my earlier footplate career at Newport I was, in effect, an apprentice driver for nearly ten years and had learnt the trade during this period. However, now that the role of secondman/driver's assistant had been abolished, the new way of training drivers was to throw them in at the deep end and hope that they would quickly learn how to swim and I believed that I could give them a least a little of the help that I had previously received. I also said, candidly, that the additional pay would be welcome. (My basic rate of pay at this time was £207.55 per week and a minder's allowance was an extra £6.70 a day.) I was then asked some questions regarding rules, regulations and traction knowledge and, although I struggled with a few, I must have done enough to convince them that I was suitable as I was appointed to one of the positions. My duties were to ensure that, on completion of their course, my trainees would be judged competent to drive both freight and passenger trains. I became a 'Minder Driver' (later changed to 'Instructor Driver') in June 1992 and, after attending a week-long training course, I was allocated my first trainee, Dave Hooper, in

August (see photo). Dave and I got on very well and I am pleased to report that he successfully qualified and today not only is he still driving, he is also a driver's rep at Westbury on the freight side of the industry.

Over the following years, many more trainees passed through my hands including colleagues Julian Ashford, Dave Fleck, Dave Drew, Steve Clarke, Darren Collins, Adrian Watts, Yvonne Le Sueur, Fred Forsyth, Jerry Cole, Francis Guard, Mat Thorley and several others on the odd day or two when their usual instructor was not available for whatever reason. They all coped well with their respective, very intensive driver training courses. Knowing the pressure they were under, I very much doubt if I would have been able to deal with the stress as well as most of them did.

When a trainee driver's position was advertised, a huge number of applications would be received and so the management rigorously enforced a screening process as they naturally only wanted the most suitable candidate to progress to the next stage of the long and detailed recruitment process. Just how fair this whole procedure was I'm not certain. All I know is that when eventually the trainees came to me, they were generally quick learners and all very keen.

The instructor would work his (there were only male instructor drivers at Westbury during my time) normal turn of duty and the trainee was required to shadow his/her (the were several female trainees) instructor's position through the link. The instructor was required to complete a detailed report every day recording the trains worked, the time the trainee spent driving during daylight or the hours of darkness, how they performed with the many different aspects of driving, the practical application of the rules and regulations that they had previously learnt in the classroom and recording any abnormal events such as being authorised to pass a signal at danger. Basically, it was a detailed daily log of the trainee's performance as judged by their instructor.

On one occasion, I was allocated a trainee driver who was based at Fratton (Portsmouth) just for one day and he was so good I assumed that he must be nearing the completion of his practical handling part of the course so I asked him how many weeks driving he had completed. When he answered, "Four." I called him a liar and, as we had never worked together before, he did not know if I was joking or not. I quickly explained to him that his driving was excellent and that if he had achieved such a very high standard after only four weeks of practical tuition, he must have a natural flair for the job and should pass his practical driving exam without difficulty. He then understood the reason for my tactless comment and the rest of the day went well.

There was a general debate at that time as to whether it was more beneficial for a trainee driver to be allocated to a single instructor throughout the entire period of their practical train handling or if it would be better for them to experience training with several different instructors. I argued that the former was the best approach, as this would give both instructor and trainee the opportunity to build up a better personal working relationship, and the instructor would become familiar with any areas that the trainee needed extra help with in order to concentrate on those in particular. A mix of instructors could confuse the trainee as we all had slight variations in our driving techniques. I conceded that if there were to be a clash of personalities that could happen on rare occasions, then the trainee should be allocated another instructor.

Inevitably, there were occasions when things went wrong and then the instructor had to 'carry the can' as, ultimately, the safety of the train was his responsibility, provided, of course, that the trainee had acted responsibly and promptly carried out any instructions received.

On 2nd July 1993, my trainee and I were onboard loco 59 102 (named 'Village of Chantry') and working 6A40. This was a loaded air braked train from Whatley Quarry with the leading 24 x 100-ton wagons ultimately bound for Dagenham and the rear 36 x 50 tonners heading for Angerstein Wharf. We were doing about 30 mph and still on the Whatley single line branch when we experienced an unsolicited emergency application of the brake that brought us to a halt. I half suspected what had occurred so, after advising the signaller of the situation, my trainee and I walked back to investigate and sure enough, as I feared, the train had parted with the last two wagons some distance back from the rest of our train. My poor tuition had resulted in a snapped coupling. However, this served as a clear albeit accidental demonstration of how long a brake application took to release on the rear-most wagons on a very long and heavy train and the danger of applying too much power too quickly. We eventually took the leading portion onto Westbury while the two remaining stranded wagons were hauled back into the quarry.

On another occasion, a different trainee was driving our passenger train to Southampton Central when we were on the approach to the last signal gantry before the station. At the time, this gantry had three signals on it, all for up trains. The left-hand signal applied to trains departing from the up loop, the middle one was for trains running on the up fast and the signal on the right would apply to our train as we were on the up slow line. There were another three lines to the right of us that were primarily for trains running in the down direction. All six lines gently curved to the left in the up direction. Our previous signal was a single yellow and so my trainee had correctly reduced our speed to enable us to easily stop should our next signal remain at danger. As we approached the gantry, all three signals were initially at red but then, as we got closer, the centre one that applied to trains on the up fast line cleared to a single yellow. My trainee released the brake and applied power; he had misread the signals. We were now perilously close to our signal that remained at red. I felt that I would not have time to explain to my trainee the fact that he had made an error so I jumped up, crossed the cab and reaching over him pushed the brake handle to the emergency position. We stopped in time but my trainee was surprised by my actions. He did not understand why I had stopped the train until a service to Waterloo then ran past us on our left under the single yellow and into the station. Then the penny dropped, he realised that he had reacted to the wrong signal. He was not the first to do so at this location and signals on this gantry were classified as being multi SPADed. He apologised for his error and then, when our signal did eventually clear, we proceeded slowly in to Southampton Central station with no more dramas but a lesson learnt.

During my time as an instructor, I had two female trainees. Both impressed me at first and they both passed out successfully. However, their ability to maintain the required high standards when driving on their own proved to be very difficult for them. Both experienced several safety of the line incidents and, despite help and retraining, they were eventually removed from driving duties. I am not saying that this was a direct consequence of their gender, as I am pleased to say that there are now many, though still too few, female train drivers employed in the industry today.

All experienced drivers, whether instructors or not, would normally allow a driver colleague to ride with them up front when road learning. It was also not uncommon for the driver to hand over control of his/her train to a route learner as this was by far the best way to get to know the intricacies of the route concerned. However, the booked driver would still retain overall responsibility for the safe operation of his/her train. I, like almost all other drivers, tried to assist any route learning colleague; after all, we had all been in a similar position ourselves before and would be again if a new route was required at some future date. I would always ask a route learner how many times he/she had been over the route and, if it was only once or twice, I would not offer them the controls but, if they were more experienced, I would ask them if they wanted to drive. I only had two experiences with route learners when this policy proved to be problematic.

The first occurred when I arrived at Southampton with a Portsmouth Harbour to Cardiff Central train formed by a GWR class 158 unit. A SWT driver, whom I did not know, asked if he could learn the road with me to Westbury. I invited him into the cab and he sat in the non-driver's seat. We departed and almost immediately he suggested that he should drive. I thought that this was very presumptuous and declined his proposition. He then seemed to go into a sulk and was unresponsive when I pointed out certain aspects of the route as we proceeded with the journey. As we approached Romsey, only 10 minutes from Southampton, he suddenly said to me, "Well if you're not going to let me drive, I might as well go back in the train."

"That's up to you," I replied. And with that he upped and left the cab. Strange chap, I thought to myself and didn't see him again.

The second time was on 23rd May 2012 when a fellow Westbury driver met me at Bristol TM and asked if he could learn the road with me to Taunton. I asked him how many times he had been over the route and he told me that he intended to sign it off the following day so I did not hesitate and offered him the driver's seat. All went well to Taunton and I was able to relax, safe in the knowledge that he knew the road well enough. However, on the return trip we were rapidly approaching our Bridgewater station stop but he was not braking at the usual point. I was reluctant to criticise but had to say, "Don't forget Bridgewater." With that he applied the brake. Too little, too late, I thought and shouted, "Go to step three!" (This was the maximum brake pressure available on our class 150 unit.) His reply was very worrying.

"I'm already in step three!"

Oh shit," I thought. "This is going to be very close." With our speed dropping but the station fast approaching I could picture us sailing through with all the implications that this involved. Would we stop in time? Yes! No! Maybe! We could do no more. Luckily the rail was dry and the brake blocks dug in. After what seemed an eternity, we just stopped in the platform.

"I'll have to change my braking point" was all he said as we both recovered from the trauma.

From that day until I retired, I never offered another route learner 'the seat'. Although I felt a bit mean at times, I reminded myself of my 'Bridgewater experience' and that I could make my own mistakes thank you.

# STEVE'S TOP TEN P DRIVING TIPS

When I was an instructor driver helping to train colleagues to become qualified drivers, I compiled the following unofficial and personal set of basic guidelines that I hoped would give my trainees an insight into what I thought would help them to prioritise certain aspects of their training.

## 1. PREPARE:
- Book on for duty in good time after adequate rest.
- Wear full uniform.
- Ensure you have your personal ID and safety critical cards.
- Collect your current periodical, weekly and late notices.
- Check all notice boards for anything new.

## 2. PLAN:
- Confirm your station stops with the guard or departure screens.
- Note and display prominently on the driving desk all booked station stops, the maximum permissible speed and number of coaches of your train.

## 3. PROCEED:
- Always use 'press & call' and risk triggered commentary driving.
- Use brake step 3 whenever necessary – but not habitually.

## 4. PRIORITISE:
- Safety before punctuality.
- Station stop – red signal – speed restriction;
  all three may be approached at the same time. Decide on the priority, and act accordingly – but you need to remember the others.
  Concentrate & use the DRA on the move when permitted.
- Unsolicited emergency brake application? – Check TPWS first.
- Possible low rail adhesion? Brake earlier – brake lighter and allow WSP to work (158 only) or release and reapply brake.
  Use the emergency brake if necessary.
- Ensure that your cab door is not blocked by passengers, luggage, pushchairs, bikes etc. before proceeding – it is your only exit in an emergency. If necessary, ask the guard to assist.
- If you need toilet facilities en route, use them at your next station stop that has such amenities, irrespective of any delay to your train. However, you must advise the guard or station staff or signaller (and later control), as appropriate, the reason for the delay.

5. **PARLEY:**
- Good communication is vital. Talk to the signaller and control. Always ask for advice if uncertain. Use phonetic alphabet when necessary and always repeat back safety messages.
- Switch off your mobile phone/s when in the cab.

6. **PERSEVERE:**
- You will make misstakes – everyone does! So, don't be overly critical of your-self but be sure to learn from your errors. In time and with more experience, the high standards of driving you set for yourself will become the norm.
- Set yourself the same standard at 03:00 with an empty stock shunt move as you would at 17:00 with a train full of commuters. Such an approach is important and demonstrates professionalism.

7. **PROFESSIONAL:**
- You are a professional – so think and act in a professional manner.

8. **PRUDENCE:**
  If you have a poor working relationship with any manager or colleague (some personalities clash) avoid them whenever possible and keep a low profile. Remember managers – and TOCs – come and go.

9. **PRIDE:**
- Take pride in the job. If you give your passengers a smooth ride and get them to their destination safely and on time, give yourself a pat on the back because no one else will!
- You are one of the team of dedicated railwaymen and women who work around the clock every day of the year in all conditions in an essential major industry.

10. **PAY:**
- You've earned it, so spend it wisely but enjoy it!

# 13
# Driver Error

Everybody makes mistakes and train drivers are no different. Obviously, any errors that we make could have disastrous consequences but with all the modern safety equipment that has now become an integral part of the industry, the opportunities for serious errors have been considerably reduced although not eliminated altogether. Early in my career, providing no one was injured or damage done, most errors would simply go unreported, though it must be said that a conscientious railwayman would learn from their mistakes and thereby greatly reduce the likelihood of a reoccurrence.

It is almost impossible to describe the combined feelings of shock, dread, fear and apprehension a driver will experience when, for example, he or she belatedly realises their error and that the red signal or station at which they are required to stop will be overshot because the train is still moving at considerable speed despite the fact that they have made an emergency brake application. It is a sensation that I have never experienced outside a train cab but too many times inside.

If a comprehensive list of all my errors were compiled, they alone would nearly fill a book – and I was considered to have had a reasonably good safety record. Please bear in mind, however, that I am talking about a period of very many years and probably tens of thousands of individual trains driven.

I will list just a few as examples:

1. On 23rd February 1993, I was driving 7A09 from Westbury to Acton, London. The 62-wagon 4,619-ton train would divide at Acton and the three parts bound for Luton, Crawley and Angerstein would be taken forward separately. The signalman had routed my train into the up loop line at Theale, west of Reading, to allow an express train to pass. I drove slowly up the long loop

line towards the signal at red that would prevent me from rejoining the mainline. However, on the final approach I misjudged the distance and, despite making an emergency application of the brake, my train only finally stopped when the front half of my class 59 (005) locomotive had passed the red signal. After a considerable amount of swearing at myself, I climbed down from the cab to contact the signalman via the telephone fitted to the signal post. He answered and said that there appeared to be a fault as he was unable to change the mainline signal to green for the up express to pass me. I immediately confessed that the cause of his technical difficulty might be down to the fact that I had passed the loop signal at danger. There was a pause in the conversation and I could almost hear him thinking. I knew I would be in trouble if he reported it so, when he then asked me if I could reverse my train the short distance back to be the correct side of the signal, I immediately said yes, climbed on board and did so. This, of course, was against the rules but, after I had done so and stopped my train, this time in the correct position, I phoned the signalman to update him.

"Right oh," he said. "Let's have another go." And with that, the trap points moved to their correct position and, a short while later, the up London express passed by. No one was hurt, no infrastructure damaged, no reports made, but a lesson was learned as, after that, I approached every red signal more cautiously.

This would not happen on today's railway as every safety conversation is recorded and it would be very detrimental indeed to the career prospects of any staff who might be tempted to 'cover up' such an incident. Indeed, employees are now expected to report (or 'shop' as I would consider it) colleagues who commit any misdemeanours whatsoever whether they are accidental or not. I can honestly say that I did not report any individual colleague to management throughout my entire career on the railway – however, there were times when I was sorely tempted to do so.

2. Nearing Taunton on 14th February 2011 with a train from Bristol, I received a yellow signal meaning the next would be red. Unconcerned, I let the train coast, as I knew that the relevant red signal was at the far end of the long platform at Taunton where the train was due to terminate anyway. Wrong! I forgot about an intermediate signal and, when it came into view, it was at danger and although I made an emergency brake application, the TPWS activated and so, even though no SPAD had occurred, I was then obliged to report the circumstances to the signaller.

3. On Tuesday 8th March 2011, I was driving a train from Bristol to Westbury with Bath Spa as the first scheduled station stop. The following day, I was driving the same train with consequently the same stopping pattern. However, on the Thursday I was again driving a train from Bristol to Westbury but this particular service was different and scheduled to stop at all stations en route. I forgot this and, with the previous two days' journeys acting as a mental template, I approached Oldfield Park station at speed; it was only when I noticed a considerable number of people on the platform that I realised that they were waiting for my train to stop. No chance! Despite my application of the emergency brake the platform slid past my train. We stopped with a severe jolt and I phoned the signaller who answered my call with the words, "What have you done?" I advised her of the situation and, after a short delay, she gave me authorisation to drive back into the station where I was met by some applause from the waiting crowd as I had now managed to stop, albeit at the second attempt.

There was a local enquiry into both incidents number 2 and 3 above and I was temporarily removed from driving duties pending a CDP being drawn up for me. Being told that my train-driving license was being withdrawn, even if only on a temporary basis, was an upsetting experience. It was a severe blow to my self-esteem with the realisation that I was not as good at my job as I thought I was. As both incidents had taken place less than a month apart after many years of (officially) error-free driving my managers were naturally concerned that there may be an underlying cause impacting on my concentration levels. I was asked if I had any personal, family, financial, or health issues. There were none at that time – it was just a coincidence. Eventually I convinced them of this and I was returned to normal driving duties but only after a couple of weeks being accompanied by Westbury instructor driver Mike Jackson who reported back that he considered that there were no issues of concern with my overall standard of driving, but I was advised by my local manager that for the next year I would be more closely monitored than would be normal for a driver with my experience and it took a long time for me to regain my self-confidence when 'in the chair'.

Most large organisations produce an in-house magazine and FGW produced several that came and went over the years. One such period-ical was called 'Motion' and was produced in 2012. The then Operations Standards Manager, Matt Collins, submitted an article on the subject of SPADs, parts of which I considered to be drivel. The editor of this august publication was another FGW Manager, Simon Telega, who, in his editorial, asked for feedback, comments or articles for future editions so I sent him my response to the nonsense that was the Matt Collins article. Not surprisingly perhaps, I received no reply from the editor. However, several weeks later I was driving a train from Bristol to Cardiff when, out of the blue, he turned up and asked if he could ride in the cab with me. I agreed and during the journey he finally acknowledged that he had received my correspondence but said that he would not include it in the next edition of 'Motion' as he considered it "a bit strong". He then produced a greatly watered-down version that he had concocted and asked me if I would put my name to that instead. I told him he had a nerve, accused him of censor-ship and refused to support his proposal. We had a discussion and, in the end, I generously agreed to take a detailed look at his version and possibly resubmit a more diplomatically worded version of my own. I then wrote to him again still refusing to support his proposed wording but submitted an edited version of my original criticism. For compar-ison my original version is below and is immediately followed by my second submission.

I have recently read the Autumn 2012 edition of 'Motion' and generally found it to be interesting and helpful. However, I believe that the feature headed "SPADS – A Personal View" by Operations Standards Manager Matt Collins contains some comments that should not go unchallenged.

Matt refers to what he calls the SPAD myth that is "As long as you have a human at the controls of a train, you will always have SPADs". Matt, this is not a myth it is a fact. That is why you will hear it a lot from drivers. You and some of your management colleagues need to come to terms with this fact and get a grip on the realities of train driving. You need to understand that from time to time there will arise a unique set of adverse circumstances that conspire to result in driver error and consequently sometimes a SPAD. I am sure you know and understand just how devastated a driver feels after his/her error has resulted in a SPAD. The sudden and dramatic fear of the potential consequences not only of the immediate effect but also for the longer term can be a frightening experience. The loss of self esteem and the realisation that you are not as good at your job as you thought you were because of one mistake is a personal blow that the professional and conscientious driver may take some time to recover from.

I would suggest that the company try to boost driver morale rather than continue to highlight driver errors thereby further embarrassing the individuals concerned.

Should we work collectively to try and reduce the number of SPADs? Of course we must. Can SPADs be totally eliminated? No, and the sooner we all accept this fact and concentrate more on helping the driver to cope with and recover from the consequences of simple human error the better. We all make misstakes. Please remember that when working at a conventional desk it is just a matter of pressing edit and delete and your error is undone but when at the controls of the desk in a train cab, one lapse of concentration could result in the loss of your career, or worse.

If there were a magic formula to eliminate SPADs it would have been found by wiser men than us and implemented long before now. SPADs have occurred on the railways ever since trains moved and signals were invented to try and stop them – literally in their tracks.

I believe that a main contributor to safety of the line incidents, including SPADs, is the pressure that FGW puts on its drivers to reduce/eliminate time delays. While we are told (correctly) that safety is always the number one priority, we are also bombarded with 'every second counts' and 'delays cost money' type propaganda and may even get asked for a written report for a delay as brief as a single minute: yes, this does happen. Delays do cost money but how much does a SPAD cost! This mixed message puts drivers under conflicting pressures and encourages potential short cuts to be taken to ensure punctuality. It also contributes to stress and therefore fatigue.

I would also like to see greater collaboration between TOCs and Network Rail in an attempt to reduce 'SPAD traps' (one signal has been passed at danger 15 times) and a speedier repair to faulty signals; I am aware of at least one signal that has been defective for very nearly a year. These examples should be unacceptable in an industry that claims operational safety to be its number one priority.

Steve Davies
FGW Driver, Westbury.


I have recently read the autumn 2012 edition of 'Motion' and generally found it to be interesting and helpful. However, I believe that the feature headed "SPADS – a personal view" by Operations Standards Manager Matt Collins contains some comments that should not go unchallenged.

Matt refers to what he calls the SPAD myth that is "As long as you have a human at the controls of a train, you will always have SPADs". I believe this to be not a myth – but a fact. From time to time there will arise a unique set of adverse circumstances that conspire to result in driver error and consequently sometimes a SPAD. Of course, we should work collectively to try and reduce the number of SPADs but I do not believe that they can be totally and permanently eliminated. This is not defeatist but pragmatic. If there were a magic formula to eliminate SPADs it would have been found by wiser men than us and implemented long before now. SPADs have occurred on the railways ever since trains moved and signals were invented to try and stop them – literally in their tracks.

I would suggest that the company try and boost driver morale rather than continue to highlight driver errors with such things as SPAD graphs and tables as these only serve to further embarrass the individuals concerned. We all need to appreciate just how distressed a driver may feel after his/her error has resulted in a SPAD. The sudden and dramatic fear of the potential consequences not only of the immediate effect but also for the longer term can be a very distressing experience. The loss of self-esteem and the realisation that you are not as good at your job as you thought you were because of one mistake is a personal blow that the professional and conscientious driver may take some time to recover from. There needs to be a much greater emphasis on helping a driver to cope with and recover from the consequences of simple human error.

When working at a computer and you realise that you have made a mistake it is just a matter of pressing edit and delete and any error can be removed. But when at the controls of a train one lapse of concentration could result in the loss of your career or worse.

I believe that a main contributor to safety of the line incidents, including SPADs, is the pressure that FGW puts on its drivers to reduce/eliminate time delays. While we are told (correctly) that safety is always the number one priority, we are also bombarded with "every second counts" and "delays cost money" type propaganda and may even get asked for a written report for a delay as brief as a single minute. This mixed message puts drivers under conflicting pressures and encourages potential short cuts to be taken to ensure punctuality. It also contributes to stress and therefore fatigue.

I would also like to see greater collaboration between TOCs and Network Rail in an attempt to reduce "SPAD traps" (e.g. signal SN63 at Subway Junction has been passed at danger 15 times) and a speedier repair to faulty signals; I am aware of at least one signal – W156 at Castle Cary – that was defective for almost a year. These examples should be unacceptable in an industry that claims operational safety to be its number one priority.

Steve Davies
FGW Driver, Westbury

The fact that neither of the above were published for all FGW employees to read clearly indicated to me that the company was not prepared to accept criticism and, despite its claims, the only feedback it actually wanted from its employees should consist of questions, suggestions, or support for its policies and certainly not any strident condemnations of management philosophy.

I was not surprised, just a little disappointed, at their failure to engage further on this issue.

When I started on the footplate, there was a commonly held belief that there were only two acts that a driver could commit that would lead to his instant dismissal. One was punching a manager on the nose (fair enough) and the other was the far more serious act of entering a single line without the correct token.

On Sunday 19th February 2017, due to engineering work, the line between Castle Cary and Yeovil Pen Mill was closed and so up trains from Weymouth to Westbury/Bristol were terminating at Yeovil PM and, consequently, down trains to Weymouth were starting their journeys from Yeovil P.M. Passengers were obliged to use the dreaded bus replacement service to and from Castle Cary on the West of England main line.

I booked on duty and was taken by taxi to Yeovil Pen Mill to work one of these trains to Weymouth. When I arrived at Yeovil, my 2-coach DMU 'Sprinter' 150 108 was shut down and the bus with the passengers had yet to appear. I started the engines and prepped the cab so at least I was ready to depart. Eventually, the bus and the guard turned up and we all waited for the scheduled departure time. The signal cleared and so now I only needed two on the buzzer as the right away signal from my guard and we could set off onto the single line towards Maiden Newton. Then, just seconds before we were due to depart, there was a knock on my cab-side window. I lowered it and there stood the signalman who handed me the Yeovil Pen Mill to Maiden Newton single line token. I had forgotten all about it! I was completely staggered by my dreadful error. I took the token, received the departure signal from the guard and we left the station. I kept thinking that if the signaller had left his signal box just a few seconds later or the guard had acted just a little earlier, the consequences for me would have been dire. While there was no possibility of colliding with another train on the single line as a token had been removed and the signal had been cleared, nonetheless I believe that I would have been sacked. Nothing was reported, as no rules had actually been broken. The conductor and signalman did not know that I would have departed without the token. So why had I made such a basic mistake? Lack of experience? Hardly; this event occurred during 2017 and I had signed the road in 1988! The real reason was because the service was starting from Yeovil Pen Mill on the up platform and not the usual down platform and so my normal routine at Yeovil, i.e. stop, collect token, wait for two on the buzzer, check signal, and only then depart, had not been applied, combined with the fact that I was eager to get the train away. It just goes to show that the most basic of human errors can occur to anyone at any time.

Of course, it is not only drivers who make mistakes. When a train is stopped at a station platform that has a departure signal, before the driver is authorised to proceed, first the platform staff (where provided) then the guard and finally the driver must visually check that the relevant signal is displaying a proceed aspect. So, at Southampton, for example, three members of staff are involved in this procedure, at Romsey two (no platform staff) but if the train is DOO then obviously it is all down to the driver.

There have been several occasions when I have received the right away signal of two on the buzzer with the signal at red. In the past, the driver would (hopefully) not move the train and consequently the guard may then realise their error, call the driver on the cab-to-cab phone to apologise and wait for the signal to clear before giving the right away signal for the second time. And that would be the end of it.

On one occasion, I was on the Brighton run when my guard gave me two at a platform red signal. I did not move the train but on this occasion the guard did nothing, so I called him up on the cab-to-cab phone and pointed out his error.

"It's your job to check the fucking signals!" he shouted back.

He may have been having a bad day but he clearly did not know me very well. I left the cab and walked back down the platform to his position. I pointed to the still red signal and told him what I thought of both his actions and his attitude. During our 'conversation' the signal eventually cleared and our journey recommenced. When we arrived at Brighton, he finally apologised and explained that some passengers had upset him a little earlier. Although I did not report him, I was sorely tempted to do so not because of his error but because of his attitude.

The last time I was given the two-buzzer signal to start my train at a red aspect was as late as 2017 and this was at Romsey station while working a train to Portsmouth Harbour. I didn't move the train and waited for the guard to contact me but he failed to do so and after about another minute went by, the signal finally cleared and so after I double-checked that the doors were still secure, we departed. I was now in an awkward situation because we were all aware that recent company policy was that we should all report each other for any breach of the rulebook no matter how minor and if I did not and the incident came to light, both the guard and I would have been in deep trouble. I quickly decided not to report it but then had to choose whether to tell my guard what had occurred at Romsey or not because he was still blissfully unaware of his error. If I did tell him, he may not have believed me, or he may have mentioned it inadvertently at some later time and the resultant gossip ended up at a manager's desk. The other reason I should have told him was that he would have probably double-checked that particular signal in future. In the end I decided to take no action whatsoever and, to this day, no one except me, and now you, are aware of this incident.

# 14

# Alarming Experiences

This chapter recalls some disturbing and potentially very dangerous incidents that I was involved in during my career at Westbury.

Italics indicate that the wording is from reports that I was asked to submit by my manager or the BTP following such events.

On 1st February 1983, I was the assistant driver on three locomotives (56 036 + 47 283 + 37 266) being transferred from Bristol Bath Road depot to Westbury when we encountered the Bradford Junction (Bradford-on-Avon not Bradford in Yorkshire!) distant signal at caution. The home semaphore signal then lowered as we slowly approached it and, when the section signal came into my view, it was also 'off', i.e. in the proceed position. (Due to the right-hand curve of the line at this location the driver was able to see the section signal from his side of the cab before I could and he later told me that he actually saw it lower from stop to proceed.) With the line clear, or so we thought, my driver powered up but as our speed slowly increased to about 30-40 mph we both saw a sight that astonished us. About 200 yards ahead and on our line was the tail end of a freight train that was also moving towards Westbury. There were now two trains in the same absolute block section! There was no chance of a collision as both the freight train and our light engines were travelling in the same direction at relatively low speeds. Initially, however, we were closing the gap until my driver reduced power and then the tail end of the freight train receded into the distance. Less than a mile further on when we reached Trowbridge station my driver stopped our locos in the platform and phoned the Bradford Junction signalman. We were instructed not to move until the signalman at Westbury North had advised his colleague at Bradford Junction that the freight train had fully cleared the section.* After

---

* At this time Westbury North was the next manned signal box as Hawkeridge Junction signal box was switched out of use.

some delay, we were advised that the section WAS now clear and it was safe to proceed. After being assured, we continued on our way, but when we arrived at Westbury North, my driver went into the signal box and spoke directly with the signalman concerned. On returning to the cab, all he would say was that it had been sorted and the matter was closed. I was a little angry and frustrated at this and although I would never report any matter that my driver decided not to officially pursue, I felt that I too was owed at least an explanation because, if the circumstances had been only a little different, there could have easily been a collision.

I later made some discreet inquiries of my own through a signalman that I personally knew. However, because I did not fully understand all the relevant signaling procedures nor the rules and regulations that had to be applied to ensure the safe passage of trains from one semaphore signal box to another, it was difficult for me to understand the chain of events that resulted in having two trains in one absolute block section. However, my understanding was that, earlier in the day, the signalman at Bradford Junction had some difficulty in 'pulling off' his section signal; however, he eventually did so to allow the freight – stone empties from Wootton Bassett – into the section towards Westbury. Then we came along with our light engines also heading for Westbury so the Bradford Junction signalman immediately sent the appropriate bell code of 2-3 to Westbury North asking again for 'section clear'. If he had stopped to think, he would have known that he couldn't possibly yet receive the section clear reply from Westbury North as he had only very recently sent the Wootton Bassett empties into the section and it was impossible for them to have reached Westbury North in that time. But when the Westbury North signalman received the 2-3 light engine bell code, he interpreted it as 5 bells (the code for a class 6 freight train) believing wrongly that the Bradford Junction signaller was still having difficulties in releasing his section signal and was again asking section clear for the Wootton Bassett empties to proceed, and consequently he, again, gave section clear to his colleague at Bradford Junction who, without thinking logically pulled his section signal off again, this time for our light engines. This suspected chain of events made sense to me and explained how the incident occurred. I may have misunderstood the exact details and if there are some of the older signalmen reading my account, I expect they may be shaking their heads at my flawed analysis. Be that as it may, there were two trains in the section at the same time and something had clearly gone wrong somewhere. To this day I don't know if there were any later consequences for the staff involved.

One of the regular trains we worked at this time commenced its journey at the Westbury Cement Works and ran to the distribution sidings adjacent to Exeter Central station. Returning with the empties on 12th March 1981, our engine was 47 095 and we were running at our maximum permissible speed up the Frome avoider line when we passed the distant signal for Clink Road Junction semaphore signal box at green and my driver and I were confident that we would be back in Westbury before midnight. However, the home signal was at danger! My driver made an emergency brake application while we rapidly agreed that the distant had definitely been in the 'off' position. I told my mate that I didn't care if we passed the home signal at danger as long as we stopped short of the junction. Had the signaller changed his mind and would we meet another train going across our path at the junction? We did pass the home signal at red but managed to stop before the junction. My driver told me to go and speak to the signalman. I got down from the loco and walked to the signal box. Up the steps I went and opened the door. The signalman sat relaxed in an armchair reading a newspaper. He greeted me by saying, "Hello mate – what's up?"

"That's what we want to know," I replied.

"Why have you stopped?"

"Well it might have something to do with the fact that your home signal is on."

"No, it's not!" he resentfully replied. "Look!" and he pointed to what must have been the relevant signal leaver in the frame. Sure enough, the leaver was pulled forward to its off position.

"Well I'm telling you that it is. You Look!" I stood aside from the still-open signal box door and together we both looked down the up line, past our train, to see the back of the home signal in the horizontal position.

"Good God!" The signalman seemed genuinely surprised. "The wire must have snapped!"

He went on to explain that when on the rare occasions signal wires do break, it is always at the time that they are under their greatest strain and that is when the signaller is in the process of pulling the lever. The snap would result in the normally heavy and stiff signal leaver instantly becoming totally free and this sudden reduction in resistance could result in the signalman falling backwards so what had occurred was obvious. But on this occasion, the wire must have snapped sometime after the signal was operated. He said that he had never known this to happen before. So, in a way, we were both correct. He assured me that it was safe for our train to proceed and that his section signal was definitely 'off'. I rejoined the train, reported the situation to my driver and we proceeded. It was an experience all three of us could have done without.

Before the class 59s arrived at Westbury, all loaded stone trains bound for southern destinations such as Eastleigh, Fareham, Botley and Totton required the services of an assisting engine on the rear of the train due to the gradient encountered immediately on departure from Westbury. This banking locomotive would then be detached at Warminster and return the short distance back to Westbury light engine. Upgraded from relief driver to driver for the day on 4th November 1985, I was allocated such a turn. All went well until our return run. My assistant was young and comparatively inexperienced so, in order to help him gain more practice, I told him he could drive back to Westbury. It was a distance of less than five miles and with no wagons or coaches to concern us what could possibly go wrong? After we had changed ends on our loco 47 125 at Warminster he got in the driver's seat. He was keen to do so and he set off on full power. I was not concerned until we reached Upton Scudamore where the gradient became 1 in 70 falling all the way to Westbury South Junction. We were due to go back into Westbury down yard so I knew that our next signal should be displaying a single yellow; and it was. I told my mate to apply the brake and he did – a little. However, due to the falling gradient, our speed was not reduced. I told him to make a full application, as I was getting apprehensive. Again, he did and, at last, we began to slow but it was too late. The red signal seemed to rush towards us and we passed it by some distance. When we eventually stopped, although we were well past the signal, we had still not reached the junction. I told my colleague not to move and I walked back to contact the signal-man on the signal post telephone. I immediately informed him of the situation and that we had accidently passed his signal at danger. He simply replied with, "Yes, so I see. I was in the process of setting the road for you into the down yard but you beat me to it. Wait there a minute."

After what seemed an eternity he then said, "You're okay to proceed into the yard now." And that was that. We heard no more about it.

It was literally years later when I found myself in the messroom with the same assistant driver although by now he was a relief driver. Completely out of the blue he said to me,

"Remember that day when we came back with the banker and had a SPAD."

"Yes," I replied, "I am unlikely to ever forget it."

"Well it did me some good."

'It didn't do ME any good!" was my response.

"What I mean is I slowed down a lot after that. It was a valuable lesson learned."

So, something was gained from such a bad experience after all, I thought.

On 23rd November 1987, I travelled 'on the cushions' from Westbury to Newport and relieved the driver of 6B19, a train that consisted of 18 tank wagons hauled by 47 220. I was then required to take the train the short distance to East Usk sidings where 6B19 was due to be recessed. I was then booked to work 6E91 from East Usk back to Westbury via Hallen Marsh in Bristol to pick up any additional wagons that needed to head south.

6E91 was an air braked train and so after the shunter had coupled my 47 to the leading wagon, I changed ends and immediately fully applied the loco's straight air brake to ensure that no train movement could take place. Then I unlocked the driver's control desk and used the brake valve to create the necessary air pressure (70 psi) so that the air brake system would be pressurised and the wagon brakes would release. So far so good. It was then necessary for me to 'trap' at least 60 psi within the braking system of the train in order for the shunter to carry out the required brake continuity test. This trap was achieved by a rapid operation of the brake handle to its 'locked out' position. I checked the gauges and with the loco straight air brake still fully applied, I advised the shunter that I was ready for him to carry out the brake test and so he started to walk back along the train. He was required to check that every wagon was coupled up correctly and that the flexible red brake pipes were also connected and their isolating cocks were all open to ensure that the brake pipe pressure ran the full extent of the train. When he reached the last wagon, he needed to place a tail-light on the rear-most bracket, and fully open the red isolating cock to allow all the air pressure to be exhausted. This action would result in the brake pressure gauge in my cab dropping from about 60 psi or whatever I had managed to previously trap in the system, to zero. I would then be assured that brake continuity had been achieved throughout the entire length of the train and, as a final assurance, the shunter would check that the brakes on at least the last three wagons had applied. I sat relaxed in the cab with one eye on my newspaper and the other on the brake pipe gauge waiting for it to rapidly drop to zero when suddenly there was a sound like an explosion and the whole train surged forward. The force knocked my feet off the desk and pushed me backwards into the seat. For a second or two I could hear the wheels on my 47 skidding as a force propelled it forward but the wheels couldn't turn as the straight air brake was still fully applied. The train stopped moving forward and, as the dust started to settle, I thought "My God, where's the shunter," as I knew that he could have been in-between wagons when the whole train moved. I jumped down and ran back towards the rear of the train, half expecting to see him seriously injured or worse but I heard him walking forward on the other side of the wagons.

I called out to him, "Are you okay?"

"Yes fine," he calmly replied.

"What the hell just happen?" I shouted.

"Oh, that was my mate at the west end just doing some loose shunting."

Apparently, his mate needed to put a couple of wagons onto my line but instead of instructing the pilot driver to proceed slowly and place the wagons well clear of the rear of my train, he decided it would be quicker to uncouple the wagons from the class 08 and instruct its driver to "Hit 'em up!" He was right, it was quicker, but also a very dangerous practice and I told my shunter to give his west end colleague a bollocking from me and that I was not impressed by his method of working.

To my knowledge, amazingly, there was no significant damage done – other than to my nervous system.

I was always wary when venturing on to the Southern Region because I was then in electric 3rd rail territory. I didn't like it and tried to avoid being trackside as much as possible. On 18th November 1988, I was passing through Eastleigh station with 56 042* light engine when my concerns became justified. At the London end of the station I had to pass through the low speed junction to access the branch line to Romsey and, as I crossed over the first of four lines, there was a bang and a flash that lit up the night sky. I stopped and immediately looked back to see smoke slowly drifting up the bodyside of my loco. I phoned the signalman, advised him of the situation and said I would call him again after I had investigated the cause of what appeared to be a small explosion. Armed only with my bardic lamp, I found myself shaking as I gingerly climbed down from the cab. The complex multi-crossing junction that I was now stuck on seemed to have rails running in all directions many of which were electrified. To be on the safe side I was determined not to step on any rail whatsoever. This was not easy; however, I eventually walked the short distance back to where part of the lower body side of the loco had been blackened. I used my lamp for an initial inspection and found that one of the air tank drain cocks had been all but destroyed. It was almost unrecognisable in its blackened and melted state. It was obvious that it had touched or at least came close enough to arc across to the third rail. I had seen enough and returned to the safety of my cab. After testing for power and a quick brake test, I updated the signalman and told him

---

\* 56 042 was the odd one out of this class as it had a different design of bogie, the type that was eventually fitted to the class 58.

that, with his permission, I would carry on towards Westbury. He told me that the third rail current was still operational and that all was well from his point of view. Back at Westbury, my entry in the repair book for 56 042 made for interesting and unusual reading for the maintenance staff who were then tasked with trying to replace the severely damaged valve.

On 21st December 1988, I found myself working 7W10 the 14:27 from Whatley Quarry to Westbury with a train ultimately bound for West Drayton in London. I had loco 56 052 and the load slip informed me that the train consisted of 41 wagons and weighed 2,256 tons. After the mandatory continuity brake test at the quarry, I departed and progressed slowly along the single line to Frome North Junction where I was stopped by a red signal. After a short delay, it cleared to green and so I released the brake and powered up. Then, with the speed at about only 10 mph, the whole loco gave an almighty shudder as it passed over the facing points for Frome sidings and this was immediately followed by a loud bang and an extreme jolt. I shoved the brake handle to its emergency position but before the brakes had a chance to fully apply, the loco started to bump and crash along, obviously off the rails. I held on tight, stayed in the seat and rode it out. Eventually the train stopped and my first thought was to protect the main line even though the signaling system should already be preventing any possible conflicting train movements. This was a DOO train and so the loco was fitted with one of the original type of radiophones, the display of which indicated that it was set up correctly and working. It wasn't, as I discovered when I hit the emergency button but failed to connect with the control office. So, I jumped down, still a little shaken and reported the derailment to the signalman on the signal post telephone who assured me that no additional protection of the line was required. Nevertheless, we did agree that I would place a red flag in the four-foot and place three dets on the line adjacent to signal W 295 at Frome North. I then returned to my loco, stopped the engine and inspected the damage while arrangements began to be put into place to eventually clear the line. I found the leading wheels of my 56 were actually still on the rails but not on the correct line! They had taken the route into the sidings while all of its other wheels had not and were derailed. The leading wagon was a new ARC owned 100-ton prototype on its very first revenue-earning excursion and it too was partially derailed. It had travelled less than five miles. All the remaining wagons were still on the road but there was considerable track damage on the branch line and some in the sidings.

I was interviewed by the BTP who were investigating the possibility of vandalism as being the cause of the derailment. This proved not to be the case as, a month later, I received a letter from the Area Manager at Bristol stating that he had been advised by the Area Civil Engineer that the derailment was caused by the track at this point being defective and 'wide to gauge'.

Merehead quarry is a little over 15 miles from Westbury and is reached via a single line branch that leaves the main line at East Somerset Junction (previously known as Witham). The branch is about four miles in length and includes some steep gradients so a driver has to be very mindful of this fact when working loaded trains, that could weigh anything up to 5,000 tons, down from the quarry towards the main line. At the Witham end of the branch, there are two ways to access the up main line, either through a lead directly from the single line or via the up loop in which, if necessary, allows trains to be held awaiting a pathway to join the up main line.

On one occasion, I was working a heavy DOO train down the branch when I was stopped by the last signal on the single line that protected the connection onto the up main. Still on the falling gradient, I bought my train slowly to a halt about 100 feet before the signal and waited for it to clear, but it didn't so I climbed down and walked to the signal with the intention of using the SPT to contact the signaller. I was just about to lift the handset when I heard a noise that terrified me as I immediately recognised the sound – my train had started to move! I spun round to see my train inching forward with no one on board. How to stop a freight train weighing thousands of tons on a falling gradient from ground level? There was only one way. I stepped into the four-foot and walked quickly head-on toward the front of my train. There was little chance that it would knock me over as its speed was still less than walking pace. I grabbed the red handle isolating cock of the brake pipe on the front of my loco and pulled it open. The air pressure immediately escaped and the train eventually stopped. I left the brake pipe air still venting and returned to the cab. I took one look at the controls and immediately realised my error. Although the straight air brake was fully applied this alone was insufficient to hold the weight of the train on the falling gradient and the wagon brakes had gradually released while I had walked to the SPT as I had carelessly left the auto train brake in the release position. I then correctly applied it, climbed down from the cab, closed the brake cock on the front, returned to the cab and just about managed to compose myself before the signal eventually cleared.

On the morning of 17th July 1997, I was booked to take a South Wales & West 2 car class 150 DMU from Westbury to Weymouth but when the train arrived it consisted of two 2-car 150s. I called control who belatedly advised me that the leading two cars were to remain at Westbury to form a later service and I was to have the remaining set (150 233) for my Weymouth train. I detached the rear two cars and when the leading set had been shunted clear by another driver, off I went. The maximum line speed was only 40 mph for the first couple of miles so I had to carry out a running brake test at this comparatively low speed. (The regulations covering running brake tests later changed.) My first stop was at Frome station that also had an approach speed of only 40 mph; however, in order to stop at the correct part of the platform, I had to select brake step 3, the maximum brake pressure available. I thought little more about it and put it down to a minor misjudgment on my behalf and the fact that some train brakes are more effective than others. The next station stop was Bruton and that was approached at a fast line speed on a falling gradient. I applied brake step 1 earlier than normal and then increased to step 2 but we were not reducing speed quickly enough so I selected step 3, left it in that position and hoped to stop in time. It was touch and go and the first half of the leading car eventually overshot the platform. It was then clear to me that there was a fault with the braking system so I called the signaller and told him that I would be travelling at no more than 50 mph for the rest of the journey. I advised my guard of the circumstances who, in turn, phoned control to inform them of the situation and that we would be late into Weymouth as a result.

When I arrived at Yeovil Pen Mill, the signalman said that he had received a message from control that he must not let my train depart before I had phoned them. I did so and they advised me that my 150 had been fitted with a new set of brake blocks the previous night at Cardiff Canton depot and the poor braking may be due to the new blocks not yet having worn enough to bed in properly. (I knew that new brake blocks were less efficient before they had worn in but I doubted that this was the cause due to the exceptionally poor retardation.) So, while I was waiting for the single line token, essential for the next part of our journey to Maiden Newton, I got down to take a look at the condition of the brake blocks myself and sure enough they all looked new with little sign of wear. However, that was not the problem. I then discovered that even though I had fully applied the brakes before I left my cab, none of the blocks on the last bogie were pressing against the wheels. This meant that the brake force of the train had been reduced by 25%, hence my difficulty in stopping within the normal distances. I reported my findings to control and I advised them that now I knew what the cause of the problem was I was happy to take the train forward but at a reduced speed and this was agreed. They allowed me to use my discretion as they quite rightly judged that I and not them were best placed to decide. I know that they would have also supported my decision if I had told them that, in the circumstances, I considered it unsafe to continue with the journey and the service must be terminated. However, I completed the journey safely, albeit late and the train was taken out of service when we returned to Westbury.* If a similar situation were to happen today, the driver's judgment would not be the deciding factor and the kneejerk reaction by the control office would be to order the driver to terminate the

---

* 150 233 was taken out of service at Westbury and later subjected to investigation at Cardiff Canton maintenance depot the same day. Additional tests were then carried out at Exeter on both 28th and 29th July and it remained out of service until 7th August when the train was examined again, this time by the brakes specialist engineer at Canton. Finally, the cause was put down to the brake actuators failing to adjust automatically due to 0.1 bar of residual air brake pressure caused by a defective brake relay valve. This fault had not materialised before and had never been experienced by the brakes engineer or any of the SW&W maintenance team. Appropriate actions and procedures were then put in place to ensure that such a fault would not recur on any other unit.

service immediately with all the disruption that this would cause.

I believe that the reason why the brake fault didn't become apparent until after I left Westbury was because the incoming driver who bought the train from Bristol had two class 150s; therefore, the reduction in brake force available to him was only on one bogie out of eight but when I took only two cars forward it then became one in four, a different scenario altogether.

On one occasion I was driving an engine and stock train from Bristol to Weymouth and stopped at Westbury. I was aware that we were allowed a few minutes recovery time there and so I was a little surprised when the signal cleared and, almost immediately, the RA (Right Away) also illuminated. That was the signal to advise me that all the necessary station duties had been carried out and the train should immediately depart. I checked the scheduled departure time on my diagram and looked at my watch. Two minutes early? I crossed the cab and looked back down the train and saw that several of the coach doors were still open! I stepped down onto the platform and spoke to the station staff, one of whom had pressed the RA button not realising the potential implications of her actions. She thought that pressing the RA button only advised the signaller that the train was ready to start where as it actually instructed the driver to depart providing the signal had been cleared, which it had. She should have pressed the TRS (Train Ready to Start) button. If I had set the train in motion, as I was fully entitled to do without looking back first, the consequences could have been appalling.

The lack of any form of streamlining on most DMUs results in a build up of air pressure on the front of the train as it accelerates. This pressure is instantly and considerably increased whenever a train enters a tunnel as the air is forced between the train and the walls of the tunnel. The driver can often detect this effect, as more power is required just to maintain the same speed. I've likened the sensation to colliding with a giant marshmallow!

On 11th May 2007, I was driving sprinter 158 776 with 1F10, a Portsmouth Harbour to Cardiff Central service when, upon entering the Severn Tunnel at the maximum permitted speed of 75 mph, there was an alarming whoosh sound accompanied by a metallic bang and a continuous rush of air. When I landed back in my seat, I put on the cab light and instantly saw the cause of the commotion. In the centre of the floor in the cab of a class 158 there is an access point to the securing pin of the coupling bar underneath, and this six-inch square hole is covered by a hinged metallic flap. In this case, the increase of air pressure proved too much and the flap shot into the air and the resulting hole created the considerable draft. I had to live with it until we stopped at Newport where I put the flap back into place and put my kit bag on top of it and that proved sufficient until we arrived at Cardiff where maintenance staff carried out a temporary repair that allowed the unit to remain in service. After that experience and in order to try and prevent a possible repeat performance, my kit bag then always had its own reserved space in my cab – sitting on top of the access point cover.

The 'leaves on the line' excuse for late running is well known and, not surprisingly, perhaps ridiculed by members of the public. However, from a train driver's point of view, 'low rail adhesion' whether caused by leaves on the line or for any other reason can result in drivers experiencing major difficulties trying to control the acceleration and, potentially far more dangerously, the braking of their trains both of which can have a knock-on effect resulting in delays to many services.

The following was my report when my passenger train 'ran away' on 2nd November 2009.

*I experienced low railhead adhesion levels from the start of my journey with 2090. This was not unexpected due to the time of the year, the weather conditions (although dry, the cold night air was causing condensation to accumulate on the ground and railhead) and the fact that my train was the first booked service of the day between Westbury and Salisbury.*

*The earliest indication of <u>exceptional</u> low rail adhesion occurred when braking for the 50 mph permanent speed restriction at Wishford. Further on I used the rising gradient to help reduce the speed of my train on approach to Wilton Junction (40 mph – green signal).*

*The next signal was single yellow. This was usual as the following* signal SY 52 (the last before the station) must initially be at red due to the diagrammed attachment of a SWT class 158 at Salisbury station. As the gradient then changes to falling between Wilton Jn. and Salisbury I attempted to brake the train early and only in step one. However, when I did so the wheels immediately locked and the speedo dropped to zero although the actual speed of my train had not reduced at all. I released the brake and tried again, and again, but to no good effect. Aware that a SPAD or even a collision was now possible I gave up on this subtle braking technique, made an emergency brake application and pressed the sanding button. Again the wheels locked up, and the speedo returned to zero and this new tactic had little effect in reducing the speed of my train. I now became increasingly concerned and considered how best to warn the signaller of the fact that 2O90 was out of control and in effect, a runaway train. I pressed the "E" button on the NRN phone (the first time I have had cause to do so) and almost immediately Network Rail Control at Waterloo answered. I advised them that it was an emergency call and explained the situation. I could now see signal SY 52 was displaying a red aspect but with the position light signal ('dots') and Junction Indicator No. 4 cleared. As Waterloo control was repeating my message the train passed over the AWS magnet (I deliberately did not cancel it – every little helps!) and then the train started to slow substantially and then eventually stopped well before reaching signal SY 52.

I advised Waterloo control accordingly and informed them that I would now contact the Salisbury signaller directly. I informed my conductor of the situation and walked forward to use the SPT.

I reported to the Salisbury signaller that I had experienced exceptional low rail adhesion on approach to Wishford and between Wilton Junction and signal SY 52 and was concerned about being routed towards another train in platform 3. However, after the signaller had taken all the relevant details I agreed to take my train forward at VERY low speed into the station. I advised the conductor accordingly and proceeded at walking pace into the station — eventually coupling up as booked.

The return journey to Westbury was less eventful due to the increased brake-force and WSP on the second unit; however, I reported to the Westbury signaller that I experienced exceptional low rail *adhesion on approach to Warminster and carried out my slowest ever approach speed on the falling gradient to the Dilton Marsh request stop!*

*I would like to make the following comments and observations:*

- *These were the worst railhead adhesion levels I have ever experienced in over 27 years of driving.*
- *I was impressed by the prompt reply by NR at Waterloo.*
- *I have been advised that the previous night another driver experienced exceptional low rail adhesion at this location. If this is so, what action was taken to improve rail head conditions and why wasn't I, as the first driver over the same route the following day, cautioned if no rail head cleaning had been carried out? Limited railhead cleaning may have taken place on immediate approach to SY 52 – hence my ability to stop – but if so this should have been done over a much greater distance.*
- *At no time during the wheel slide taking place on the approach to signal SY 52 did I apply power – irrespective of what the OTDR may indicate.*

The following is the report I submitted following an incident when the train I was driving struck a road vehicle on the line.

### 3rd February 2010

*My train, 1F29 from Cardiff Central to Portsmouth Harbour was running approximately 15 minutes late due to signal delays at Newport and Severn Tunnel Junction and later additional delays that occurred due to overcrowding at Filton Abbey Wood, Bristol Temple Meads and Bath Spa. 1F29 ran as a two-coach class 158 (766) and not the three-coach train as booked.*

*At approximately 19:40 after running on green signals through Wilton Junction at the maximum permitted speed of 40 mph I accelerated the train onto the up line towards Salisbury – the next station stop. Though dark with some drizzly rain I observed the tail-lights and flashing hazard lights of a road vehicle that I initially thought must be a Network Rail van parked in the up side cess. (This is not an uncommon sight for train drivers as such vehicles are frequently parked line-side and off public roads to enable NR staff or contractors to get as near as possible to the site where they are required to work.) However, as my train got closer I could see that the vehicle was not in the cess but partly on the up line. This was confirmed by the driver of a passing down train who flashed his headlights at me as a danger signal.*

*I estimate my speed to be about 50 mph when I made an emergency brake application and sounded the horn. It soon became evident that my train would hit the vehicle and so, as I could do no more in the cab, I rapidly vacated it and advised several passengers who were stood in the vestibule area to hold tight as we were about to hit a car.*

*After the impact I re-entered the cab as the train came to a halt and used the NRN to make an emergency call to Waterloo control to advise them of the situation requesting all emergency services (At this time I did not know that the road vehicle was not occupied at the moment of impact) and that I would carry out initial protection of the down line with a track circuit clip, which I then did. (I later discovered that this was unnecessary, as the passing down train had stopped within the signal section – though out of view from my position.) I then contacted the Salisbury signaller using my mobile phone who assured me that both lines were blocked and protection had been provided. I then walked back to the crash site (about 200 yards) and spoke to police who were already on the scene. A police officer advised me that the vehicle, a large black Ford Ranger 4x4 pick up, had crashed off the road and onto the line but was empty when struck by my train and asked if anyone on the train was injured to which I replied, "None that I am aware of."*

*I then briefed the MOM and a RIO who had soon arrived. The conductor spoke to a paramedic who had boarded the train. Two members of SWT maintenance team arrived to check if the train was safe to continue – at least to Salisbury. I also spoke to a per-way inspector who was required to inspect the track to ensure that it was safe to run following trains.*

*Westbury Conductor Competence Manager Trevor Deacon also attended at the scene and checked that my conductor, the customers and I were all okay.*

*The front-end damage consisted of a large section of yellow fibreglass cowling that had been hit off, the BSI coupling was badly out of alignment and one horn was missing (see photo). I was surprised that I could get both brake release and power without the isolation of any safety equipment and so after all concerned gave permission, I was advised that the train could then proceed to Salisbury. I drove 1F29 slowly to the station accompanied by a SWT Driver Manager who had previously walked to the crash site from Salisbury station.*

*At Salisbury all passengers were detrained and some, despite their ordeal and delay, actually thanked me. I then, still accompanied, shunted the empty train into platform five and was relieved by West- bury Driver Robin Lane. Westbury Guard's Manager Clive Sturgess then drove Adrian Webb and I back to Westbury, and in my case directly to my home, for which I was grateful.*

*Please note that my Conductor Adrian Webb acted in a calm and professional manner throughout the incident. Immediately after the impact he came to the front to find out if I was okay and that protection was being carried out. He repeatedly checked that no passengers were injured, made reassuring and informative announcements and liaised with FGW Control – advising me accordingly.*

The following is a report I submitted after an incident on 1st July 2014 that occurred when I was driving three-car 'Sprinter' 158 954 to Portsmouth Harbour.

*Whilst driving 1F19 at the maximum permitted line speed of 75 mph I passed signal SY 68R at green on the approach to Wylye. Then, as I neared signal SY 68 (this signal is located under the A303 road bridge and was also displaying a green aspect) I observed an object on the track adjacent to the signal. I applied the brake and as I got closer I could see that a Network Rail portable stop board/red light had been placed on the left hand running rail. I applied the emergency brake and sounded the horn continuously to warn of my approach and impending collision. My train hit the stop board at approximately 50-60 mph and then exploded three detonators that had also been place on the left hand running rail.*

*My train stopped about 250 yards passed signal SY 68 – before Townsend accommodation crossing and adjacent to Teapot Street, Wylye. As I was unaware of the circumstances that had resulted in protection of the line being in place but with the associated signal showing line clear, I pressed the emergency call button on the GSM-R and immediately reported the situation to the Salisbury signaller.*

*After a brief conversation to clarify the circumstances and the location of my train I was told not to move 1F19 and to await further instructions. This was agreed. By this time the guard had come to the front of the train to ascertain what had occurred, to check that I was unharmed and to offer assistance, a (medically qualified?) passenger then also kindly offered to help if anybody had been injured. I thanked him but advised him that no one was hurt.*

*I then decided to inspect my train for potential damage while the guard dealt with passengers' concerns and liaised with FGW control. I could find no obvious impact damage as the life/rail guard situated in advance of the leading axle must have done the job it was designed to do. As I neared the rear of the train on the cess side I could see a Network Rail employee who was standing near to signal SY 68. I continued to walk back and asked him – not very politely – what was going on. He indicated that he did not know as he had received no instruction to remove protection that was in place due to work being carried out at Hindon Road accommodation crossing (this crossing is situated approximately 1¼ miles in advance of signal SY 68). I then returned to the leading cab and again contacted the Salisbury signaller. Apparently there had been either a breakdown in communication or a misunderstanding between the person in charge of possession, the signaller and the person responsible for carrying out protection. The signaller asked if I was okay and if the train was able to proceed. I reassured him that both the train and I were in a fit state to continue. He then gave me permission to proceed but to approach Wylye AHB crossing – situated approximately one mile in advance of SY 68 at caution and not to proceed over this crossing until I was satisfied that it was safe to do so. I advised the guard accordingly and proceeded very slowly towards Wylye AHB crossing and sounded the warning horn long and loud. This was just as well as I then observed several vehicles and one pedestrian zigzag around the half barriers. One vehicle actually drove onto the track and then reversed clear. (I believe that my train had stopped after activating the AHB Starting sequence and consequently the crossing traffic had been considerably delayed.)*

*My train then passed safely over Wylye AHB crossing and then Hindon Road crossing where a work gang was situated and evidence of repair work being carried out.*

*On arrival at Salisbury, SWT and NR managers asked if I was okay and after I confirmed that I was they asked what had occurred. I briefly related the facts to them and then proceeded to Portsmouth Harbour with 1F19 then running about 25 minutes late.*

*Personal observations:*

*The Fratton based Conductor working 1F19 with me was very proactive, helpful and professional.*

*I am also grateful for the concerns expressed for my welfare, not only those reported above but additionally I received a phone message from the 'On Call' Manager Trevor Deacon and was met on my return to Westbury by my Line Manager Sally Wiltshire.*

*Even though this incident was unfortunate and obviously should not have occurred at least it was a 'right side failure' as my train had been stopped – rightly or wrongly.*

This was my report concerning a near miss during the summer of 2015.

*On 11ᵗʰ June 2015 I was driving 2086 from Westbury to Weymouth. My train consisted of a two-car sprinter D.M.U. no. 150 232 and as I drove towards Pound Lane Crossing\* at approximately 50 mph (maximum line speed at this location is 75 mph and is a single line) I observed a large yellow JCB plant machine emerge from my left and onto the crossing. I immediately sounded the warning horn and made an emergency brake application. The JCB then stopped with the leading 'bucket' type attachment out foul and in the path of my train. It then immediately reversed clear. My train stopped approximately 50-75 yards past the crossing. I briefly informed my guard (Westbury Conductor Mark White) as to what had occurred and advised him that I*

---

\* This crossing is situated at 147m 10ch between Yetminster and Chetnole stations and is one of several farm/accommodation user-operated gated crossings on this route with direct line telephones provided to the controlling signaller and signs instructing vehicle users to obtain permission before crossing etc.

*would walk back to speak to the JCB driver. By the time I had got back to the crossing the JCB had crossed over the line, stopped clear, and its driver was in the process of closing the gates. Before he could drive away I called to him and said,*

*"I want a word with you!"*

*He replied with "I'm fed up with you people!"*

*We then had a brief but heated conversation during which I asked him four times if he had contacted the signaller for permission to use the crossing. He did not confirm that he had and repeatedly referred to "good visibility". He also called me son, which I took personal offence at because (a) I am 61 years of age and (b) my dad passed away some 10 years before.*

*I used the crossing telephone myself on the same side from which the JCB had crossed to check that it was in working order (it was) and to report the incident to the Yeovil Pen Mill signaller who advised me that he had not received a request from anyone to use the crossing. I noted that the registration number of the JCB was E944 LHW and that the drivers name was Mike Bird (according to the name embroidered on his shirt) and so I reported these details to the signaller. I also asked the signaller to report the incident to the British Transport Police. He asked if I was okay to continue. I said that I was, returned to my train and continued with my journey to Weymouth where I spoke to the FGW Duty Senior Controller. We discussed the incident and he asked after my welfare. I then had my PNB and drove 2E24 back to Westbury where I was met by Westbury Driver Competence Manager Colin Grieg who again checked on my welfare and asked for brief details, which I provided.*

*I advised Colin that I would submit a detailed report the following day and I included in that report the additional following paragraph ...*

**As the JCB driver clearly demonstrated such blatant disregard to safety by not only putting his and my life at risk but also those of my guard and all of our passengers I now expect the BTP to do all they can to ensure that he is prosecuted, found guilty and punished appropriately. I believe that my report, the YPM signaller's statement and the appropriate download from the train's forward-facing CCTV camera should provide sufficient evidence to result in a conviction.**

I later watched the train's CCTV pictures and I considered that they reinforced my version of events. However, after a considerable delay and a thorough police investigation, the BTP advised me that they believed that the bucket leading on the JCB did not actually encroach over the railway line; therefore, there was insufficient evidence to prosecute Mr. Bird, notwithstanding the fact that, in his own statement to the police, he admitted he did not at any time get authorisation to use the crossing and only stopped his machine and reversed clear when he heard me sound the warning horn. I could not believe what I was being told and insisted on a face-to-face meeting with the relevant senior BTP officer. This meeting took place at the BTP office at Southampton. I was accompanied to this meeting by my Manager Sally Wiltshire and an ASLEF rep. Brian Corbett (a network rail representative was also invited to attend but failed to turn up). A full and frank exchange of views took place but to no avail. The police considered there was insufficient evidence but I considered their inaction as being a dereliction of duty and said so.

I later made enquiries through my trade union if it was possible to pursue a private prosecution against Mr. Bird but I was advised that it would be very unlikely to succeed if the crown prosecution service had already considered it not viable and there were also the legal costs to consider. It was a dead end.

Subsequent to this sorry episode I wrote to my union's internal magazine 'The ASLEF Journal' and they printed a shortened version of the following on their letters page.

### Level Crossing Safety

*D.O.O. passenger train drivers are repeatedly reminded of the safety risks to members of the public at the train-platform interface. While this aspect of operations is undoubtedly critical and requires continuous vigilance to reduce the number of incidents, I believe that the greatest risk to all drivers and on-train passengers alike is from the misuse of level crossings by members of the public.*

*All road/rail level crossings are equipped with some combination of physical barriers either remotely or automatically controlled and red flashing lights that are usually accompanied with an audible warning.*

Users are made fully aware that a train is about to pass and so would obviously be at risk should they still chose to ignore all of these warnings.

However, in country areas farm accommodation type crossings are far more basic and may consist of little more than self operated gates and a Network Rail notice board with information concerning the correct method of crossing usage. I have driven trains over such rural routes for many years and have encountered several instances of dangerous practices at remote crossings.

My last near miss was potentially catastrophic as a JCB driver attempted to cross in the path of my train after failing to contact the signaller for permission to access the field on the opposite side of the line. I am certain that I am not alone and that many other drivers can relate similar instances of either a near miss or even a collision.

I am aware that Network Rail have done a lot of good work in recent years by closing many little used crossings and continually monitoring and assessing others in an attempt to make them as safe as realistically possible. However, the biggest problem is that crossing users may be lulled into a false sense of security by believing, sometimes wrongly, that due to the infrequency of trains telephoning the signaller for permission to cross is unnecessary and inconvenient. Also, as the approach speed of the train will be slow there is little risk involved especially during periods of good visibility. They may also leave the gates open for their own convenience to save stopping the next time. As practical railwaymen and women we know how potentially dangerous this attitude is.

I would ask all drivers who observe any misuse at any type of level crossing to report the same to Network Rail and their TOC in order to maintain an accurate record of repeated problems at specific crossings with a view to appropriate action being taken either by Network Rail or the British Transport Police.

At small and little used crossings it may be possible to install some form of gate locking mechanism (operated remotely by the signaller) on a new design of self-closing gates. While this would require a not inconsiderable amount of money due to the high number of such crossings it should be considered as an investment in safety – always a worthwhile cause.

This was not my first or last level crossing incident. Many years previously, on 7th April 1995, I was driving a train to Weymouth when between Castle Cary and Yeovil Pen Mill I saw a tractor and trailer pass over the single line about half a mile in front of me at Thorny Marsh Lane crossing near Sparkford, Somerset. This is another of the many user worked farm accommodation crossings found on rural lines and is not for public use but provided for the farmer to gain access to his fields on the other side of the track, but only after gaining permission from the signaller using the phones provided at the crossing. Luckily, the railway line is straight on the approach to this crossing and although my speed must have been about 60 mph with a full application of the brake, I was able to stop my train on the crossing, by which time the tractor and trailer had crossed and its driver was closing the gates behind him. I got down from the cab and asked the young farmhand if he had telephoned and asked for permission to cross the line. I was surprised when he answered, "Yes" because if the signalman had authorised the use of the crossing, a major error had occurred that would have put my train in jeopardy. So, I then asked him what the signaller had said to which he replied in a broad West Country accent, "E zed thur wur a train coming."

Now I was even more astonished and said, "But you crossed anyway?"

"Well I couldn't see one," was his response.

We then had a five-minute discussion on the correct procedures he had to adopt in future.

Unfortunately, such an attitude has led to many collisions and even more near misses in the past throughout the network and will no doubt also do so in the future.

Most 'sprinter' type DMU trains are fitted with end gangway connecting doors that can be opened when two or more units are coupled together that then provide a walk-through connection between the sets. When not in use and situated at the very front or rear of the train, they must be kept shut and locked at all times and it is the responsibility of the traincrew to carry out this procedure whenever necessary. These metal end gangway doors are very thick and heavy but they or the doorframe can still distort and cause problems with either opening, closing or with the locking mechanism. Whenever I changed ends on such a unit, as part of my cab preparation practices, I would normally double-check that the end doors were correctly locked as to have the door come open at speed was an alarming experience indeed. It happened to me twice during my career. On both occasions my speed had reached between 60 and 70 mph for the first time in the journey when all hell broke loose. The end door burst open with a loud crash like an explosion, the cab was instantly engulfed in a tornado and the other door from the cab into the vestibule also suddenly burst open. Anything not secured in the cab would take off in the turbulence and all the dirt and dust, of which there was a great deal, would create an instantaneous mini sand storm. The train had to be stopped no matter where it was at the time because it was physically impossible to push the door shut against the air pressure at the front of a moving train. If that was a shock for the driver, just imagine what a poor unsuspecting punter on a crowded train would have experienced. One second, he was standing in the vestibule minding his own business reading a 'Metro' and the next it was blown from his hands as the door from the cab burst open and he could see the track ahead!

During my many years of representing ASLEF in general and individual driver colleagues in particular, one of my proudest moments occurred on 20th October 1994 during an enquiry into a major derailment that had taken place on 5th September of that year.

Westbury Driver Brian Eastman was working 6A18 under DOO conditions. This was the 05:45 Whatley Quarry to Southall and consisted of 43 x 100-ton wagons, hauled by 59 001. When 6A18 was on the up main adjacent to Hungerford up loop and travelling at about 35 mph Brian observed the air brake pipe pressure gauge drop rapidly and that, consequently, the train started to slow and then stopped. On looking back Brian saw a huge cloud of dust coming from his train and it was then obvious to him that a derailment had occurred so he immediately carried out full protection of the down main and informed the controlling signaller at Reading of the situation, as a result of which an approaching passenger train was halted.

The subsequent meticulous joint enquiry concluded that nine

wagons had derailed and the cause was a broken axle on the 22nd wagon. Photos taken at the site showed that the down main line was blocked by ballast and several concrete sleepers dislodged from the remains of the up main line, such were the forces involved.

During the enquiry, its chairman Mr. R. Atkins interrupted Brian when he was giving his evidence by getting up, crossing the room to shake Brian's hand and personally thanking him for his prompt actions on the day of the incident.

To quote from the report:

> *The Chairman spoke for the Panel when he told Driver Eastman, during the Inquiry hearings: "Both the action that you took and the promptness of your action were fully in accordance with the highest traditions of railwaymen. The Panel wish to commend your promptness in carrying out your actions, which prevented an accident from becoming a disaster".*

Brian said that he was only doing his job but given the shock and the pressure he must have been under, all agreed that his actions were exemplary and possibly lifesaving.

# 15
# Faults and Failures

As every railway commuter knows only too well, trains occasionally breakdown and the challenge for the industry is how to reduce the number of failures and to minimise delays when they do.

During BR days, drivers were expected to be very hands-on when dealing with any sort of traction fault or failure. So much so, in fact, that when a driver initially qualified and passed his driving exam he was provided with a tool kit that he was expected to utilise and, if possible, repair any fault that occurred during the journey. My MP12 driving course in 1981 was the first such group not to be issued with the standard BR tool kit and since then drivers have seen a slow reduction in their capability and expectation to repair faults en route. The policy is now if you have a fault don't touch anything but call maintenance control for 'expert' advice and instruction. Most drivers have accepted this dogma and may wait for a considerable time for orders when they could possibly have quickly corrected the fault themselves.

GWR, like most other TOCs I presume, employ mobile technicians who roam their areas troubleshooting and, whenever possible, carry out repairs to trains while they remain in service. These individuals are worth their weight in gold and many passengers have reached their destination safely and on time, unaware that these 'flying fitters' were responsible.

Minor problems may have been repeatedly reported by drivers in the fault/repair book that is carried in every driving cab. It was not uncommon to see the same fault report repeated time and time again. The primary causes of defects remaining unattended to are:

- Insufficient time for maintenance staff to carry out fault diagnosis and repairs as the train must reenter service as soon as possible because no others are available to replace it.

- Shortage of staff to undertake the repairs.
- Shortage of spare parts.

I recall that, in frustration after one particularly long, tiring and troublesome shift, I wrote in the repair book under the column headed:

DESCRIPTION OF DEFECT: 'Driver worn out; replacement required'.
   When the train next entered a maintenance depot, the fitter on duty continued my flippant theme and simply wrote in the column headed: ACTION TAKEN BY MAINTENANCE STAFF: 'None in stock'.

In no particular order, the following is an incomplete list of why trains maybe cancelled or delayed:

- Defective signaling
- Track faults
- Mechanical or electrical problems with the train
- Staff shortages
- Obstructions on the line
- Vandalism
- Cable theft
- Trespass
- Fatality
- Overcrowding
- Disruptive or poorly passengers
- A lineside fire or emergency services attending to an incident
- A 'bridge bash'
- Level crossing incidents
- Overrunning engineering operations
- A landslip
- Flooding
- Terrorist incident

I have even known disruption caused by an unexploded bomb and a suspected gas leak. I could go on (and on!) but I suspect that you get my drift. With regard to obstructions on the line, I have personally come across stray animals, a wrecked car, old bikes (both motor and push), a supermarket trolley, a fence post, a wheelie bin, a pile of rumble and a load of rubbish. It sounds like a list of booby prizes on the conveyer belt for the Generation Game's losing team!

With all the things that could go wrong, it's a wonder to me that any train ever runs on time.

The old BR phrase used to explain all instances of late running was the classic and all-encompassing 'Operational Difficulties'.

There have been many occasions when my train has broken down. Sometimes a member of the maintenance team or I have been able to overcome the fault but, at other times, there was nothing we could do to remedy the situation, a few examples of which include:

- A triple pump failure on a class 47 loco when my freight train had to be dragged back into Salisbury.
- Frozen air pipes on a class 150 DMU that resulted in a cancelled service and a tow back to Bristol TM from Bristol Parkway.
- Brake problems between Weymouth and Upwey stations that ended with an SWT class 442 EMU unit No. 2415 towing my train – 37 407 and five coaches – back into Weymouth. (This was on 16th August 1999 and made for a very rare sight and possibly unique combination of trains.)

Failing at a station was bad enough but breaking down in remote countryside is another thing altogether and especially embarrassing when a crowded passenger train is involved.

My worst experience by far with a broken-down train occurred on Saturday 19th August 1995 when I was working 2096, a BR Regional Railways service from Westbury to Weymouth. This train had started from Cardiff Central at 06:10 and our two coach DMU 'Sprinter' 150 249 departed Westbury at 08:07 some 16 minutes late and already busy. We picked up more passengers at Frome and Castle Cary and, at Yeovil Pen Mill, the train became full with many passengers forced to stand. The weather forecast had proved to be accurate and the day was dry, sunny and eventually very hot indeed. It was at Yeovil that I first noticed something amiss. The main air reservoir pressure gauge in the cab was reading low at 5-6 bar. However, as we were now running 20 minutes late and heading onto the single line to Maiden Newton with the token already in my possession, I hoped that the air pressure would rise with increased engine revs. (The air compressors were directly driven from the diesel engines.) This proved not to be the case and just a few miles outside Yeovil, the low main air safety device did the job it was designed to do and instigated an emergency brake application. (This was to prevent the possibility of a train running with insufficient air pressure in reserve to operate the air brakes.) A driver's first action in such circumstances is to activate the compressor speed up switch as this would substantially increase the engine revs and thereby make the compressors run faster but not supply any power to the axles. This I did but it made no difference. The air pressure didn't rise and so I could not release the brakes. I phoned the signalman at Yeovil PM to explain the situation and told him that my guard and I would check the train for possible air leaks in the system. The guard walked through the train listening for any air leaks and I did the same on the outside. We both failed to discover any. By now the ambient temperature was high and the train had stopped on a small raised embankment in full sunshine, and so, with no through draft that the small open windows would have supplied if the train was moving, the inside temperature was higher still and increasing by the minute. (There was no air conditioning on these trains at this time.)

I was reluctant but forced to declare my train a total failure and I reported this to my control office and the signaller. After some considerable delay with the temperature still increasing and tempers now beginning to fray, it was decided that 2V70 – a service from Weymouth to Bristol – would be allowed onto the single line without the token that was still correctly in my possession to assist my train from the south end. So, I walked forward and put down protection in the form of three detonators on the line and displayed the mandatory red flag as an additional safety precaution. Eventually, 2V70 consisting of another two-car DMU 'Sprinter' 150 244, turned up. I explained the problem to its driver and rode with him the short distance back to my train. I left his cab, reentered mine and we coupled up our two trains.

I expected my air pressure gauge to immediately react and show an increase – it didn't! I advised the assisting driver of this worrying and unexpected development who, in turn, reported to me that the air pressure on his train had remained static. We both got down trackside to make sure that the automatic mechanical, electrical and pneumatic couplings had been correctly made. They had and as both the air supply isolating cocks were also open, we could not understand why the air pressure on my train stubbornly refused to rise. Together we then both walked round all four coaches looking and listening for air leaks. We detected none and found that all other systems were apparently working correctly.

Every time I rejoined my train to consult or update the signaller, at Yeovil PM, the control office at Swindon and the maintenance department at Cardiff Canton, I was questioned by passengers who were now, not surprisingly, becoming increasingly frustrated at the prolonged delay, but with no obvious end in sight, I could not honestly reassure them. Everyone was sweating in the increasing heat and then things got considerably worse.

A Railtrack employee, first name Bill, who had been called out to assist had what we first suspected to be a heart attack after he had injured his arm on a closing power operated door and had collapsed on the track sweating profusely. I ran back to the cab to call an ambulance and the guard used the public address to ask if there was a doctor or qualified first aider on board. Luckily, there was a nurse on board 2V70 who kindly volunteered to help attend to Bill and discovered that he had in fact fainted with the heat and the pain in his arm.

After much further delay, it was agreed by all parties that our passengers would transfer to 2V70, the two trains would then uncouple and 2V70 was to return to Weymouth with all the passengers. The plan was that the original passengers on 2V70 would then travel forward in hastily arranged road transport. I correctly retained the single line token throughout all this time and confusion.

A Railtrack Mobile Operations Manager now appeared on the scene and again, after much discussion with all parties concerned, it was decided that the following service to Weymouth, sprinter 150 233, would detrain all of its passengers at Yeovil PM, proceed onto the single line, again without the token to try and assist my train, this time from the north end. Again, I was required to protect my train with detonators and a red hand signal as an additional safety precaution in these very unusual circumstances. 150 233 duly arrived on the scene coupled up and immediately the air pressure on my unit started to rise. Then, with the signaller's authority, our two 2-coach train ran empty stock back to Yeovil PM and terminated in the sidings. I then uncoupled the units and shunted 150 233 into the station to work forward to Westbury with 2V74 that had been cancelled from Weymouth to Yeovil Pen Mill.

I never did find out why the air pressure system on my train failed so dramatically.

I drove class 59s regularly from June 1986 until March 1995 and they were so reliable that, in all that time, only once did I experience an engine stop fault when on the main line. It was 11th September 1989 and I was driving 6A29 with 59 004 (then named 'Yeoman Challenger') from Westbury to Theale when, about an hour into the journey and without any warning, the engine simply stopped running. Fellow Westbury Driver Ken Spiller who was booked to relieve me at Theale accompanied me in the cab. (Ken was very knowledgeable concerning all types of traction and later deservedly went onto become a popular driver manager.) Luckily, we were on a falling gradient and so we decided to let the train coast as far as Hungerford. We chose this location to stop the train and investigate as there was an up loop line at Hungerford and if we were unable to remedy the fault then at least trains would still have been able to pass us. The only problem with this cunning plan was that, as the engine had stopped, so too had the air compressors and we had to maintain air pressure to prevent the air brakes from applying automatically. It was a case of whether we would reach Hungerford before the air pressure dropped too low? We made it and, even before we got there, Ken had found the fault. The engine governor had tripped out for some reason. I stopped the train, Ken reset the governor, I restarted the engine and away we went. Total delay less than 10 minutes. It tripped out once again when we were on our way home with the empties; same fault, same remedy, same brief delay.

"Severe lateral oscillation", that was the phrase used in a repair book by Westbury Driver Mike Badger one day to describe the ride on a class 143 'Pacer' unit. He was right to report it and summed up in three brief words the awful ride quality of many a class 142 and 143 at speed. Basically, these two-car DMUs consisted of a bus body mounted on a chassis designed for rail freight wagons and so they had only a single axle at the end of each coach and no air suspension. I found them dire to drive but still preferable to a single class 153; the only reason being that, at least with a class 143, I had two engines so if one failed, I might still be able to limp along and get home or at least to a location where assistance could be forthcoming. But if the one and only engine on a class 153 stopped and would not restart, I would be a dead duck.

11th June 2004 was a very pleasant day weather-wise and I was driving 2M85 the 14:23 from Swindon to Westbury; it was my last train of the shift. My single car 153 308 had performed faultlessly all day and I had departed Chippenham in good spirits when on approach to Thingley Junction and the single line to Bradford Junction, there was a slight hiccup from the engine and then everything went very quiet. Damn! My one and only engine had stopped but, apart from checking the banks of circuit breakers on the cab wall behind me, I took no immediate action and managed to coast to the junction signal. I then tried to restart the engine but without success so I called the signaller and arranged for the up line to be temporarily closed as this would allow me to safely examine the exterior of my train in an attempt to find the fault. Meanwhile, Guard Dave Chamberlin informed our passengers why it had all gone quiet and that I would try to fix the problem. He also advised our control office in Swindon of our predicament. I climbed down and went into fault-finding mode. Fuel? Yes, plenty in the sight glass. Engine lubricating oil? Again, the level seemed adequate. Engine coolant? None in sight!

The single coach class 153s were originally built as two-coach class 155 units but most were converted into two single-car 153s and although this 'doubled' the number of trains, it did not double the number of seats available and the additional cab that then had to be grafted onto one end of each coach was terribly small for traincrew use. Furthermore, should the one and only engine stop due to lack of coolant, for example, this would render the train a total failure. So, in an effort to provide a portable water supply, it was very common at one time to find a full watering can in the cab. When necessary, some drivers would use this very basic bit of kit but others would not as they deemed it to be a task for maintenance staff, many of whom had, by this point, been made redundant at Westbury. After one incident, when a member of staff was scalded attempting to top up the coolant, it became company policy that the job must only be carried out by appropriately trained maintenance staff wearing the correct safety kit that included gloves and goggles. Then someone somewhere came up with an ingenious way to overcome this problem. The toilet water gravity feed tank was fitted within the roof space so, in an emergency, why not use some of this water to refill or at least top up the engine radiator coolant? So, a new connecting hose was installed on these units and a stopcock fitted on the outer bodyside just above the radiator filler cap. I had never used this emergency procedure before and was very skeptical about whether it would work; however, I had nothing to lose so I gave it a go. I heard the water flowing down from the internal toilet water header tank and into the radiator but it sounded like the smallest of trickles. I thought to myself that I could pee more into the radiator, although that would have been extremely difficult from ground level! I then returned to the cab, prayed and pressed the engine start button. No one was more surprised than me when the engine restarted immediately! I updated the signaller and away we went on a wing and a prayer. At Trowbridge, a passenger thanked me for my efforts, as he said he had expected a major delay (as did I) when the engine had stopped. I arrived back at Westbury with no further problems and only 13 minutes late.

I booked on duty at 06:30 on 1st August 2005 and my first task was to prepare 153 318 for service but, when I arrived at Westbury holding sidings, I found that its batteries were boiling and giving off a considerable amount of acid fumes. The unit was obviously not fit for service and so, in an attempt to prevent any further damage, I held by breath, walked into the gas cloud and operated the battery isolation switch. I advised maintenance control of the situation and they managed to find another unit for me. At the end of my shift, I was asked to submit a written report, did so and forgot all about the incident. Many years later I became aware that for a £10 fee, any employee was legally entitled to read his/her personal file held by their employer. So, just out of curiosity, I asked my boss if I could read mine and a few days later I was advised that it was now available to me but that no fee was required. It made for interesting reading and some of it was factually correct! The most glaring error referred to my alleged transfer application from Didcot. This obviously concerned another S. Davies and possibly his file contained some of my employment history. However, the most telling paper in my file was a copy of my report dated 1st August 2005 describing my actions when dealing with the battery fumes from 153 318 because, at the end of my report, an anonymous manager had added a hand-written note that read:

*"We must expect to receive a claim for compensation from Driver Davies."*

If only I had known that at the time, I would willingly have fulfilled their expectations!

On 14th March 2014, I was driving two-car 'Sprinter' 150 266 with the last train of the day from Westbury to Weymouth when just 10 minutes into the journey, we stopped at the first station, Frome, and got no further! My guard on this occasion was Conductor Dave Cornwell (see photo) who was working his final train of the day and was on his way home as he was based at Weymouth. I, on the other hand, had just started my night shift. At the correct time, Dave attempted to close all the sliding passenger doors ready for departure and they all closed except for one pair of double doors. We tried everything we could think of to get them secured including checking the electrical and air supply and using an alternative set of door controls but all to no avail. So, we thought that we would simply isolate them manually, and then close and lock them out of use for the rest of the journey. No good. They still wouldn't budge an inch and, as far as we could tell, neither door had come off its runner, which was another possibility.

I advised the signaller and FGW control at Swindon of our predicament and they put me through to maintenance where I was talked through the process of fully draining the air supply from all the doors as this would make them 'floppy' and they could then be simply pushed closed by hand and, when the air pressure was then restored, all would be well. Even that drastic action failed to work. They remained immovable. It was only then that we discovered the problem. We spotted a small metal bracket on the floor that could have only come from the door control mechanism situated above the doors. Part of the opening/closing mechanical linkage had fallen off. This meant that the only way the train could be moved was by isolating the relevant safety devices and this would mean that the train could not remain in public use. We were forced to admit defeat and so, with no practical alternative, Dave sprang into action. He liaised with control to get as many taxis as possible to take our passengers forward after speaking to every passenger individually. The three for Castle Cary could all travel together in one taxi. Eight for Yeovil? Then two taxis would be required and so on. His organisational skills combined with his genuine concern for the welfare of his customers was exceptional. We had one passenger who must have boarded at either Westbury or Frome who told us he was travelling to Plymouth. "Don't worry sir, we are obliged to get you there," we advised him. However, this individual then told me that he would spend the night with friends at Frome, as he didn't have a ticket anyway. End of obligation!

Eventually, Dave made sure that he was the last to depart for Weymouth in the final taxi and I took the empty train back to Westbury – still with a pair of open doors.

Dave earned my admiration that night and I was very pleased for him when he eventually fulfilled his ambition to become a driver, albeit with Scotrail in Dumfries.

The country railway line from Westbury to Weymouth passes through some picturesque parts of Somerset and Dorset. Much of this rural route is single line but, for long stretches, trains still hurry along at 75 mph. Wildlife is in abundance and consequently animals are, unfortunately, often killed when they stray into the path of a train. The usual victims are birds, predominately pigeons and pheasants; however, larger animals such as deer may also suffer a similar fate. 14th June 2017 turned out to be an unlucky day for me for several reasons. During the first half of my shift, I drove to Portsmouth and back to Westbury but my three-car unit (158 955) was only powering on two engines. This was not an uncommon occurrence. We were then further delayed at Southampton on the return trip due to overcrowding (again not a rare event) so, by the time I arrived back at Westbury, it was off one train and immediately on to my next job to Weymouth. I relieved the incoming driver on 2O86 with unit 150 261 and set sail for the south coast. All went well until my train struck a deer at 75 mph between Yeovil and Maiden Newton and so I reported the incident to the signaller.

Then, when we arrived at Weymouth, an alighting passenger approached me and said, "Are you the driver?"

"Yes sir," I replied.

"Did we hit anything?"

"Yes, a deer."

"I thought so. I was sitting near the front, heard a bang, felt a bump and for the rest of the journey the train rode rough."

"That was probably due to my driving," I joked.

"No. I think you've got a wobbly wheel."

"A wobbly wheel?"

"Yes," he seriously replied.

"Okay sir. Thank you for letting me know," I said. And with that, off he went.

I was convinced that it was all in his imagination as a deer alone could not cause such a serious defect and I had not suffered from 'wobbly wheel syndrome' even in the leading cab.

Nonetheless, I asked my guard if he had noticed anything wrong with the train, and he hadn't. So, I then carried out a visual examination and found that the remains of the deer were spread a little over the front but mainly down the lower left-hand side of the leading coach. Not only did it look dreadful but also it was beginning to smell vile in the heat of the summer sun. The wheels, however, looked fine. I reported the situation to our control office in Swindon and, while I did not want or expect them to take the unit out of service there and then, I asked if a unit swap could be carried out a Westbury on the return run to Bristol as the sight and smells would be unpleasant for both passengers and staff alike. I was advised that there were no spare units available and 150 261 would have to soldier on and remain in service for the rest of the day. So, we departed Weymouth on time with 2E24 the 13:08 to Gloucester. However, fate was not done with us yet. Less than 5 minutes into the return journey, I was unable to regain power after carrying out a running brake test. I just managed to coast the train into Upwey, our first station stop. When it was time to depart, the engines, although both running, would not produce any power. So, after consulting with Guard Rob Franklin, I tried to power up from the rear cab and, as this test was successful, it proved that the fault could only lay with the controls in the leading cab. I returned to this cab but it took many attempts to persuade the engines to start moving the train forward again.

I advised the signaller of our problems and Rob informed our maintenance control office. Our next stop was Dorchester West and, again, this frustrating intermittent fault occurred. I informed the signaller that we were stuttering along on a wing and a prayer so he must expect us to take longer than normal to clear each section of line. The fault became progressively worse with it taking longer and longer to regain power. We managed to claw back some time at Maiden Newton as we were scheduled to wait there for 16 minutes for a down train to clear the next section of single line. Unfortunately, we had to stop at Yetminster (a request stop) and we were stationary there for a considerable time before I was able to regain power. I then decided that the train would have to be terminated at Yeovil Pen Mill (if we got that far) as the alternative would be to risk a total failure on the single line between Yeovil and Castle Cary or worse still, we could possibly block the up West of England main line somewhere east of Castle Cary Junction. My guard, our control office and the signaller were made aware of my decision but our passengers were not advised until we knew what arrangements were to be put in place for their onward travel. At Yeovil Pen Mill, it was quickly decided that taxis were not viable due to the number of passengers involved and we were told that no local coaches or buses were available at that time as they were all setting out to take school children home. So, we waited at Yeovil and eventually a GWR mobile fitter turned up by road to find and, if possible, fix the fault. If he had rapidly diagnosed the fault and found a simple remedy, I would have been made to look incompetent. So, in one way

I was glad when he too couldn't get the engines to power up although, to be fair, he rapidly found the fault. This he traced to an electrical feed under the driver's control desk from the power handle that had been arcing and this had caused further damage that would require new parts and a significant time to repair. The only way to move my train was to have assistance from the front. So, arrangements were put in place for the following up train (2E26 the 15:08 from Weymouth) to run through Yeovil PM station on the down line to pass us and then reverse onto the front of our train, couple up and depart as two trains in one towards Westbury; this was carried out reasonably quickly given the abnormal operations required. My train was timetabled to depart Yeovil PM at 14:10 but we actually left at 16:25. I eventually booked off after 11½ hours on duty.

Of course, it is not only trains that breakdown from time to time. Signaling and points can also be subject to failure. From a driver's perspective, a 'technical SPAD', as it was called, can be an upsetting occurrence. This is when a signal should be displaying a proceed aspect of green or at least a yellow but is at danger. This affords the driver little opportunity to stop if approaching at speed and so the train may technically pass the signal at danger. The reason a signal may be showing red when it should not be, is often as a result of a track circuit or axle counter failure indicating to the signaling system that a train is present in the section ahead when, in fact, there is not. This is known as a 'right side failure' as the system is designed to 'fail safe.' However, the driver must always be aware that the equipment may not have failed but that the signaller may have deliberately switched the signal to red in an attempt to stop the train due to some immediate danger ahead. I have experienced several technical SPADs over the years, all of which were unsettling.

A typical example happened to me on 11th May 2011. I was driving 1F19 comprising a 3-car 'Sprinter' DMU 158 956 from Westbury to Portsmouth Harbour when I passed the last signal before Warminster station that was displaying a green aspect. We stopped at the station and then departed as normal. With the speed approaching 50 mph and full power applied, the next signal (W 308), situated at Beechgrove, came into view. It was red! I made an emergency brake application but we passed it by some distance. Shaking a little, I called the Westbury signaller who, until then, was apparently unaware of any problems. He advised me that it must have been caused by a track circuit failure. We exchanged all the relevant details as we were both required to submit reports later and, after asking me if I felt able to continue, he instructed me to proceed with caution and check that both my down line and the adjacent up line were clear. I was then to stop at the next signal (SY 72) and report my findings to the controlling signaller at Salisbury.

I advised my guard, the confident and competent, Daphnie Heywood of the situation and proceeded at caution. Daphnie then correctly advised our passengers that there would be a slight delay due to a signaling fault. I found nothing untoward in the section, reported the same to Salisbury and we proceeded on our way.

# 16

# Danger on the Line

Working on the railways has never been safer than it is today. Statistically employees are far more likely to be injured or killed on a road journey to or from their place of work than when actually on duty. Having said that, you have to have your wits about you when you are working on or about the line when great big lumps of metal weighing hundreds of tons are hurtling along at high speed.

Personally, I have escaped possible death and certainly serious injury on two memorable occasions both of which were my fault.

The first occurred during my time as a secondman at Ebbw Junction. We were working a train of empty coal wagons from Margam back to Newport when we were brought to a halt due to a red signal on the approach to Miskin Loop west of Cardiff. I contacted the signalman on the signal post telephone (before in-cab radio communications or even mobile phones this was the only way of contacting signalmen whose panel signal box could be many miles away) who told me that he had received a report from a member of staff at Llantrisant who had noticed a possible defect on one of our wagons as we passed by the sidings on the up main line. The signalman told me that, to be on the safe side, he would now route our train into the passing loop where the guard could examine the train for any possible defect. I reported this to my driver and, as he drove the train very slowly towards the east end of the up loop, I said that I would get off and advise our guard of the situation. I jumped off the loco and onto the ballast okay but I got off the mainline side. That was mistake number one. I started to walk back towards the guard's van at the rear of the train when, around the curve in the distance, a Swansea to Paddington express came into view. Although it was approaching me at a considerable speed, it was still some distance away and this allowed me plenty of time to decide whether I should remain between our train, that was still moving very slowly, and the up main line on which the express was approaching or cross both main lines and stand well clear while the up passenger train passed. I chose the former. Bigger mistake! The driver of the up London sounded his warning horn and I acknowledged it in the correct way by holding one arm high above my head. I was still not concerned as I considered that there was plenty of room for the express to pass, with me between it and our train. Wrong again! The train to Paddington rushed past and, for about a second or two, all was well but then the slipstream hit me and knocked me off my feet. Luckily, very luckily, I bounced off the side of one of our coal wagons and I continued to walk back to carry out my mission. When I reached the brake van, I could hardly stand my legs were shaking so much. The guard took one look at me and said, "What the hell is the matter with you? You're as white as a sheet."

"The up London nearly had me," I mumbled and sat down on the ballast to try and regain some composure. I recovered quite quickly – I was young then – and, ironically, the guard could find no defect with our train. The original report had been a false alarm.

A lesson learned, yes, but there was still a second though, thankfully, final occasion when I nearly got struck by a train. This was many years later at Westbury. I was walking from the station to the diesel depot, a short distance but one that required crossing over several lines. The authorised walking route was along platform three to the south end of the station, down the platform ramp, turn right, cross over platform no. 3 line, then across two other lines; this was the up reception and the back road as it was locally known, and then you were within the depot limits. All lines were bi-directional. On the day in question, as I walked south along platform three, an up High Speed Train bound for Paddington arrived and stopped at the same platform. Because of the length of the train, the rear power car was then blocking the official walking route. I should have waited for the HST to depart and moved clear of the walking route but, instead, I walked around the back end of the HST and almost directly into the path of the up yard pilot that was carrying out a shunting maneuver in the down direction but on the up reception line. I didn't see it because it was approaching from behind the HST power car and I didn't hear it for the same reason. Luckily, I reacted in time with a quick step back-wards. The driver on the pilot didn't see me and to this day remains unaware of my lucky escape.

Over the years, I have seen many instances of trespass on the railway. (I am ashamed to say that I too was also guilty of a few going back to my trainspotting days.) On one memorable occasion, I was the driver of 2097, the 17:49 FGW service from Bristol Temple Meads to Weymouth on 31st January 2012. I had stopped my train at Upwey, the last station before the south coast terminus, when, out of the shadows, my headlight picked out a dark-clothed figure staggering along in the four foot towards my train. I got out of the cab and called to him but got no response. He just kept on coming. I dashed back into the cab and made an emergency call to the signaller to ask him to stop all trains and arrange to have electrical power to the third-rail cut off. I then joined my Guard Adrian Webb on the platform and we called to the trespasser to try and alert him to the danger he was in. By now, he had reached the end of our platform but we still got no reaction. I jumped down onto the line and could now see that he was a young man clearly in a state of distress, disheveled and apparently oblivious to his surroundings. I grabbed him and tried to make sure that neither of us fell onto the third-rail as I didn't know if the power had yet been switched off. He was incoherent, in tears and uncooperative but, between us, Adie and I managed to manhandle him up onto the plat-form. Again, we tried but again we failed to get him to understand the situation. He was either unwilling or possibly unable to communicate rationally and started to wander off. We were at a loss as what to do next. I judged that the immediate danger had passed so I called the signaller again and told him that the trespasser was now clear of the line; trains could restart and third-rail power should be restored. I requested police attendance as it was possible that the poor chap could return and either accidently or, through a deliberate act, be killed. If my train had not been booked to stop at Upwey, we would have surely wiped him out but the last we saw of him, he was wander-ing across the fields in the dark but, at least, it was away from the railway. His identity and the reasons for his actions remain a mystery to this day.

Stockton crossing is situated between Salisbury and Warminster and, on the 2nd May 2012, my train 1F10, the FGW 08:23 service from Portsmouth Harbour to Cardiff Central was approaching it at the usual speed of 75 mph. I had sounded the warning horn on approach, as required by the rulebook, when I saw an elderly gentleman start to walk over the crossing. I blew the horn again and expected him to either stop or walk faster to clear the crossing before my train reached him. To my alarm, he did neither. He just kept walking slowly forward, head down and directly into the path of my train. I started to apply the brake and sounded the horn continuously. There was still no reaction. I slammed the brake into emergency and could do no more. He didn't even look up. I thought that impact was inevitable and my train was now so close to him that I had to stand up and lean forward over the control desk to see if he would get clear in time. He did, but only by the smallest of margins. Even if he had poor eyesight and bad hearing to explain his lack of reaction, he must have felt the slipstream of air from my train and then perhaps he may have realised just how close to death he had been. My train eventually stopped with a jolt and I called the signaller to report the situation. While I was making the call, Rod Langfield my guard came to my cab to find out what had happened. I briefly explained to him what had just occurred and he told me that the colour had drained from my face and we could both see how much I was shaking. After a while and with support from Rod, I managed to regain my composure a little and, when I had reassured the signaller that I had recovered enough to carry on driving safely, we went on our way.

This very near miss was bad enough but what really shook me up more than anything else was the resemblance that this elderly gentleman had to my own father. His build, the slight stoop in his gait, the use he made of his walking stick and even his clothing and headgear all made him look remarkably like my dad who had sadly passed away seven years earlier.

If a train driver has a long career like I had then statistically he/she is more likely than not to be involved in at least one fatality on the line. This could be a suicide or accidental death. Either could be considered an occupational hazard for train drivers. Anne and I had talked over the possibilities of me being involved in such a fatality and she believed that, knowing I was a bit of a softy, if I ever did experience a death involving my train, I would not be able to overcome the emotional experience and drive a train again. I had a different view. I thought that if I experienced a clear and obvious case of suicide, I would cope, as the victim would simply be using my train as a weapon and if it was not my train then it could just as easily have been the train in front or the one behind. It would simply be a matter of chance as to which train and driver would be involved. However, if it involved an accidental death such as a trespasser on the line, or worse a child or fellow railway employee, Anne could have been right and my driving days could have ended. Late in my career when I was rapidly heading towards retirement, I was hopeful that I would not suffer such an incident but this did not prove to be the case. The following is a copy of my report and is self-explanatory and basic as it was all the police required from me.

*My name is Stephen Davies. I am 60 years old and have been a train driver since 1981. I am currently employed by First Great Western and based at Westbury.*

*On Saturday 12th April 2014, I was the driver of 2U32, the 20:17 service from Taunton to Cardiff Central.*

*My train departed Taunton platform 3 at 20:18 and was formed of a 2-coach diesel multiple unit No. 150 219 with car no. 57219 leading. The weather was dry and the visibility good although, by this time, it was dark. As my train increased speed to approximately 50 mph, I saw a man walk briskly out of the dark from my left, directly into the path of my train's headlight and onto a public footpath crossing. He then stopped, stood between the two rails, turned his back to me and held up both arms into the air as if in a gesture of surrender. My train immediately hit him full on. From the time I first saw him until the moment of collision I estimate that no more than 3-4 seconds had elapsed.*

*I observed no other persons nearby.*

*I can't recall if I sounded the warning horn at that time but even if I had had the opportunity to do so I believe that the outcome would have been the same given the very brief time window. I made a full brake* application, my train slowed and then stopped. I pressed the emergency call button on the GSM-R (cab-fitted radio communication equipment) and reported the situation to the controlling signaller at Exeter as best I could, given that I was distraught. The train's guard, Bob Lock from Exeter, then came to my cab to ascertain what had occurred and to help accordingly. The signaller and I worked out the exact location of the crossing concerned (it was public right of way foot crossing No. 5/13) and the emergency services were summoned.

After carrying out the necessary safety conversations and procedures with the signaller and the FGW control office in Swindon I called the British Transport Police fatality line and reported the details as requested. The first of the emergency services to arrive on the scene were the police and an officer joined me in the cab and made notes based on my answers. She was followed by a Network Rail employee and then a paramedic who asked me if I required any medical treatment. I advised him that I did not.

The paramedic then confirmed what was certain to me that a fatality had indeed occurred. A BTP officer then also attended the scene.

I was advised that an on call FGW manager and an Exeter driver were on their way to me and, after a considerable delay, both appeared on scene. I then relinquished control of my train to my colleague from Exeter who drove the train back to Taunton station. A taxi was then arranged for me to be taken home to Westbury.

**Approximate timings:**

| | |
|---|---|
| 14:55 | I reported for duty (Westbury turn 2230) |
| 18:53–19:58 | I drove the 18:53 from Bristol TM to Taunton (2C87) |
| 20:18 | I departed Taunton with 2U32 to Cardiff Central |
| 20:22 | Collision occurred |
| 20:23 | Emergency call made / all trains stopped |
| 20:45 | First emergency services arrived on scene |
| 22:20 | Relieved by Exeter driver |
| 22:35 2U32 | arrived back into Taunton |
| 23:00 | I departed Taunton station by taxi |
| 00:30 | I arrived back at Westbury |

There are now a couple of issues concerning the above that I would like to expand upon.

Firstly, my thanks to the Guard, Conductor Bob Lock, whose assistance and calm approach helped the situation more than he probably realised. He repeatedly checked on my welfare, liaised with our control office and kept our passengers up to date and so they were remarkably patient given the long delay before they ended up back at Taunton to restart their journey all over again.

Secondly, on the approach to the public footpath crossing there is a **W** signpost to instruct drivers to sound the train's warning horn in order to alert anyone about to use the crossing that a train is approaching. I couldn't remember and was worried that I may not have sounded the horn at this point and that it could, therefore, be construed as a contributing factor in the young man's death. The only way to find out for certain one way or another was to obtain a download from my train's data recorder, i.e. a black box type device that records many parameters of a train's operation. It took weeks but, eventually, the British Transport Police advised me that the relevant data recording had been analysed and it was found that the horn had been sounded at the **W** board as required by the rule-book. I was mightily relieved.

I was supported by my family and my employer and, at my request, I returned to normal driving duties a few days later. I then had an important decision to make. Should I attend the inquest? I did not have to do so as my written report was considered by the BTP to be adequate, and the facts were not in dispute. However, I felt that if I did, it might help me to find some sort of closure to this tragic event. My son Gareth accompanied me to the inquest that, after a considerable delay, finally took place in Taunton on 15<sup>th</sup> January 2015. It was a very sad affair as many family members of the young man who had committed suicide were in attendance. My statement and others were read out and a BTP officer briefed the coroner who then sought background information from the deceased's family. It is not appropriate for me to go into any further details here. The coroner then, as expected, returned a verdict of suicide.

Immediately after the inquest, I was asked who I was because, although it was open to members of the public, Gareth and I together with a local reporter were the only 'outsiders' in attendance. I told the family members that I was the train driver involved and I braced myself for a possible adverse reaction to me being there, as emotions were naturally running high. I need not have worried. They were very kind, sympathetic, understanding and even thanked me for attending. As I was the last person to see him alive, I was asked by the young man's mother if I believed he had suffered when he died. I assured her that, given the circumstances, it must have been all over in an instant, at which point our emotions got the better of us and we both shed some tears.

As a direct result of this suicide, I received a payment of £1,000. I must now immediately explain how this apparently strange situation came about. While suicide is not illegal in the UK, trespass on the railway is so, in the past, when a driver experienced such an incident, a claim for compensation, normally with the assistance of ASLEF, could be made with the government's Criminal Injuries Compensation Board and reparation may have been paid to the driver, depending upon to what degree he/she suffered. It must be borne in mind that some drivers undergo great emotional and mental anguish, may need a considerable time off work and, in extreme cases, have found that they cannot drive again – with the consequent loss of income. However, the government has now changed the compensation rules and, as a result, train drivers are no longer covered by the scheme. Various train operating companies have some sympathy with their employees who experience fatalities when on duty and, following negotiations with ASLEF, agreed to grant a fixed payment of £1,000 to any driver who experiences a fatality. This is what happened in my case. I did not claim it, I did not ask for it. It was simply paid to me as part of my wages one week. After the normal deductions, it amounted to about £800. Anne and I talked it over and we soon decided that we would use £400 to have a short break away together and the remaining £400 we donated to the Samaritans to help them in their good work trying to reduce suicide rates. I hope, dear reader, that you consider this reasonable in the circumstances.

The following is my report of an incident that befell me just three months after I experienced my first and only suicide and, although no one was killed this time, it had a greater emotional impact on me because I became personally involved. I also felt a little guilty as I promised the woman concerned that she would receive support to help her overcome her problems, but I don't know if she ever did. I often wonder what became of her.

*On Saturday 19th July 2014, I was the driver of 2C30 – the 18:42 Gloucester to Frome FGW service. It was formed of three-car unit no. 150 921 (52121 leading) and I was scheduled to drive it from Bristol TM to Frome.*

*The train was running about 6 or 7 minutes late due to an incident earlier on in the journey when an ambulance was called to attend to a passenger at Keynsham. When we departed Trowbridge the weather was warm, dry and sunny with good visibility but I did not attempt to accelerate to the line speed of 70 mph due to a restrictive signal (UT 106R was at yellow – though UT 106 showed green when it came into view) and because I was also aware of two temporary speed restrictions that were in operation on my line ahead – one at Yarnbrook (40 mph) and another at Hawkeridge Junction (20 mph). Between Trowbridge and Yarnbrook viaduct there are two public footpath rights of way that cross the line. As we approached the first of these, I observed a woman stood in the down side cess near to, but not at, the crossing. Initially I assumed that she was just a trespasser taking a short cut but then I saw something black on the ground near her that I thought was a dog that had either been hit by a previous train or that the woman was trying to get back under control. However, as I got closer, I could see that the object was not a dog but in fact a black coat.*

*I braked quickly but the train stopped about 50 yards past the woman. I looked back out of the cab right-hand drop window and called to the woman but got no response. It was only then I thought that she might be intent on self-harm.*

*In order to stop any approaching train on the adjacent down line I pressed the GSM, Rail Emergency Call button and switched on the red lights on the front of my train. Another train did then approach but stopped well short of the crossing.*

*I reported the situation to the Westbury signaller and then walked back along the down line to speak the woman who at first kept walking away from me. However, I soon caught up with her as she then decided to sit down on the ballast shoulder.*

*She was clearly very upset, agitated, shaking and crying. I sat down next to her and tried to engage her in conversation. This was very diffi-cult as she was reluctant to speak to me. I told her my name from the outset but she would not tell me hers. However, after some time and only then in response to my persistent but I hoped gentle questioning she told me, in fragments, that she lived in Trowbridge, was 26 years old, had nothing to live for and wanted to kill herself. She had a bandaged left wrist that was apparently from a previous attempt at suicide only the day before. I asked her about the reasons she felt like that and she said that she was alone as her boyfriend had recently died from a drugs over-dose and that she had hoped to get married and have kids with him but now no one cared if she lived or died.*

*Although she did not initially tell me her name, she eventually gave me a bankcard (which I returned) with the forename of Lucy\* and this helped our conversation along.*

*She repeatedly told me to go back to my train, as my passengers would be eager to get home. (I think she wanted trains to start running again.) I told her they could wait and that she was more important than all of them. At this comment she smiled for the first and only time.*

*She got to her feet several times during our one-sided conversation because when she heard a lorry passing by on the nearby main road she thought that a train was approaching and that she may still be able to carry out her plan.*

*Initially, during the time I sat with her, the train crew from the down train that I had stopped approached on foot to help but I waved them away as I did not want to put Lucy under any more pressure. She smoked a couple of cigarettes during our time together but was shaking and quietly crying almost constantly.*

*I knew that the police and or ambulance services would have been called by now and so I just tried to keep her calm until professional help arrived.*

---

\* I have changed her name for this book.

*After what seemed a very long time – though in fact it must have been about 20-30 minutes – several policemen arrived and I was glad to see a couple of policewomen on the scene together with a paramedic. I introduced them to Lucy and briefed them on the situation. I feared that she might react badly to their appearance but as they were calm, friendly and promised her help she was co-operative and quietly went with them. As we all walked up the line towards the crossing Lucy called me to her and then thanked me. I found this very touching. We hugged each other and I wished her well.*

*After speaking to the train crew of the down train we agreed to contact the signaller separately to advise that the line was now clear and that with the signaller's permission trains could start running again.*

*My Guard's name was Jay Harrington who told me that he had recently qualified and was based at Bristol. He was very calm, professional and helpful throughout.*

*It was suggested to me that he should ride in the front cab with me to Westbury as I was emotionally drained by this time and not a little upset. Jay kindly agreed to do so and after getting permission from the signaller and authorisation from the senior controller on duty we proceeded at reduced speed to Westbury where we arrived about 55 minutes late. The train was terminated and I was met by station staff under the 'chain of care' procedures. I was offered a taxi home but declined. I was asked to phone my control's office when I reached home to confirm that I had arrived safely and this I did. I also called my Line Manager Sally Wiltshire who had left a message on my personal mobile concerned about my welfare.*

As a little aside to the above, the reference to the young man who had previously been taken ill on our train is that, after we stopped at Keynsham, I didn't receive the signal from the guard to depart so I looked back along the platform to see my guard 'assisting' a young man off the train in a robust manner. I walked back to offer any support that may have been required but none was. My guard had the situation well in hand and the very drunk young man was hauled off our train and onto the platform. My guard explained that he had been acting in an anti-social manner, been very sick and unable to stand and, therefore, he had called for an ambulance. I could see from the state of our would-be passenger that my guard had a valid point and so we moved him away from the platform edge as far as possible. However, he would insist on getting up to try and rejoin our train. We were never going to allow this to happen and the guard suggested that he closed the doors and we should depart without further delay. I pointed out that if we did so and our erstwhile passenger later got to his feet and staggered over the platform edge where non-stop trains passed though at high speed, he may be killed and if so, we could be regarded as failing in our duty of care. Luckily, an individual who was waiting to meet someone on the next stopping train was a witness to the whole scene. He introduced himself as an off-duty fireman, showed us his identification and offered to keep an eye on our former customer until the ambulance arrived. Satisfied that no further harm would befall the young man, we thanked the fireman and promptly departed. I heard no more about that incident. I don't know if my guard ever did.

The following is a report I submitted concerning another trespass incident that I became involved in on 30th March 2016 when driving 2089 comprised of 2+1 car Sprinter units (150 248 + 153 372) from Westbury to Weymouth, but this time there was a much happier ending.

*As my train neared the point indicator signal on the approach to Maiden Newton station I observed a trespasser stood in the cess on the up side. I estimate that the speed of my train was, at this first sighting, to be less than 30 mph. I was concerned that this person may have been about to cross the line, but I was able to stop my train a short distance before reaching the trespasser who turned out to be a girl that I would guess to have been no more than 10 years old.*

*I crossed the cab and dropped the side window to speak to her who I now noticed was crying and clearly very upset and possibly frightened. She was holding a length of rope with a loop at the end that transpired to be a makeshift dog lead. She explained between sobs that her dog had escaped. I told her not to move and after briefly explaining the situation to my guard (Weymouth-based Conductor Steve Hayles)*

*I put on my high visibility jacket and exited the train from the train-crew door.*

*I asked the young lady if at any time she had crossed the line and she said that she hadn't. I tried to calm and reassure her that she had been good in not doing so and was not in any sort of trouble. I asked her if she knew the whereabouts of her dog and what size and colour it was. She told me its name, that it was white in colour and pointed to the top of the opposite embankment. I looked up but was not able to see it. During this brief conversation there were two other girls shouting and screaming in alarm on the other (safe) side of the boundary fence. I told the first girl not to move. I crossed the line in front of my train and scrambled up the short but steep and muddy embankment and through thick bramble bushes that damaged my uniform in several places. (It's a good job my new GWR uniform issue was imminent!) After a brief search I found the dog (a small white terrier type) that appeared to be seeking out rabbits from a small burrow. With some difficulty and several scratches to my hands from the bramble bushes I was able to grab the dog by the scruff of its neck. Luckily for me it did not put up a fight. I then, surprisingly, managed to clamber/slide down the embankment without falling arse-over-head and still maintained a firm grip on the troublesome dog.*

*Steve my guard was now also trackside to offer any necessary assistance. The original young lady trespasser had now been joined by one of her previously hysterical friends who then, at my insistence, both clambered back over the fence and into the adjacent field. I passed the dog to them who was then immediately secured back onto its makeshift lead at my recommendation. The girls were now a little calmer and thanked me for my efforts. I reminded them never to cross the railway line, rejoined my train and drove into Maiden Newton station where I carried out the necessary single line token protocol and also advised the signaller at Yeovil Pen Mill the reason for the delay (about 10 minutes) to my train.*

I believe that trespass on the railway is not now as prevalent as it once was. There may be many reasons for this. Better boundary fencing is probably the main explanation. Also, kids spending more time at home playing computer games and not risking life and limb by playing 'chicken' on the line could be another. Placing objects on the

246 | RIGHT AWAY!

line just to see what would happen when a train hit them was another common occurrence and it still does occasionally occur today. It is not only children who trespass. Instances of adults breaking down fences to access a short cut home from the pub have also been known and the thieves who cut and steal lineside cable for its copper scrap value not only put themselves in danger but are responsible for huge delays to trains and many cancelled services.

Kids or sometimes adults throwing stones at trains or dropping objects from a bridge as a train passes under can be an alarming occurrence for the driver. I have experienced such incidents myself but nothing compared to the horrific events that a former colleague of mine suffered.

The following is an extract of a letter I wrote to the FGW Chief Operating Officer in my role as an FGW Company Council Representative:

*Dear Mr. White*

*I am taking the unusual step of writing to you directly as I am very alarmed about the recent and repeated attacks that took place on the FGW 15:30 Taunton to Cheltenham Spa service (2G20) on the mainline west of Bristol.*

*On THREE consecutive days (30th October – 1st November 2007 inclusive) this train came under missile attack from a stone throwing vandal as it passed under a road bridge east of Flax Bourton tunnel at speeds of between 80-90 mph. Unfortunately, the same driver was at the controls on all three occasions.*

*The first time Westbury based Driver A. Brown\* was driving two-car sprinter 158 865 and was very lucky to escape serious physical injury or possibly death as the missile was of a substantial size and weight. This object was pushed off the parapet of the bridge and struck the end gangway door with such a force that it tore the hinges off and forced the door open into the cab. (To get an appreciation of the degree of impact needed to do so much damage I would invite you to closely inspect a class 158 end gangway door. It is a very substantial, thick, robust and weighty*

---

\* I have changed his name for this book.

*piece of metal with a heavy duty locking mechanism.) The driver's wind-screen is made of toughened and laminated glass; however, given the weight of the projectile and the speed of the train, should the rock have been dropped only a foot or two to the left it would have undoubtedly smashed through the window. Despite the inevitable shock he was suffer-ing from, Driver Brown immediately made an emergency brake application and an emergency call to Network Rail control centre on the NRN radio-phone system to report the incident. Eventually he took the train forward to Bristol Temple Meads where he was diagrammed to be relieved. He submitted a written report later the same day.*

*The following day (31ˢᵗ October) he was driving the same train when at the same location and at approximately the same time and speed his train was again targeted. Fortunately, on this occasion the stone, about the size of half a house brick, missed the train and landed in the six foot. Our colleague reported the incident to the Bristol signaller stopping especially at signal B19 to do so via the signal post telephone. Again, he submitted a written report.*

*The very next day (1ˢᵗ November) Driver Brown was again driving the same train, when at the same location and at approximately the same time and speed his train was again targeted. This time the brick size object struck the end gangway door. Yet again he made an emergency brake application and reported the incident to the Bristol signaller and also to the British Transport Police. It became apparent that although the BTP were in the area on this third occasion, they were positioned on the wrong over-bridge and so not only failed to prevent this attack but also failed to arrest the culprit. I am advised that this is because they do not recognise railway lineside mileposts as an appropriate method of geographically locating possible crime sites. If true this is unacceptable.*

*As the BTP are a specialised force I would expect them not only to be familiar with railway jargon in common use such as "four/six foot" "main/relief lines" "up/down lines" they should also be aware of the significance of lineside mileposts. Also, are BT officers trained in personal track safety?*

*I have spoken directly with Driver Brown and he is naturally angry and upset that no successful action appears to have taken place to appre-hend the individual/s who attempted to kill him.*

*I am left with the impression, wrongly I hope, that if this attack had taken place on three consecutive days from a road bridge over the M5 motorway the culprit would now be under lock and key awaiting trial for attempted murder. But because it was 'only' another stone throwing incident at a train it is just another crime statistic to be filed away.*

*I would be very grateful if you could reassure me and all my driver colleagues by advising what actions the company has taken to date or intends to take following the above incidents.*

*I am sure you will agree that Network Rail also has a responsibility to do all they can to prevent such attacks taking place. There are many over rail bridges that have been fitted with a physical barrier to prevent stone throwing onto trains passing beneath. Could this be considered at this location?*

*Finally, the failure by the BTP to stop the second and third incidents would I suggest warrant investigation to see if lessons can be learned that could result in a safer railway not only for drivers but also for other traincrew and our customers.*

'Trespass' by animals is still a regular occurrence and any large creature such as a horse or cow has the potential to derail a train so drivers are obliged to make an immediate report, stopping if necessary, should they encounter any such animal on or near the line. Previously, it was up to a driver to use his/her discretion in deciding whether or not smaller animals such a sheep, pigs or goats needed to be reported immediately or not. However, in recent years, in an attempt to reduce delays to services, it was deemed that fewer than six sheep did not constitute a risk to trains but more than half a dozen did! What criteria if any was used in selecting this apparently arbitrary number is anybody's guess. I and many other drivers simply ignored it and would always immediately report sheep on the line as mowing down animals was an unpleasant experience not only for the driver but also for those staff who were required to clean up the mess and, of course, for the farmer concerned.

Returning from Portsmouth on 1st June 2010, I was accelerating my train after stopping at Romsey station and was approaching 80 mph when I spotted some sheep grazing contentedly on the railway embankment but within the boundary fence. I decided to stop and report the situation and called the signaller accordingly.

He asked me, "How many sheep are there?"

I replied, "At 80 miles per hour it was hard to estimate."

He persisted, "Take a guess; I need to know."

"Several," Was my response.

"That's no good to me; was it more than six!?"

By now I had had enough and said, "Well I started to count them but I fell asleep."

## PHONETIC FAMILY FUN

Good communication is vital in the rail industry in order to maximise safety and minimise delays and so the FGW management introduced the use of the phonetic alphabet that we were then required to use when, for example, referring to specific signals. So, signal UM 120 had to be said as "Uniform, Mike, One, Two, Zero" and, while this made good sense and is in common use today, some of us initially found the 26 phonetic words used to represent letters hard to remember. To try and assist my fuddled brain, I made up as short a story as possible using every one, but that still made some sort of sense.

The following was the best I could come up with:

During **N**ovember in a **H**otel near the **A**lpha **D**elta in **I**ndia, **R**omeo and **J**uliet would **F**oxtrot and **T**ango while **M**ike the **Y**ankee shouted,
"**B**ravo, you both deserve an **O**scar!"
"I **E**cho that." agreed **C**harlie in his **U**niform.
**P**apa then suggested "Why don't we all go to **L**ima in my **S**ierra."
"No" replied **V**ictor "Let's go to **Q**uebec in my **G**olf instead."
"Well I can't go," said the **Z**ulu "I've drunk a **K**ilo of **W**hisky and need an **X**-ray!"

Did this help? Well sadly no. I found the best way to remember them all was by the repeated practice of phonetically reciting to myself passing road vehicle number plates as I walked to work.

# 17
# Odd Jobs

In this chapter, I recall some of the more unusual train operations that I have been involved in during my footplate career at Westbury.

On 6th March 1981, I was assistant to Westbury Driver Fred Tucker. Fred was a quietly spoken gentleman and a pleasure to work with. We were rostered to work a special that turned out to be the royal train. We booked on duty at 04:00, travelled to Yeovil Pen Mill station and relieved the previous footplate crew who were on duty all night while the train was stabled and Prince Charles slept on board. This was the first time I had seen armed police officers. We came across one as we approached the train on foot in the dark and we were challenged. We rapidly explained our presence and so escaped being shot!

Charlie was the only member of the royal family on board[*] a train that must have cost a substantial sum to run just for one individual. As a republican, I was not impressed because all of the considerable costs involved were ultimately met by the taxpayer.[†]

Our locomotive was the immaculately turned out 47 500 named 'Great Western'. We took the train to Dorchester station where Charlie boy got off to visit nearby Poundbury, Dorset – one of his pet projects. We then took the train to Weymouth and ran round to take the empty stock back to Westbury where we were relieved by another crew. Naturally, Fred drove throughout. That was my first and last dealings with the royal train.

The class 59 was and I suspect still is a major attraction for enthusiasts when exhibited at open days or railway festivals that occasionally

---

[*]  At that time, Charlie and Diana were engaged and would be married later that year.

[†]  Today, as a result of rail privatisation, a German-based rail freight company, DB Cargo UK, a subsidiary of Deutsche Bahn, operates the royal train, the costs of which are still met by the UK taxpayer.

take place at various locations throughout the country. (Even Westbury had an open day on 5th May 1985.) One such event was a 'Diesel
Weekend' that took place on the Severn Valley preserved railway
during May 1988. On Sunday 8th, I was booked to go there and fetch 59
001 'Yeoman Endeavour' light engine back to Westbury. I had never
visited the Severn Valley Railway before, either on or off duty, but that
day I made a mental note that I must do so as it looked a very interesting set-up. (I'm ashamed to admit that 30 years later I still haven't
been.) I booked on duty at 15:51 and travelled 'on the cushions' to
Kidderminster and was made welcome in the signal box where I had
a cup of tea. No driver at Westbury knew the road throughout and I
only signed the road as far as Gloucester and so a driver from that
depot was provided to act as my pilotman for the first part of the
journey. We departed at 19:20 and, after dropping off the pilotman, I
arrived back at Westbury at 21:45.

A similar arrangement took place a year later, on 12th August 1989,
when Foster Yeoman kindly loaned another of their class 59s for a rail
fete exhibition. This time it was their latest purchase from GM: 59 005
named 'Kenneth J. Painter'. I left Westbury at 07:02 and ran light
engine to Newport station where the display was to take place. Ivor
Mason, representing the owners, accompanied me and we believed
that this was the first time that a 59 had passed through the Severn
Tunnel and into Wales. After showing my son Gareth (he was then
nine years old and staying with his grandparents in Newport for a few
days), the cabs of the 59 and 37 038 that was also on display among the
many other exhibits, I travelled back home to Westbury.

On 5th September 1990, I was to drive 7A30 from Westbury to the
stone distribution depot at Theale in Berkshire. There were two
drivers rostered on this particular turn so that the second driver could
relieve the first at Theale to enable him to have his PNB. In this way,
the unloading operations need not be halted. My colleague on this day
was driver Dave Francis and we walked to the up reception line and
relieved the incoming driver who had just arrived with our train from
Merehead quarry. Our loco, 59 005, was hauling 30 wagons giving a
total train weight of 3,187 tons. When we entered the cab, we were
surprised to find Traction Inspector Mike Cheesley on board together

with a cameraman who was to film the journey. We departed at 15:04, were held in the up loop at Woodbourgh for 13 minutes and arrived at Theale at 16:48. I was not fully aware that the sounds from our in-cab conversations were also being recorded. Consequently, should you ever view Railscene Cabride XTra No. 2 (Merehead to Theale) you may just about hear me above the sounds of the engine taking the mickey out of the inspector by suggesting that the blisters on his hands were not a result of gardening as he was claiming but from repeatedly counting all of his money!

One of the more unusual workings that Westbury drivers became involved with for a short period was hauling withdrawn former British Rail southern region electric third rail powered units to Margam in South Wales for scrapping by Gwent Demolition (see photo of one of these trains). I drove this train on several occasions. The first time was on 9th January 1992. This was a Thursday, which was payday on the railway at this time. (This fact will become more relevant as you read on.) My train was made up of loco 33 019 (named 'Griffon') towing three withdrawn 4-coach units nos. 5418 + 5417 + 5182 with a train weight of 482 tons and a headcode of 5Z45. I departed Westbury at 16:43 and arrived at Cardiff Central at 18:35 where I picked up a pilotman for the final part of my journey to Margam. However, 33 019 was feeling poorly and the engine stopped several times en route suffering from low oil pressure. I discovered that I needed a longer dipstick as the one fitted failed to reach the engine oil level! Luckily, it restarted every time and, after abandoning our train to its inevitable fate in the sidings, we managed to limp along to Margam diesel depot, arriving at 19:50, for much needed oil for the engine and tea for its crew. While our loco was receiving appropriate attention from the maintenance staff, I made myself a brew in the messroom and, while it cooled, I decided to phone home to tell Anne that I may be late getting back.

Now this may be hard to believe for readers of a younger generation who should now brace themselves for the following shocking statement of fact: "At this time nobody had a mobile phone!"

So, I looked for a phone with an outside line, as most railway phones were for internal use only. Peering through a glass partition in an office door, I spied what I was looking for on a desk. I knocked on the door, got no response and so I tried the handle. It was unlocked so in I went. I called Anne and was in the middle of explaining my situation when I was joined in the office by an individual who was not in uniform or overalls so I assumed, correctly as it transpired, that he was a supervisor of some sort. He looked me up and down and realising that I was not local, he asked me what I thought I was doing. I carried on talking to Anne and held up my hand to try and signal to my newfound co-worker that we would talk when I had finished my phone conversation. I was shocked at his response – he almost exploded! I have never seen anyone lose their temper so quickly and totally. He went very red in the face and started to shout at me at the top of his voice. How dare I come into his office and use his phone! I would have liked to point out to him that it was neither HIS office nor HIS phone, as British Rail owned them both. However, I could just about hear Anne asking what on earth was going on. I ignored my still ranting colleague and finished my phone conversation. I continued to be verbally attacked. I was amazed as the cost of my phone call was perhaps 10p so why all the drama? He still didn't calm down and repeatedly yelled at me to get out of his office and he then tried to justify his actions by saying that there were dozens of full wage packets in the desk waiting for the night shift staff to collect. His responsibilities had clearly overwhelmed him. I genuinely feared for his heart and rising blood pressure so I left the office. However, as I departed, I suggested that perhaps in future he should take the quick and effective security action of simply locking the door every time he left the office unattended. I made my way back to the mess room. I needed a cup of tea more than ever now. There were several of the Margam depot maintenance team sitting around the messroom and, as I entered, they all burst out laughing. They had clearly heard the commotion and my face must still have been showing some signs of shock.

"You've met Dai Red Pen then?" one asked me.

"If that was the bloke yelling at me – then yes."

"He's always doing that – take no notice. He normally just uses a red pen to give vent to his feelings but you got the verbal version."

"He'll give himself a heart attack. I only wanted to phone home."

This remark only made them laugh out loud again, and even more so when one of them called me ET! I managed a smile, finished my tea and rejoined my class 33. I knew that Margam would not want to hang on to it even if they were short of engines as there would be no local drivers who would have the relevant traction knowledge. (It was a southern engine based at Eastleigh.) My pilotman and I then headed back light engine to the Welsh capital. I thanked him as he got off and I took the loco back to Westbury arriving at 23:13.

On 1st April 1993, I was allocated to work a special train headcode 2Z96 from Westbury to Cardiff. This was officially a DOO train but I was far from alone. The train had originated at London Waterloo and was bound for Derby via Cardiff. It consisted of a two-car hybrid class 158 formed by 57716 and 52774. This was a test train with a team of British Rail engineers from Derby on board who had wired up their equipment to carry out stress tests on the class 158's aluminum body. To make the test more realistic, many of the seats were occupied, not with passengers but with bags of sand to replicate weight distribution. Unfortunately, we were severely delayed when we were turned into the down loop at Pilning on the English side of the Severn Tunnel behind two freight trains. A previous train had reported some sort of problem in the tunnel and the line through 'the hole' had to then be examined to ensure it was safe for the passage of following trains. We arrived in Cardiff exactly two hours late but none of the 'customers' complained! I was relieved by a Cardiff-based driver and travelled back to Westbury on the 19:30 service.

On one memorable occasion, I was the driver on a special service to Weymouth. A private company wanted to run a train once a week on Wednesdays during the school summer holidays of 1993 to Weymouth Quay and, as this involved the novelty of a train passing through the streets of Weymouth utilising the old tramway line to the quay, it was hoped that such a journey would appeal to adults, children and rail enthusiasts alike. This, when combined with a meal on the train, made it an interesting enterprise. I worked the train on a couple of occasions, the first time being for a publicity run that took place on 3rd June 1993.

I travelled to Weymouth as a passenger on the 09:48 from Westbury and relieved the driver on the same train that consisted of class 37 408 (named 'Loch Rannoch') hauling six coaches weighing 196 tons. We departed Weymouth (Town) station at the planned time of 11:35 and ran empty stock through the streets of Weymouth at walking pace. The weather was good and crowds gathered in large numbers to see this unusual sight. I was told that it had been four years since a train had run over these metals. Unfortunately, our slow progress came to a halt altogether when we encountered an unattended Porsche parked and partially blocking the line (see photo). The police attended and it was eventually towed away. I had offered to slowly nudge it to one side with my loco but the police thought this a bad idea – the spoilsports. The owner of the Porsche would have come back to find his car missing, a parking fine and a towing fee to pay. Eventually we arrived at Weymouth Quay at 12:40 some 25 minutes late. After running round, we departed at 13:00 now 15 minutes late with customers on board, a bagpiper marching ahead and even more people lining the streets to observe our stately progress past houses, shops, pubs and even the bus depot. We rejoined the main line and I applied full power to ascend the steep incline up to Bincombe tunnel. Then it was down hill to Dorchester West station where we were held for ten minutes because, unbeknown to me, we had left our bagpiper behind in Weymouth! He eventually turned up in a taxi looking a little disheveled with bagpipes, bearskin and alarmingly his kilt all needing adjustment before he regained his composure and rejoined the train. We arrived at Yeovil Pen Mill 15 minutes late at 14:25, ran round the train again and were relieved by another Westbury driver who took the train with its then dining passengers back to Weymouth. This time the bagpiper was not abandoned!

Dilton Marsh station was made famous by the poem 'Dilton Marsh Halt' by Sir John Betjeman and serves a village of the same name between Westbury and Warminster. It is a request stop with one platform for up trains and another serving the down line, though they are not opposite one another. Both platforms are less than one coach in length and must make up the smallest station in England with two platforms. British Rail wanted to close it rather than spend money when its wooden construction deteriorated to such a degree that it would soon become unsafe for public use. There was strong local opposition to this proposal and, eventually, BR relented. It was closed but only temporarily while it was rebuilt during the spring of 1994. To celebrate its rebirth, a special return train ran from Dilton Marsh to the seaside at Weymouth on Sunday 22nd May.

I was allocated to work the very last part of the return run. I booked on duty at 17:33 and detached the Dilton Marsh portion off a regular service from Weymouth. I then departed Westbury at 18:03 with 1Z29 sprinter unit no. 158 863. Less than five minutes later we arrived at Dilton Marsh but, due to the very short platform, every passenger had to alight from a single door. As the two-coach train was full with what appeared to be half the population of the village, this took considerably longer than the time I had been driving it! Eventually, the celebrating sea-siders all went home and my guard Graham Mabbet and I took the empty train to Warminster in order to access the nearest crossover and return to Westbury via the up line. I had completed all the work allocated to me for the day and so, after checking that I was no longer required, I went home. Total time on duty 1 hour 24 minutes. Total payment 10 hours 15 minutes (guaranteed minimum payment for a Sunday turn with such a booking on time). Happy days!

A small but classic example of the difference in the way British Rail conducted their operations compared to a private TOC can be demonstrated by a train that Westbury crew were scheduled to work towards the end of their shift.

The last train from Bristol was among several that were cleaned overnight at Westbury before being checked and prepared ready for service the following morning. But this train didn't officially terminate at Westbury. It called in at Westbury but then made the short journey to Frome where the service officially terminated before immediately returning empty stock back to Westbury for the night. In British Rail days, if there were no passengers on board travelling to Frome when it was about to depart from Westbury, the train was simply terminated there and then as it was accepted that to run empty to Frome and then empty back again was just a waste of time and resources. This 'cancellation' was arranged locally between the traincrew, station staff and signaller. It could not take place until the very last minute, of course, as a passenger might turn up at Westbury or already be on the train correctly expecting to be taken to Frome. BR managers were happy with this procedure and accepted the logic of it.

Initially the privatised company too did not object to this arrangement, possibly because I suspect that there were few managers to been seen on Westbury platform at 1 o'clock in the morning and so what they didn't know wouldn't hurt them was our approach. However, after many years of ignorant bliss, Wessex Trains management became aware of our antics when they started to be fined for a cancelled service. No matter that it carried no customers: a cancellation had to be avoided whenever possible. So, from March 2004 this ghost train frequently ran with just a driver on board because the guard went home, as, clearly, he/she was not required to perform any duties. Even the passenger doors were not released at Frome. The driver simply changed ends and retraced his/her journey back to Westbury. What an absurdity.

The FA cup final took place at the Cardiff Millennium Stadium (since renamed the Principality Stadium) for six consecutive years from 2001 while the redevelopment of Wembley Stadium took place. The 2004 final on 22nd May was between Manchester United and Millwall and additional trains were provided to help transport some of the 71,000 fans who attended the game, in particular, the Man. U. contingent who, I suspect, were more widely spread throughout the country than the Millwall supporters.

I booked on duty at 13:52 and travelled to Cardiff Canton depot with my Guard for the shift, Conductor Ian Middleton. We had loco 31 128 (named 'Charybdis') leading four coaches with 31 454 at the rear. 5Z62 from the depot became 1Z62 from Central station and we departed 12 minutes late at 18:07. We called at Newport, Severn Tunnel Junction, Bristol T.M., Bath Spa, Bradford-on-Avon, Trowbridge, Westbury, Warminster and terminated at Salisbury. We then returned empty stock to Westbury and berthed the train in the up holding sidings at 21:10. (PS Man. U. won 3 – 0.)

Here I would like to pay my respects to my guard on that day, Ian Middleton, who sadly passed away several years later. Ian was a popular, friendly, knowledgeable and as helpful a colleague as anyone could have wished for. We only fell out once. Ian used to buy *The Times* newspaper most days and, as I was too mean to buy my own copy, I would frequently 'borrow it' – when he had finished with it, of course. However, my supply seemed to dry up suddenly and, when I made enquiries, my personal newsagent told me that he had taken out an online subscription to the paper to read off his laptop so a paper copy of the newspaper was no longer available to me! I was unhappy at this development and told him so too but he only laughed and suggested that I buy my own copy. The cheek of the man!

On Saturday 7th August 2004, I booked on duty at 06:19 and travelled 'on the cushions' to Bristol TM where I was rostered to drive 2087 the 08:58 departure to Weymouth. I was advised that my train had been stabled in platform 2. This was a bay platform, situated at the west end of the station and not in public use (see Chapter 10 Passengers Not Customers).

My train consisted of loco 31 454 named 'The heart of Wessex' leading five passenger coaches with loco 31 128 named 'Charybdis' at the rear and, although the two locos were not directly coupled, they were still operating in multiple mode as the coaches had been adapted to accommodate all the necessary through connections.

2087 was to depart from platform 10; however, due to the track layout at the west end of Temple Meads, it was impossible to gain direct access to this platform from platform 2 in a single reverse direction operation/shunt. I needed to drive the train forward into Pyle Hill sidings, change ends and drive the train onto the up through line in the station, change ends again and drive my train until it was in clear of the west signal gantry, change ends yet again and finally drive forward into platform 10. This maneuver was called a double shunt and was very time consuming because, in total, I had to visit all four cabs four times in order to ensure that the correct head and tail lights were displayed. This was due to the fact that, although the headlights could be switched on or off from what was to be the leading cabs, the switches to operate the necessary tail lights were then situated in the cabs adjacent to the coaches and, therefore, both cabs on both locos had to be visited prior to each change in direction of travel.

Not surprisingly, all this messing about meant that the train was late departing by some 11 minutes and it was not the last time I needed to carry out such a performance that summer.

For the duration of the summer 2010 timetable, Westbury drivers had a turn of duty that included running an empty unit, usually a single-car 153, from Bristol TM to Weston-Super-Mare but unusually via Highbridge and Burnham. Our unit was normally to be found berthed in platform 2 at Temple Meads station. I was allocated this turn one hot and sunny day and, when I opened the cab door of 153 372 to prepare my little train ready for departure, the heat inside hit me like an oven as it had been standing in the sunshine with all of its doors and windows closed for a considerable time. I opened both cab windows, took off my uniform jacket and hung it on the only coat hook available that happened to be behind the non-driver's seat adjacent to the now open right-hand cab window.

Any reader who may be familiar with the class 153 will be aware that cab number 1 is original but number 2 is not and is very small indeed. I just happened to be driving from the number 2 end. I advised the signaller when I was ready to depart and, after a quick shunt to access the down main, I powered up. As my speed slowly increased, the cab heat slowly decreased as the internal hot air was being drawn out of the cab and through both of the open side windows. My jacket started to gently move about in the breeze but, as the speed increased, it gradually became more and more animated until it looked like a demented ghost having a fit was wearing it. I glanced over with some concern and was just thinking to myself, "I hope it doesn't blow..." Too late! With one final flourish the ghost jumped out of the window, still wearing my jacket. Should I stop and retrieve it, write it off or perhaps pick it up on my return run to Bristol. I made an instant executive decision and put the brake into emergency. When stationary, I looked back and could see my errant garment spread over the rails of the up main like the ghost was trying to commit suicide. A bewildering concept! I switched on my company mobile phone that had all signal box numbers stored in its memory and called the Bristol signaller. As it was ringing, I left the cab on the safer cess side and started to run back. The signaller answered and I tried to explain why my train had stopped and the bizarre situation I was now in. Not surprisingly perhaps, he asked me to repeat the message, as by then I was panting for breath. I tried again and this time I knew from his laughter that he now understood the situation. I retrieved my jacket luckily before it was run over by the next up train and returned to my cab. I called the signaller again to update him and, after he had congratulated me, my journey to Weston-Super-Mare continued but now with only the driver's side window open.

The summer of 2012 saw the Olympic & Paralympic Games officially come to London, although some events, notably the majority of the football matches and all the sailing competitions, actually took place outside the capital. Weymouth and Portland hosted the sailing competitions between 28th July and 11th August.

In anticipation of great demand, additional trains were laid on including CrossCountry return services from Birmingham and Manchester and whenever possible FGW strengthen their services from Bristol (see photo). Initially, FGW also operated an HST on the route, but this additional service was curtailed when demand did not reach the anticipated levels.

A new relief road together with a park and ride had been especially built and these facilities must also have helped with the transport arrangements of the crowds who did attend.

I visited Weymouth five times during this period, four on duty and once off duty with Anne. The atmosphere was wonderful. Good-natured crowds populated the sunny seafront enjoying not only the Olympics but also the multitude of other attractions on offer. For those keen on the sailing and all the other sporting events, huge free-to-view TV screens were located on the beach and, just a short walk away on the other side of the river Wey, you could observe part of the course that the multitude of colourful yachts were racing over.

Like many others, I was, initially, a little skeptical in the build up to this huge international event imagining all sorts of problems from summer storms to transport chaos and even a possible terrorist attack. However, from the little that I personally saw, especially at Weymouth, it was an unqualified success.

Occasionally, train crew had to be provided with road transport, as it may have been the only practical method of starting a service or returning staff to their home depot at the end of their shift. This normally involved the company hiring taxis. I hated this and, given a choice, I would always do all that I could to avoid them. Comfortable and relaxed taxi journeys were as rare as hens' teeth due to the poor and sometimes alarming standard of some of the drivers. Three journeys in particular stick in my mind. In all three instances, I was being transported back to Westbury after the last trains of the day had departed from Bristol, Portsmouth and Weymouth respectively.

The first, from Bristol TM, departed at about 01:00, so with very little traffic about the driver decided to make the most of it but every corner seemed to take him by surprise as we lurched left and right. He was almost permanently in the wrong gear with the engine either revving very high or struggling to the point of stalling. He told me that he frequently made this journey under contract to FGW so I assumed that, when we reached Keynsham where a 30-mph zone was policed by a speed camera, he would be well aware of it and at least slow down then. Not a bit of it. We flew passed the camera and sure enough flash, flash, he was caught. His reaction was only one word that he repeated over and over again.

"Shit. Shit. Shit ...", eventually he added

"You do realise the money I'll get for taking you home will now all have to go to pay the speeding fine."

Apparently, it was all my fault!

The taxi journey from Portsmouth to Westbury was an adventure! First, the driver had no idea where Westbury was and when I told him it was north of Salisbury but south of Bath, he was clearly shocked as he told me that he only did local trips within the city and that he shouldn't have been given the job by his boss. Not a good start I thought to myself but, in an attempt to be helpful and to get home in a reasonable timescale, I told him that I could give him a postcode to put in his sat nav; he told me that he didn't have one. "Okay," I said, "I'll show you on a road atlas," thinking that he would at least have one in the car. He didn't. He then advised me that his fuel tank was almost empty so we would have to stop at a 24-hour service station, which we did, though he only put a few pounds-worth in the tank. Eventually, we set off but, as I had also never driven by road from Portsmouth to

Westbury, it was very much a case of the blind leading the blind. We found the motorway and soon came across a slip road exit signposted for Romsey. This was good, as I knew that the train at least went through Romsey en route to Westbury so we followed the signs into the night, eventually coming across the town but then we became completely lost. The driver noticed a police station so he stopped and asked for directions. The journey was becoming more and more bizarre. Eventually we found our way onto the A36 and, when we reached Salisbury, I knew which road to take. He repeatedly apologised for the time the journey was taking so, in the end, I began to feel sorry for him. It should have taken about 1½ hours but it was nearly double that by the time we reached Westbury. He dropped me off, did a three-point turn and drove away only to immediately head off in the wrong direction! I never knew if he eventually found his way back to Portsmouth or if he ran out of fuel trying to do so.

The journey by road from Weymouth to Westbury includes some dangerous highways, or at least they can become dangerous when being driven along by a taxi driver in a Cavalier with a cavalier attitude. It was a late winter's night and the rain was torrential when we sped out of town. My driver clearly new the way and appeared intent on stopping for no one. The county roads became more flooded as time went by but this fact appeared to be lost on him. As I became increasingly alarmed, we rounded one corner and hit a pool of water with such force that the steering wheel was nearly wrenched from his hand (note the singular). I had bitten my tongue long enough.

"You need to slow down mate!"

I couldn't believe his reply when he said, "It's okay, I had a new set of tyres fitted this morning."

"New tyres or not, you're going to lose control completely in a minute."

He slowed down a little but for the rest of the journey there was an awkward silence between us. Luckily, I lived to tell the tale but felt that, on his way back to Weymouth, he was heading into danger despite his four new tyres.

# 18

# Winding Down and Retirement

As I got older my enthusiasm for my multiple roles as train driver, instructor driver and staff representative began to noticeably diminish. Jointly, the three positions I held began to take their toll and I wanted a simpler and less stressful life. While I was happy to retain my train driving position, the other two roles had to go. I gave my Local Manager Sally Wiltshire notice that I intended to resign as an instructor on 31st December 2008 and she put the wheels in motion to find a replacement. I was far more concerned about who would replace me representing my depots on FGW Driver's Divisional Council. I knew of only one person who stood out as potentially the best candidate. The question was whether I could persuade him to throw his hat into the ring. Howard Rugg was the FGW driver's local rep at Fratton (Portsmouth) depot and we had worked together on and off for some time. I considered him to be dedicated, reliable and trustworthy and he was also well respected by his Fratton-based colleagues. Two problems – was he prepared to stand in an election to find my successor and if so who, if anybody, would also put their name forward? I told Howard (or 'H' as he was known) that I intended to resign and I hoped that he would try for the position. We discussed the role in detail and, some while later, 'H' agreed to be nominated. I was pleased and relieved because I knew that if elected, he would do a good job. I did not want to leave the position in the hands of someone whom I considered to be unsuitable. Obviously, it was not up to me to choose my replacement but I was content that 'H' would at least be on the ballot paper. I need not have worried, he got the job and, at the time of writing this, he still has it!

I was very moved at the end of the last DDC meeting I attended when I was thanked by all present for my efforts and contributions to the council over the many years that I had represented my constituents. I was presented with a large card with appropriate messages from all my staff side colleagues and members of the management team alike. I was also given a model of a class 153 DMU (153 303 in Regional Railways livery).

In return, I took the opportunity to bestow a 'medal' around the neck of Dick Samuels one of my HSS DDC colleagues who, whenever he had a victory (however minor), would praise himself and joke that he deserved a medal much in the same way as the cartoon character 'Muttley' demanded from 'Dick Dastardly'.

I was now able to wind down a little and was content with my lot. All I wanted was to be left in peace to carry on simply train driving. My thirst for new routes and/or new types of trains to drive had been well and truly quenched over the years. While my interest in the job had considerably subsided, I still loved train driving and wanted to carry on. I started to rely more and more on my experience and less on my knowledge and I found it hard to keep pace with the never-ending new technologies being introduced to the role. As I grew older, the shift work too was getting more difficult for me to cope with. However, there were compensations. Free time during the week and crawling into a warm bed after a long night shift in the winter were both very welcome.

In my introduction I wrote, *I have included some details relating to my personal life but only when they have impacted on my career – or vice versa.* Well, some personal health issues have indeed impacted on my career and they all started when I began to fall apart at 59 years old. By which I mean that, until I reached that age, I had been lucky enough to have enjoyed reasonably good health for nearly all of my life. The first sign of something being amiss occurred while I was walking to work one day during June 2013. I began to feel a pain to the right side of my groin. I tried to ignore it, hoping that it would go away. It didn't. Walking up steps or climbing into the cab from ground level became an ordeal so eventually Anne sensibly persuaded me to consult a GP who correctly diagnosed the problem even before he had examined me. I had developed an inguinal hernia. The doctor explained that this was very common in men of my age and that I could either simply learn to live with it, as many did, or undergo a simple operation to fix the problem permanently. I told him that I would see how things developed but, within two weeks, I was in increasing pain from doing the most simple of physical tasks like pushing a shopping trolley along the isles in Morrisons supermarket. So, after another visit to the doc, I was placed on the waiting list for an operation. Meanwhile, I was not fit enough to work and went 'on the sick'. In total, I was off work for nearly four months made up of time spent waiting for the operation and then convalescing afterwards. This was the longest period of time that I had ever been away from a working environment and I could not mentally adjust to this new concept. I felt like a fish out of water and, when eventually I had a return to work medical, I told the doctor how I felt and that I could not wait to return to normal train driving duties. He told me that this was the opposite reaction to most of his patients and that "I should be bottled." I still don't know if this was a compliment or not!

It was during this long period of forced absence from work and after I had explained to Anne just how unsettling and unnatural it felt for me that she said, "Well, you'll have to retire some time, so you had better get used to the idea of not going to work."

Retire? I had given the matter little thought up to that point.

I returned to work but immediately began to suffer with tummy problems and after a series of tests I was diagnosed with a sliding hiatus hernia. So, I was literally coming apart at the seams! The good news with this second ailment was that no operation was necessary and the resulting indigestion and heartburn could be relieved, though not cured, with simple over-the-counter medications.

Like all drivers, when reaching 60 years of age I was required to undergo more frequent examinations by the railway's medical department. At least one every year was now deemed to be essential and, as you would expect, it covered all aspects of health. The normal weight–height body mass index measurement, blood pressure checks, hearing tests, sight tests, sugar and blood in urine tests and, of course, being wired up to the dreaded ECG machine. I failed the last one three times. It's a wonder I'm still here! All joking aside, the first time (28th January 2009) that the doctor told me that there was an 'anomaly' showing on my ECG readout so I would be immediately removed from driving duties as a precaution and that the recording would be sent to a heart specialist for analysis, I was mightily concerned because this was potentially the end of my career – if not my life. I was excluded from working for five days waiting for news before I was eventually told that all was well and that I could resume train driving. You can imagine how relieved Anne and I were at this good news. On the two other subsequent occasions, my ECG readout again had to be sent off for further examination as some form of abnormality had, again, been detected. But on these two occasions, I was cleared to return to driving duties much more quickly. To this day, I don't know what the exact problem was – I was never told.

Anne has had far more serious health issues to contend with as she had been diagnosed with type one diabetes in 1981. She has to self-inject four doses of insulin every day. That totals over 55,000 jabs and still counting! Despite excellent NHS monitoring, it was beginning to affect her eyesight and she developed diabetic maculopathy, apparently a relatively common problem with this illness. She had to undergo a prolonged series of laser treatments to seal leaking blood vessels in her eyes. At one time she had these problems in both eyes and was almost blind for a few days. Then her treatment changed to include injections into her eyes. This made us rethink our work/life balance priorities and we decided that we should make more of our time together. In other words, more life and less work. We did some financial calculations but found that I could not afford to retire and live on my railway pension alone and, as I would not be eligible for the state pension for a number of years, we decided to pursue a middle way. Could I become a part-time train driver? Though very uncommon within FGW at that time as there were only a handful of drivers working to part-time contracts, I applied to become another of those at the end of January 2014 but only after confirming that ASLEF both locally and nationally had no objections. On 20th March, Anne and I had a meeting with my local manager, her boss and the local union reps and between us we agreed a way forward. I would work 2 or sometimes 3 days per week with a pro rata reduction in my pay and annual leave entitlements but otherwise there would be no change to my working conditions. I would still undertake the same shifts and drive the same trains, just less frequently. It worked out very well. I topped up my reduced wage by claiming my railway pension so the finances were okay and we had a lot more time together to do the things we wanted and to enjoy life while we could.

I was a part-time driver from 19th May 2014 until I fully retired at the end of September 2017. I gave my boss more than the mandatory three months' notice but, apart from my local union reps, none of my other colleagues were aware of my intentions to take 'early' retirement at 63 years of age and that was deliberate, as I just wanted to finish with as little fuss as possible.

The end of September emerged as the best time for me to retire. There were several reasons for this. I wanted to finish working at a time of my choosing but there were two possible reasons why others could have decided my fate and the termination date of my career. The first and more likely of the two was the fact that my annual medical would, again, soon be due (my last one had taken place on 8th November 2016) and with it the possibility of my removal from driving duties due to being deemed unfit. The second, but less likely possibility, was that my biennial rules assessment was also about to fall due (my last one had taken place on 2nd October 2015) and with it came the risk that I may fail to pass the examination. So, I decided to retire just before either of these two possibilities could occur that may have forced me to terminate my driving career.

The last time that I ever drove a train was on Thursday 28th September 2017 and what an eventful day it turned out to be.

I booked on duty at 11:58 and my first job was to relieve 1F14, the 10:23 from Portsmouth Harbour at Westbury and drive GWR three-car unit 158 959 to Cardiff Central. I had not gone far when the signaller cautioned me for cattle that had strayed onto the line between Freshford station and Bathampton Junction and, sure enough, approaching Dundas aqueduct at low speed I saw about half a dozen cows wondering along the adjacent line, apparently without a care in the world. An up train had stopped behind the cattle and its driver, along with his trainee, were attempting to round them up. After updating my guard and the signaller of the situation, I joined in and we eventually managed to guide and persuade the now skittish bovine beasts to vacate railway property and rejoin their colleagues still contentedly grazing in an adjacent field. After a minor trackside celebration and high-fiving my co-cowboys, I rejoined my train, advised the signaller that the line was again clear and proceeded with my now considerably late train to Cardiff.

All services from Westbury that are bound for Cardiff must reverse direction at Bristol Temple Meads. So, I changed ends as usual at Bristol and, upon departure, immediately became aware that the train was underpowered when travelling in this new direction. I soon discovered that one of the three engines had not reversed. It was just idling and, therefore, not providing any directional power output. On checking the repair book when we eventually reached our next station stop of Filton Abbey Wood, I discovered that this fault had been previously reported and was known to the maintenance department; however, the unit had to remain in service as no others were available and it was deemed better for the service to run late than to be cancelled. This was not an uncommon situation as many faulty units remained in service due to an acute shortage of serviceable trains and this had been an ongoing situation for very many years. When I arrived at Newport, my two brothers Dave and Roger joined my train to help me commemorate my last working day. After the inevitable late arrival at Cardiff, I shunted the empty train from arrival platform 3 to departure platform 0 and following some hurried train cleaning and preparation by staff at Cardiff, we were ready to depart, again with Dave and Roger on board, at the correct time of 14:30 with 1F23, the return working to Portsmouth Harbour. I was still sitting in the cab but talking to one of our better managers Jon Godden who was on the platform overseeing GWR services and explaining to him that this was my very last day on the railway when the in-cab GSM-R burst into life with an 'All Trains Stop' emergency broadcast. This was the first and last time that I would receive such a warning on the latest radio system but, as my train was already stationary, I was then required under the rules not to proceed until I had the appropriate authority from the signaller to do so. I was eventually informed by station staff that the emergency stop broadcast had been initiated by a driver at Heath Junction north of Cardiff who had noticed a passing train that appeared to be on fire. (I later found out that this was a bona fide emergency and that all passengers had to be evacuated onto the line-side from the 14:04 Arriva Trains Wales service from Radyr to Coryton due to an engine fire.) Despite this information I could not depart until I had received official confirmation from the signaller that it was safe for my train to proceed and so I waited, still chatting to Jon. After about ten minutes which I considered more than sufficient time for the signaller to inform all trains that were not in the area of the train on fire that is was safe to continue, I called the signaller directly myself only to be told that the call had no relevance to trains on the mainline or in the Cardiff Central area and so I was authorised to proceed as normal.

I departed only 12 minutes late and arrived at Bristol Temple Meads 8 minutes behind time where another driver would take the train forward to Portsmouth. I then had just enough time for my PNB (which included some cake provided by Jon Godden who had travelled with me from Cardiff) before working my next train 2C81 the 15:54 to Taunton with two-car unit no. 150 128.

I was then delayed twice en route. Firstly, I was advised to proceed at caution due to a report of a trespasser on the line near Highbridge & Burnham station, though I saw no one and the second delay was at Bridgewater station when the guard was initially unable to close the doors. This we eventually managed to overcome by the use of an alternative door control but not before a drunk and irate passenger had a rant at me about the further delay.

My return working from Taunton to Bristol Temple Meads was to be the last train I would ever drive. This was 2U26 the 17:06 GWR departure to Cardiff Central again with 150 128 (see photo.) This return journey was less eventful though we arrived in Bristol 16 minutes late at 18:28 where I was astonished to see my son Gareth waiting on the platform to record the event.

When I arrived home that day, Anne had conspired with Gareth to produce a celebratory cake topped with appropriate railway-related decoration that included the numbers of the very first train I had officially driven 47 309 (see Chapter 7) and my last 150 128.

The following week, I attended the ASLEF Westbury branch where

I announced to my surprised colleagues that I had now retired and that this would be the last branch meeting I would ever attend. I then read out the following.

*Thank you for allowing me the opportunity to make a personal statement.*

*I have been a member of ASLEF since 1971 and since then I have attended literally hundreds of branch meetings. This particular meeting is very special to me because it is the last one that I will ever attend. Thankfully this is not because of any ill health issues but simply because, as I retired last week, I feel that now is the appropriate time for me to bow out of branch activities. I have not made this decision lightly and I do not intend to cut all my ties with ASLEF, as I will now join the retired members section.*

*As you know I have been working part-time for the past three and a half years and though not the main reason, this was, in part, an attempt to help me prepare for the inevitability of full retirement.*

*I asked the local management and local reps that the date of my retirement remain confidential, as I wanted to just finish quietly, and without any fuss.*

*ASLEF branches are the bedrock on which our trade union is built and it is only thanks to ASLEF that I have enjoyed such a long career and thereby income since being made redundant at Newport 37 years ago. So even though I may now be preaching to the converted I wanted to say that it is essential for all members to continue to do all they can and actively support our trade union. While it is not perfect – no organisation is – it has saved many drivers' jobs, mine included, over the years.*

*I first joined the railway at the tender age of 15 and consider myself very fortunate to have been continuously employed within our industry since then. I have seen many changes over the intervening years – though not all of them for the better.*

*Looking back over my 47 plus years on the railway my personal career low points include …*

- *Unwisely transferring, albeit briefly, to Kings Cross.*
- *Being treated like shit by some local managers when I was made redundant from my original depot at Ebbw Junction in 1980.*

- *Standing on a picket line with my redundancy notice in my pocket.*
- *Being separated from my family whilst initially living in lodgings in Westbury.*
- *Receiving a letter threatening me with dismissal during the 1982 strike.*
- *Privatisation of the rail industry.*
- *My time as an ASLEF rep. when I was a member of the negotiating team that failed to deliver a harmonisation package that was acceptable to the majority of FGW drivers.*
- *Two operational incidents that both resulted in my temporary suspension from driving duties.*
- *A young man committing suicide with my train.*
- *Recent attempts to expand DOO passenger operations by several TOCs, including initially by GWR. (This policy remains fundamentally flawed and must not take place.)*

*But on a brighter note highlights include …*

- *The start of my railway employment as a messenger boy at Maesglas, Newport, in 1969.*
- *Entry into the 'footplate line of promotion' in 1971.*
- *Becoming a fully qualified driver in 1981 and my first driving turn soon after.*
- *Regularly driving the then heaviest freight train in Europe hauled by a single locomotive.*
- *The great variety of work (traction, routes, freight and passenger) prior to privatisation.*
- *My time as an ASLEF rep. when I was heavily involved in some successful negotiations; the most personally satisfying of which was not connected to collective agreements but helping to get a driver reinstated who had suffered grossly unjust treatment due to personal differences with his local manager.*
- *Assisting with the training of new drivers.*
- *Preventing a woman from committing suicide on the line.*
- *Working with colleagues who have become friends.*
- *Playing my part in getting thousands of passengers (not customers) to their destination safely and even occasionally on time!*

*Throughout my entire driving career, I have kept a daily log, recording the details of every shift and every train I have driven. I have now completed 148 notebooks – how sad is that!*

*I now hope to do more photography and not get out of bed before 07:00 ever again!*

*Looking back, I like to think that I have carried out my duties to the best of my ability and all-in-all I am content with the small part I have played within the union and the industry I love.*

*I wish you all a successful future.*

*Thank you for listening.*

*PS I would appreciate it if as many of you as possible join me and Anne in the bar after this meeting has closed as we have arranged for food and free drinks to be available for all.*

At the end of my little speech, my colleagues kindly gave me a standing ovation, which took me by surprise and left me a little emotional but we soon all got back down to earth and put the world to rights with a few pints in the bar afterwards.

Now that I have retired, do I miss the job? Yes, of course, I do but I am slowly adapting and I know that, given time, I will move on (recover?) completely.

I have many railway-related memories only some of which I have been able to include in this book. The bad ones I will try to forget but the good ones are wonderfully warming as I reminisce to myself. Seeing the winter sunrise over fields covered in sparkling frost or wild deer running in adjacent fields. Moonlight reflecting off the river Avon as I pass by; a rainbow at night and a meteor blazing across a pitch-black sky are some of the many spectacular sights I have witnessed when driving my train. There are a thousand such memories – all precious.

However, the most heart-warming scene that will forever remain with me occurred totally unexpectedly one day at Bradford-on-Avon station when I was driving a train from Portsmouth to Bristol. I noticed a woman at the far end of the platform looking in my direction with a small boy aged about four or five, who I took to be her son, standing in front of her. He started to jump up and down excitedly as I bought my train to a stop but she sensibly had both hands on his shoulders to gently restrain him. My guard released the doors and one passenger, who alighted from the leading coach and was in full Royal Navy uniform, walked past my open cab window in the direction of the small boy and his mum. This proved too much for the young man and with a shout of "Daddy!" his mum let him go and he ran as fast as his little legs would let him into the waiting arms of his father who picked him up and swung him round in a circle, both of them laughing all the time. Mum then joined them both in a group hug. My guard closed the doors and gave me authority to restart the train. As my train slowly approached the small but happy family, I heard mum say "Wave to the driver" which her son immediately did and with gusto. I waved back and gave a short toot of the horn at which point the little boy, still in the arms of his dad, gave a jump and all three started to laugh again. Then, when I drew level with them, the father shouted "Thank you!" which to me at the time felt more than a polite remark but rather a heartfelt expression of gratitude for helping him to return safely to his loved ones on the final part of his possibly very long journey. I continued with my train to Bristol all the while feeling a great deal of job satisfaction and contentment with the world in general.

I hope that you have enjoyed reading this book. If you did please feel free to contact me on stevedavies.westbury@icloud.com. If you didn't, fair enough, but I've done my best and you will be pleased to know that there will not be a second volume!

**RIGHT AWAY!**

# Glossary

The railway industry, like many others, has its own unique 'language' using words, phrases and abbreviations that will initially bewilder anyone new to the scene. I would like to think that not only railway-men and women could enjoy this book and so, in an attempt to simplify my ramblings a little, I have provided here a brief explanation of some of the terminology used.

I hope it helps.

**AHB:** Automatic Half Barrier. A level crossing that has both warning lights and half width barriers that are normally automatically activated by the passage of trains.

**ARC:** Amalgamated Roadstone Corporation Ltd. One-time owners of Whatley quarry.

**ASLEF:** The Associated Society of Locomotive Engineers and Firemen. The trade union for train drivers.

**Auto brake:** When operated by the driver, this will apply the brakes (vacuum or air) on the locomotive and on all such fitted wagons or coaches that make up the train. This brake will also automatically apply should the train accidentally divide (see also straight air brake).

**AWS:** Automatic Warning System. A safety device that will stop a train if its driver fails to react to its audible warning when approaching restrictive signals or severe speed restrictions.

**Banker:** An additional locomotive at the rear of a train that assists on rising gradients.

**Bardic lamp:** A heavy-duty torch/lamp (also equipped with red, green, and yellow shades for signaling) in very common use during BR days.

**B-B:** The wheel arrangement code for a diesel hydraulic locomotive with two bogies and four powered axles. See also Co-Co.

**B&H:** Berks and Hants. A common term for the rail route between Reading and Westbury.

**Bidirectional lines:** Railway lines on which trains may run in either direction.

**Bobby:** An old-fashioned term for a signalman as policemen originally fulfilled this role.

**Brake stick:** A wooden pole about a metre long, half of which was rounded for the handgrip and the rest squared, which was used to apply and release mechanical brakes on freight wagons.

**Brake test:** A static test undertaken by drivers or maintenance staff to ensure that the operation of the brake handle produces the correct readings on the brake force gauges in the cab. See also running brake test.

**Bridge bash:** When a high-sided road vehicle collides with a low rail-over-road bridge.

**BTP:** British Transport Police.

**Buzzer:** The on train audible sound/code communication between guard and driver.

**Caped:** A train that has been cancelled.

**Carriage key / T key:** A key with three different heads for un/locking carriage doors and various other rail industry locks.

**Catch points:** Points designed to derail vehicles to prevent a possible collision in the event of vehicles running away.

**CDP:** Competence Development Process. An individually agreed assistance and monitoring procedure introduced to try and prevent a reoccurrence of driver error (separate from the disciplinary procedures).

**Cess:** The strip of land that runs between the side of the track and the railway boundary fence.

**Co-Co:** The wheel arrangement code for a diesel electric locomotive with two bogies and six axles – each of which has a traction motor. See also B-B.

**Company Council:** The top negotiating committee within a TOC that represents both the company and all employees.

**Conductor:** See Guard.

**DDC:** Drivers Divisional Council. The top negotiating committee when dealing solely with driver related pay and conditions of employment. DDC also make up part of Company Council. See above.

**Detonators/Dets:** Small charges used in an emergency that are placed on top of the rail and will explode when run over by an oncoming train requiring its driver to stop.

**Diagram:** The daily work schedule card issued to drivers and guards listing full details of all trains to be worked.

**Distant signal:** A semaphore signal that can only display Yellow (prepare to stop at the next signal) or Green (all clear to proceed at normal speed).

**DMU:** Diesel Multiple Unit. A passenger train that is powered by diesel engines located beneath the coaches (i.e. not a locomotive hauled train) and capable of being coupled/uncoupled with others to form a longer or shorter train as necessary.

**DMMU:** Diesel Mechanical Multiple Unit. Older 'heritage' DMUs with mechanical transmission. (Newer 'sprinter' DMUs have hydraulic transmissions.)

**DOO:** Driver Only Operated. A train running without at Guard.

**DOO – P:** A Driver Only Operated Passenger train.

**Driver's vigilance device:** See Deadmans.

**DSD:** Driver's Safety Device or **Deadmans:** A safety device designed to stop the train should the driver become incapacitated. The driver is required to maintain foot pressure on a pedal to prevent an automatic emergency brake application. This device was later modified and renamed the **drivers' vigilance device** as it now encompasses a timer that sounds a warning every minute and this requires the driver to reset the pedal if the power handle or brake has not been operated within that time period. This ensures that the train would stop should the driver not react for any reason.

**EMU:** Electric Multiple Unit. A passenger train that is powered by electric motors located beneath the coaches (i.e. not a locomotive hauled train) and supplied either by a third rail or overhead wire and also capable of being coupled/uncoupled with others to form a longer or shorter train as necessary.

**ETH:** Electric Train Heating. Operated from the loco to supply heating for passenger coaches that replaced the original steam heating of trains.

**Fail safe:** See right side failure.

**Feather**: A term in common usage meaning a junction indicator.

**FGW: First Great/er Western:** A train operating company running services from Paddington along the Thames Valley, also through to Gloucester & Cheltenham, Hereford, Carmarthen and Penzance. Other routes include to Gatwick, Portsmouth, Brighton and Weymouth and all the branch lines in Devon and Cornwall. (Superseded by GWR.)

**Footplate:** This originally referred to the large metal plate, sometimes covered in wood, which formed the floor in the cab of a steam locomotive. The term survived the move from steam to diesel and electric locos and so became an acceptable alternative to the phrase 'the driving cab' when referring to modern traction and is still in use today.

**Foster Yeoman:** One-time owner of Merehead quarry and many stone distribution depots.

**Four-foot:** The space between a pair of running rails. The actual distance (standard gauge) is 4' 8½".

**Fully Fitted:** A train that has a continuous brake throughout which is normally controlled by the driver but will also automatically apply in the event of the train becoming divided.

**GSM-R:** Global System for Mobile Communications – Railway. The latest in-cab digital communication system that includes the ability for any signaller or driver to send an 'Emergency Stop' message to all nearby trains with the press of a single button.

**Guard:** Generic job title now incorporating Conductor and Train Manager.

**GWR:** Great Western Railway. Successor to FGW.

**Harmonisation:** The process of merging all rates of pay and conditions for different groups of drivers, and other grades who are all working for the same company.

**Headcode:** All trains are individually identified by their headcode, a four-digit (number, letter, number, number) code, e.g. 1F27 is the 16:30 Cardiff Central to Portsmouth Harbour passenger service.

**HSS:** High Speed Services operated by FGW/GWR.

**HST:** High Speed Train. Normally used to identify the 125 mph diesel sets.

**Junction indicator:** A signal made up of a row of five white lights that advise the driver which route his/her train will take through a junction.

**K2:** A printed weekly notice booklet issued to traincrew with updates covering such items as temporary speed restrictions, engineering works and signal alterations etc.

**LDC:** Local Departmental Committee. Made up of local managers and elected staff reps; this body negotiates all local conditions of service that include linking and leave arrangements.

**LH&SR:** Local Health & Safety Rep.

**Light Engine:** A locomotive without any coaches or wagons attached.

**Link:** A work roster consisting of a list of names with a week's work allocated to each through which staff would cycle.

**Loop:** A short section of line running alongside a main line where slower trains may be stopped to allow higher priority trains to pass.

**Loose coupled:** A freight train that has only the locomotive and guard's van brake in operation.

**Low Rail Adhesion:** When the top of the rail is slippery. This could be caused by leaves on the lines, snow, frost or even light rain that can result in train wheels spinning during acceleration or skidding during braking. See also RHTT.

**LSR:** Local Staff Representative.

**LTV:** London & Thames Valley services operated by FGW / GWR.

**MGR:** Merry Go Round. A system designed to empty coal hopper wagons at power stations that should eliminate the need for the train to stop or uncouple.

**MOM:** Mobile Operations Manager. Job title of the local NR manager frequently called out to the site of an abnormal train operational incident.

**Multiple working:** When a single driver controls more than one locomotive. See also tandem working.

**Near miss:** Any incident that, if the circumstances had been only slightly different, could have resulted in serious damage, injury or even death.

**NR:** Network Rail (previously Railtrack). The state-owned company responsible for Britain's entire railway infrastructure network.

**NRN:** National Radio Network. The forerunner of GSM-R.

**NUR:** The National Union of Railwaymen (now RMT).

**On the cushions:** Train crew travelling as passengers.

**OTD/MR:** On Train Data / Monitoring Recorder. A train's "black box" that records most aspects of its operations.

**Panel box:** A colour light signal control building operated by signallers that replaced many of the older semaphore signal boxes.

**Pilot (1):** A small low speed locomotive used for local shunting work. Usually a diesel class 08.

**Pilot (2):** To accompany and advise the driver or guard who is not familiar with the route.

**Pilotman:** Someone who is acting as a pilot (2) or additionally during degraded working.

**PNB:** Personal Needs Break. A guaranteed break from duty at agreed locations and times to facilitate traincrew rest, refreshments and the use of toilet facilities.

**Protection:** Various methods used to ensure that trains do not move or, in an emergency, are brought to a halt.

**RA:** Route availability. Each rail vehicle and each route has an RA number. Provided the RA vehicle number is below or the same as the RA route number, no additional restriction is necessary. If, however, for example, a wagon with an RA number of 10 was to be conveyed over a route with an

RA number of 8, an exceptional load certificate has to be provided that would advise the driver of any additional restrictions necessary en route.

**Railtrack:** Predecessor of Network Rail.

**Repeater:** A two-aspect colour light signal that can only display Yellow (prepare to stop at the next signal) or Green (all clear to proceed at normal speed).

**Request stops:** Some small rural stations at which certain trains will only stop if passengers advise the guard that they wish to alight or hand signal the driver to stop if they wish to join the train.

**RHTT:** Rail Head Treatment Train. A special train designed to clean the railhead and so increase adhesion between wheel and rail for subsequent trains.

**Right Away (RA):** The common phrase (and type of signal) used to indicate that a train should depart immediately.

**Right side failure:** Any form of railway safety equipment that, if it becomes defective, is designed to fail-safe, e.g. a green signal would revert to its default norm of red.

**RIO:** Rail Incident Officer. The job title of an N.R. manager called out to take charge in the event of a serious railway operational incident.

**RMT:** The national union of Rail, Maritime and Transport workers (previously the NUR).

**Road learning:** The system employed by traincrew to ensure they have a detailed knowledge of a route before operating any train over it.

**Running brake test:** A brake test carried out by the driver at the earliest practical point in a journey and additionally during snow to satisfy him/herself that deceleration of their train is satisfactory. See also Brake test.

**Run round:** When a locomotive arrives at its destination and is then detached from the front of its train, proceeds through points and along an adjacent line then through another set of points to the rear end of the same train to couple up in preparation for its return journey.

**Semaphore signals:** Old-fashioned mechanical signals operated by levers and wires from a signal box.

**Shunter:** A railwayman employed to couple/uncouple locos, freight and passenger rolling stock, marshal trains, carry out brake tests and prepare trains ready for departure.

**Sign the road:** All drivers and guards are required to sign their name next to individually listed routes to confirm that they have a thorough knowledge and are competent to operate trains over that particular route. At one time, the individual alone took full responsibility but everyone is now comprehensively assessed before they can 'sign the road'.

**Single line token:** Conflicting train movements on some single lines are prevented by a token system. The driver of any train entering onto these single lines must have in his/her possession the relevant token that has been issued to them and authorised by the signaller. Only one token can be in use at any time.

**SLU:** Standard Length Unit. Used to calculate the total length of a train (1 SLU = 21 feet).

**SPAD:** **S**ignal **P**assed **A**t **D**anger. A red signal or stop board passed by a train without authority.

**Spate:** A temporary **S**peed restriction **P**reviously **A**dvertised **T**erminated **E**arly, i.e. no longer in operation.

**Sprinter:** A class 15xxx D.M.U.

**SPT:** Signal Post Telephone. A phone located at a signal post to enable the driver to contact the signaller when stopped at a red signal. Now little used due to the introduction of GSM-R.

**Straight air brake:** When operated by the driver this will apply the brakes only on the locomotive and not on any of the wagons or coaches of the train. See also auto brake.

**SWT:** South West Trains (now South Western Railway). A train operating company with routes from Waterloo to Reading, Portsmouth, Weymouth, Exeter and Bristol. Its subsidiary also operates services on the Isle of White.

**SW&W:** South Wales and West was a 1996-2001 rail franchise. See also Wales & West.

**Tandem working:** When two or more locomotives haul a train, each of which has a driver. See also multiple working.

**T key:** See Carriage key.

**TOC:** Train Operating Company. A generic term applied to each of the many privatised passenger train businesses.

**Token:** See single line token.

**TPWS:** Train Protection and Warning System. An automatic safety device designed to stop a train if it is approaching a red signal, speed restriction, or buffer stops faster than a preprogrammed speed.

**Track circuit clip:** An emergency safety device that, when placed on two running rails, will short-circuit their low current and reproduce the presence of a train on the signaling system, thereby preventing another train from entering that section of line by returning the protecting signal to red.

**Trap points:** Points designed to derail a train in order to prevent a potential collision should a SPAD occur.

**Train manager:** See Guard.

**TRS:** The Train Ready to Start button is used by platform staff to advise the signaller that all station duties have been completed if the signal is red.

**TUPE:** Transfer of Undertakings (Protection of Employment). The legislation under which employees' terms and conditions are protected when a business transfers to a new company. (This procedure was applied to me personally on three occasions. 1996 from BR (Regional Railways) to Wales & West (initially operating as South Wales & West), 2001 to Wessex Trains and finally during 2006 to First Greater Western (now operating as GWR).

**Vacuum brake head:** When only the leading wagons of a freight train are fitted with vacuum brakes and operated from the locomotive.

**Wrong side failure:** The opposite of a right side failure. This is a very rare occurrence when safety equipment does not fail-safe, e.g. a signal displays a green light when it should be red.

**WSP:** Wheel Slide Protection. Fitted on more modern trains, WSP is a computer-controlled device that will automatically and rapidly release then reapply the brakes should wheel slide/skidding be detected during braking. Similar in principle to the antilock braking systems fitted on modern cars.

**W&W:** Wales & West. A TOC that operated the SW&W franchise.

Lightning Source UK Ltd.
Milton Keynes UK
UKHW020022310520
364100UK00002B/183

9 781789 630350